can take to succeed—a course between an absolute free market and rigid state control. The strategies require a lean government that works cooperatively with the private sector to respond quickly and flexibly to challenges in world competition. Vogel demystifies the source of Japanese success and provides a framework for achieving long-term economic leadership by thinking ahead.

About the Author

Born and educated in Ohio, Ezra F. Vogel first went to Japan for research in 1958, and he has been following East Asian developments ever since. As a sociologist, he has studied villages, families and histories, but he has also had unusual opportunities to know Japanese government and business leaders. In 1967, he became a professor at Harvard, where he has served as Director of Harvard's East Asian Research Center and Council of East Asian Studies and is director of the U.S.–Japan program.

COMEBACK

CASE BY CASE: Building the
Resurgence of American
Business

EZRA F. VOGEL

88-105

SIMON AND SCHUSTER

NEW YORK

10 9 8 7 6 5 4 3 2 1

Library of Congress Cataloging in Publication Data
Vogel, Ezra F.
   Comeback: case by case: building the resurgence of American business.
   Bibliography: p.
   Includes index.
   1. Industry and state—United States. 2. Industry
and state—Japan. 3. Competition, International.
I. Title.
HD3616.U47V64   1985   338.952   84-22232
ISBN: 0-671-46079-X

To Charlotte

CONTENTS

Part Four: American Response

PREFACE

In 1976, when I began lecturing on the urgency of America's learning
lessons from Japan, my well-meaning but skeptical listeners would ask questions like: "Professor, don't you know that in America we have antitrust laws and
an adversary relationship between government and business and that it won't
work here?"

This book is my answer to such critics. In a word, I believe that Americans
are perfectly capable of cooperation when they are convinced it is in their interest. Unprecedented changes in the world economic environment that render
other nations more competitive and increase our dependency on world markets
now make it urgent that Americans pull closer together. Unfortunately we are
not yet convinced, and this book is my effort to help narrow the gap between our
interests and our convictions.

The nation most successful in adapting to these worldwide economic changes
is Japan. To respond more effectively, we Americans need to acknowledge the
scope of its success and learn how the Japanese achieved it. Although our knowledge of Japan has grown in recent years, it remains inadequate and subject to
misperceptions. At this stage I feel that I can contribute more to understanding
by looking at concrete cases than by repeating generalizations. Therefore, during
a sabbatical from Harvard, as the first incumbent of the Reischauer Research
Professorship, I spent 1982–83 in Japan studying four industries in which Japan
became highly competitive. I report here the results.

In my view, the American response to the Japanese challenge has thus far
been woefully inadequate. I believe that an effective American response requires

new efforts in many different fields: education, business, and government. This in turn requires greater cooperation between public and private sectors, and I therefore will consider how Americans can best accomplish this. With the help of talented graduate students, I studied four cases in which American government and business worked together to achieve great results.

The reader may rightly ask why a sociologist specializing in Japan is giving advice about American policy. I do so for the same reason that many East Asians who went abroad to study in the late nineteenth and early twentieth century came home to work for the revitalization of their countries. By being exposed to a very different way of doing things, they saw more clearly and felt more keenly than the rest of their countrymen their own nations' weaknesses. The onrush of industrial change in East Asia in recent decades has transformed the world we live in, and it pains me that our nation's response to this change falls short. Many Asians who went abroad helped provide new perspectives for understanding their countries' problems, and I aspire to do the same.

Although that is my goal, I do not believe that the strengthening of America need be at the expense of other countries. I talk of the Japanese challenge to encourage a better American performance, but Japan is an ally and should not be made our scapegoat. I hope that by 1990 we will feel thankful to the Japanese for impelling us to achieve higher levels of education, productivity, and social cohesion. I hope also that thoughtful Japanese will realize a vigorous America is in their interest and that by 1990 they will be thankful they helped spur us to greater strength. A revitalized America will be in a better position to work well with all other countries, to import their goods, support an open world trade system, share technology, and contribute to international security.

I am aware that many Americans see no point in studying Japan. They feel that Japan is too different, has too many weaknesses we do not want to emulate. I make no secret of my respect for much of what Japan has accomplished, but these critics are right that Japan does many things we do not want to import and that we must fashion our own response to their challenge. Still, I am convinced that many who say "But they are different" are excusing their own inflexibility and inviting disaster. The lessons from Japan, to be sure, are not easy ones, and given the complexity of the world's problems and the difficulty of resolving them, escapism has its attractions. This book is not for those who prefer that path.

Part One

THE NEW COMPETITIVE ENVIRONMENT

1

The Continuing Japanese Challenge

1. THE UNADORNED VIEW FROM TOKYO

Many Japanese, while more interested in America than in any other foreign
country, see America's problems as more than temporary dislocations and
current Japanese successes as just the beginning. They see America as a nation
on the decline and Japan as a nation on the rise.

Japanese visitors to the United States are no longer surprised by street crime
and inner-city decay, by vandalized automobiles and trash-littered streets. They
notice elaborate security measures and fear of strangers at night. Compared to
goods and services at home, they complain that American products break, that
American service is slow and unreliable. They exchange stories about the ignorance of ordinary Americans and sigh at the incompetence of American workmen.

Japanese businessmen see in American businesses poorly motivated managers
and workers, poor workmanship, lack of knowledge of the world, outdated equipment, short-range perspectives, and lack of coordination for the public good.
Japanese government representatives see in their American counterparts ama-
teurism, political expediency, and lack of constancy. These Japanese see talented
and creative Americans all about them but believe that their abilities are channeled into litigiousness and paper entrepreneurship rather than in strengthening
government and business organizations. Large American organizations are seen
as tired and weighted down with rules, legalities, selfishness, personal rivalries,
and fear of job loss. Small ones are seen as out of touch with world developments.

Surprising though it may seem to Americans, the Japanese see in America a
lack of entrepreneurial spirit, an acceptance of mediocrity, even an unwillingness

to try. American firms seem too concerned with short-range profits and too unconcerned with long-range strategy and staff development and with applying new technology. America's failure to sell goods in Japan, in their view, arises from American inability to make quality goods at competitive prices, lack of proper preparation for the demands of the Japanese market, and impatience. In their view, the Japanese market is just as open as the American. They believe that if both markets were completely opened, if Japanese bought all the competitive American agricultural goods and competitive manufactured products and Americans bought all the competitive Japanese TV sets, steel, and autos, the trade balance would be even more one-sided than it is. In Japanese eyes, America's views of the Japanese market are the sour grapes of the loser in international competition. American official pressures on Japan are seen as attempts to replace through politics what was lost in the open market.

Present-day America in this estimate is equated with Rome in the early stages of its decline. In their analysis of international relations, Japanese see Pax Americana as going the way of Pax Britannica. America may be acting tough and waving the flag, but its illusions of power cannot conceal the growing weakness of its economic base and therefore its diminishing ability to control events around the world. Current world problems are analyzed in terms of the collapse of the American world order, and among themselves Japanese are discussing what form a Pax Nipponica might take.

The Japanese see their economic success as covering the entire range, including heavy industrial goods, consumer products, and high technology, and they have confidence in their growing abilities in areas in which America is still ahead. Everywhere they look, they see expanding market shares for Japan and declining market shares for America: automobiles, semiconductors, computers, communications, chemicals, pharmaceuticals, biotechnology, airplanes, composite materials, and the service industries.

Like earlier generations of Westerners who saw their technological superiority as proof of their moral superiority, many Japanese see their success as a sign of superior moral worth. They see Americans as lazy whereas Japanese are diligent, Americans as short-tempered and short-sighted whereas Japanese are patient and persistent, Americans as contentious whereas Japanese find ways to cooperate. Americans are perceived to be self-centered, even selfish, while Japanese are considerate of other people; Americans are complacent while Japanese are willing to learn and to adjust; Americans are careless and sloppy while Japanese are careful and attentive to detail. Americans give up easily and then complain while Japanese keep trying.

Not all Japanese agree with all these observations, and many who do are not happy with what they see. To be sure, many share the exhilaration of a team formerly far back in the pack now overtaking the front-runner. Some, like proud samurai humiliated by defeat in World War II, feel they are now avenging themselves on the economic battlefield. But many thoughtful leaders who deeply appreciate the help Japan received from America during the occupation after World War II sympathize with friends undergoing decline. Some even suggest that Japan should now give America aid as America gave Japan aid after the war. Others who think seriously about the international economic order doubt that Japan is ready for world leadership. They believe that at least for now a Pax Nipponica cannot successfully replace Pax Americana and that they must cooperate with America to maintain the current international economic order so beneficial to Japan. Many others are aware of how much the fate of Japan is intertwined with that of America and worry that America's decline will create more problems for Japan than it will solve, that Japan will catch the "American disease." Competitive juices are still flowing and the desire to win is still strong, but most Japanese want their competitor to remain healthy, to look out for himself. They are ready to applaud him if he succeeds and only regret that he appears to be declining so fast.

Americans living in Japan and observing the vitality around them tend to share many of these views. Indeed, if current trends continue, it is not hard to imagine an analysis of America in 1990 that described what went wrong more or less as follows:

2. SCENARIO OF A NONCOMPETITIVE TROUBLED AMERICA, 1990

Although some high-tech fields continued to expand, America as a whole lost economic ground through the 1980s. Not only did merchandise trade imbalances grow; the current account deficits exceeded $100 billion each year despite the increase of "voluntary agreements" by East Asian countries to restrain exports and despite the decline in the value of the dollar. U.S. budget deficits grew, and political fights between taxpayers and welfare and military advocates became more bitter. Unemployment continued to rise.

Why did competitiveness continue to erode throughout the 1980s? In the early 1980s, because Japan produced small cars much more cheaply than did the United States, Americans largely ceded this market to the Japanese. Moreover, to remain competitive, American companies in other fields increased their imports of parts from Japan even when assembly was done at home, paralleling the five Japanese auto companies with final assembly factories in the United States: Honda, Nissan, Toyota, Mitsubishi, and Toyo Kogyo. In the early 1980s, because the number of cars Japan could sell in the United States was limited by quota, Japanese car companies began producing higher-priced cars to make larger profits.

Despite some advances in manufacturing productivity in American firms and despite some labor union restraint in holding back wage increases, the Japanese sold enough large cars in America by the late 1980s to gain a quality and price edge over large American cars, as they had earlier done in the case of small cars. Political pressure from Japan caused a slight increase in the number of cars imported, but "voluntary quotas" prevented the Japanese from completely dominating the American market. Auto parts imports grew much more rapidly than did those of finished cars, but both grew. The number of workers engaged in auto and related production in the United States accordingly continued to decline throughout the 1980s not only because of imports but also because of the new labor-saving technology introduced in U.S. plants in a desperate effort to keep American-made cars competitive.

America imports most of its steel from Japan, Korea, Taiwan, and Brazil. In the early 1980s American steel companies gradually began diversifying and reducing their investment in domestic integrated steel plants, which by now have been mostly closed down. In the mid-1980s some dynamic American steel companies found niches in specialty steels where they were very competitive. However, the larger foreign steel companies with bigger incomes engaged in more research and bought more new equipment. They therefore decreased costs for specialty steels and offered products at such low prices as to make American companies suspicious of predatory pricing. American companies slowed down foreign domination of the American market by legal proceedings against dumping, but in the end they gradually ceded more niches in specialty steels to Japanese and other foreign companies.

In computers, telecommunications, fiber optics, biotechnology, pharmaceuticals, ceramics, and other new materials, Japanese companies substantially increased their world market share through the 1980s, including their market share in the United States. They increased their share of the production of the world's commercial airliners and the number of airplanes that they own and lease to other countries. As Japanese research efforts expanded, the technological gap gradually began to disappear, and Japan's greater supply of new engineers, especially electrical engineers, enabled it to expand its lead in product engineering and to move far more quickly to computer-aided manufacturing. Although a number of very prominent American high-tech firms remain internationally competitive, they do more sourcing and engineering abroad, often importing more goods than they export.

America still has a number of extremely innovative small firms, and venture capital is available to support them, but many of those active in the early 1980s went out of business. Few small firms that developed important new products were quick enough to move successfully into large-scale manufacturing. The more successful ones sold out to larger companies, many of them Japanese, able to offer attractive sums for technology useful in large-scale manufacturing.

As American financial analysts observed the record of Japanese successes in areas the Japanese government had targeted for growth, they became cautious in lending to American companies in these areas. Even in cases in which they did end up making loans, they charged more interest because of the added risk, increasing the already high cost of capital in these areas.

Despite American pressure, Japan continued to buy only a very small amount of American manufactured goods, especially in the high-tech area. Of course, in the few areas in which America still had a substantial lead, Japan bought, as before, a small number of machines, but hoped to acquire the manufacturing technology quickly so as to produce its own. Once Japanese companies developed their own products, foreign product sales in most cases dropped off quickly. Americans complained of unfair trading practices, but Japanese answered that American goods were no longer competitive, that American service was not as good as Japanese, and that American products were often not sufficiently adapted to their needs.

Japanese firms afraid of American protectionism in their sectors erected factories in the United States, but most of the advanced research, engineering, and product design work was done in Japan. Their American factories were for assembling the parts imported from Japan.

Japanese banks collaborated with American banks in lending to Japanese firms to set up facilities in the United States. As Japanese banks acquired know-how, these firms found the services of American banks less necessary and relied more on their old Japanese bank relationships. As the Japanese banks acquired experience in America, they gradually expanded their services to other American companies and then began to buy out smaller American banks to expand their services. In Hawaii, where Japanese acquired choice real estate and tourist services, and in Alaska, where they acquired rights to natural resources, Japanese banks already have gained dominant positions. Japanese banks control almost half of the assets deposited in California banks and are expanding rapidly in New York, Texas, Georgia, Tennessee, and elsewhere where Japanese companies have moved in.

Japanese trading companies originally servicing Japanese companies in the United States greatly expanded their trading operations during the 1980s, not only between the United States and Japan but also between the United States and other countries. Although relaxation of American antitrust laws made it possible for U.S. companies to form general trading companies, the long history of Japanese firms enabled each of the top six of them to remain several times larger than their American rivals. The two largest American trading firms are still subsidiaries of the big Japanese trading companies: Mitsui of America and Mitsubishi International. These Japanese-led firms made serious efforts to sell American manufactured goods abroad, not least in Japan, but the lion's share of the bilateral trade still consists of manufactured goods from Japan and of agricultural commodities and raw materials from the United States.

In the early 1980s, although the United States had unfavorable balances in merchandise trade, its great strength in services enabled it to maintain a favorable current-accounts balance. Then as in the late 1960s, it was widely believed that if the stronger yen were revalued against the dollar American exports would expand. In the mid-1980s, in the immediate aftermath of revaluation, this did indeed happen, but in the late 1980s as in the mid-1970s Japanese productivity gains were so rapid that they more than offset the revaluation. The revolutionary changes that began in Japanese service sectors in the mid-1980s enabled those sectors to begin significant overseas expansion of their network, especially in America. Japanese banks, insurance companies, trading companies, retailing companies, restaurants, consulting companies, publishing, engineering, and other service firms all greatly strengthened their foreign networks. This success is beginning to create problems in some American service sectors similar to those that began in many manufacturing sectors in the 1960s.

The decline in American competitiveness led to acrimonious debates within the United States. As American firms became less competitive, their profits declined substantially. During the early 1980s corporations were in fact paying only modest taxes, but gradually the size of the budget deficit forced increases in corporate as well as personal taxes to provide for increasing military, welfare, and other expenditures. Companies complained that this further eroded their competitiveness, and taxpayer revolts became more widespread.

Debate over how much to protect America's noncompetitive industries remained intense throughout the 1980s. Generally the administration, conscious of worldwide American responsibilities and the difficulty of keeping a relatively free world trade system, resisted protectionist measures. Congressmen representing special interests vocally defended the need to protect American jobs.

Arguing against protectionism were representatives of resource and agricultural sectors selling to Japan and elsewhere, economists advocating free trade, American lawyers and public relations firms representing Japanese clients, and American firms retailing Japanese products. As a whole they were supported by American press editorials, which vociferously defended the right of consumers to buy the lowest-priced products wherever they were made. Labor unions argued strongly for the need for protection, but their membership and power declined with the decline of American heavy industry. Many business leaders wanted to maintain plants in the United States, but when they calculated the effect on the bottom line they felt they had no choice but began to source more and more parts, if not finished products, from abroad.

Many former manufacturing firms became in large measure marketing firms for goods produced overseas. As a practical matter, therefore, they found it hard to advocate protectionism, and while individual firms in individual sectors did advocate protectionism, other firms with different interests often opposed it. The result was a haphazard and complex pattern of protectionism, but the growing number of American sectors that were not competitive led to more protectionism. Although barriers helped some sectors to remain profitable temporarily, and although many American firms tried to adapt to the new global competition, they rarely regained world competitive levels by manufacturing efforts in the U.S.

Because in areas in which they were not highly competitive the Japanese had found ways to inhibit foreign manufactured goods from entering Japan and because Japanese goods were at the forefront of competitive pressures, American spokesmen found it easy to blame the Japanese. Advocates of protectionism could point to many cases in which nontariff barriers in Japan remained where their sectors were not so competitive: in agriculture, chemicals, petrochemicals, software, and other high-tech areas where they had not yet fully caught up. The American firms concerned often found legal action (involving laws against dumping, patent infringements, unfair subsidies) a useful way to retard Japanese penetration of the American market. In some cases this did slow down Japanese penetration, providing a temporary shelter for profitable operations for American firms and those Japanese firms already well established in the American market. The Japanese continued to delay concessions until congressional action was imminent and then offered to establish cartel-like "voluntary" arrangements to limit exports to the United States.

Many Americans tried to address the problems, and much progress was made in a number of areas. Some dominant multinational firms and small innovative companies accomplished a great deal. The quality of many American products improved markedly. The government did more to ease antitrust worries in order to allow the formation of research consortia and trading companies. Pressures on Japan to support opening of the financial markets had considerable impact in realigning the yen. Attention to American educational standards and to engineering training led to some sporadic improvements in educational programs. However, the changes did not have a major impact. Few research consortia or trading companies were able to move quickly on a large scale to affect aggregate statistics on amount of research and trade. Average educational levels, as measured by standard tests, did not rise appreciably.

Successive administrations dealt with monetary and fiscal policies, but the problem of trying to forge a new national consensus to deal with competitive problems without simply subsidizing the losers seemed too difficult. Furthermore, economists within the government strongly opposed any initiatives to deal with the issues other than monetary and fiscal ones. As a result, the government provided little leadership in trying to promote competitiveness.

The Japanese, despite substantial trade surpluses and success in penetrating American markets, were greatly upset at the problems caused by the decay of the American economy. Not only did protectionism grow as a result, but the market uncertainties and the strong anti-Japanese feeling created great unpleasantness for Japanese living and traveling in America. Elaborate Japanese efforts at public relations in the United States, both through direct campaigns and through American public relations firms, backfired, for the Japanese could not understand that arguments which seemed so persuasive in Japan only antagonized foreigners, who increasingly distrusted the Japanese. Dedicated leaders in both countries, aware of Japanese-American interdependence economically and politically, managed, by great efforts, to prevent the growing mutual antagonism from leading to even greater protectionism and damaging the military alliance.

Perhaps most serious were the social effects in America. Labor unions, distressed by the decline in manufacturing, the loss of jobs to foreign countries, and the pressure for wage restraint, became more militant. The national government's disregard for their plight created enormous bitterness among those groups and regions adversely affected and strengthened cynicism and naked pursuit of self-interest on the part of others. The underclass of unemployed had sufficiently explosive potential that welfare payments did not decline, but the continued hopelessness of large groups of people led to increased crime and continued to impose enormous burdens on the society. Because company profits were down, the government eventually had no choice but to raise taxes to try to reduce the budget deficit, which nevertheless remained very large. The tax increase in turn further exacerbated the competitive problem.

3. CAN AMERICA STAGE A COMEBACK?

By 1990, whether American problems are as severe as described in the foregoing scenario or not, Japan is likely to be an even stronger competitor. The results of the superior Japanese system were little felt in the 1960s when the Japanese were still catching up. By the 1980s the cumulative effects had already transformed the international competitive environment as Japanese products overwhelmed their American competition in field after field, in the U.S. and in Third World countries. In the mid-1980s America's worldwide trade imbalances were already $100 billion per year, almost half of it with Japan.

Japan is now poised to expand its high-technology and service sectors as it once expanded its heavy industry. By 1982 Japan's exports of computers and computer parts to the United States were higher in value than comparable exports from America to Japan, and the lead was growing. Telecommunications trade is even more one-sided. Japan is producing more college graduates in engineering than the United States and since 1971 about 50 percent more electrical engineers, with half the U.S. population. In the United States in 1983, Americans took out some 36,000 patents, the Japanese 9,000, but worldwide the Japanese took out more patents than Americans.

Japan is now passing America in the proportion of GNP going for research and development. The United States still spends more on R&D than Japan, but most of America's biggest efforts are in basic research and in military areas that have little commercial spin-off while Japanese efforts are highly concentrated in areas regarded as most promising for the commercial future: semiconductors, computers, telecommunications, biotechnology, ceramics and other new materials, lasers, fiber optics, pharmaceuticals. Just as Japanese steel companies, starting from scratch, built the world's most modern steel mills in the 1970s and 1980s, so new Japanese research labs going up now have state of the art technology to work on future research problems.

Many of the reasons for Japan's success are well known: the high quality of Japanese manpower, the large number of trained engineers, the commitment of employees to a company, attention to manufacturing and especially to product engineering, the low cost of capital, high savings rates, availability of long-term funds which permit a long-term perspective, global strategy, and government incentives to business. But these factors do not work in isolation. They are part of an overall system coordinated by key government and business leaders.

There is no reason to expect that this system will be any less effective in the coming years. In fact, given the expanded capital base, the improved educational and research base, and the extended informational networks, Japanese competitiveness almost certainly will be even stronger in the future.

Americans desperately need to develop guidelines for responding to this challenge. They cannot afford to go about business as usual, ignoring the force of the competition. On the other hand, they would be foolish to imitate slavishly Japanese patterns of success, rather than fashioning solutions of their own, fitted to their own traditions and drawing on their own strengths. They need to have a better understanding of the competition, but they also need to understand what parts of their experience are most relevant to the problems they now confront.

For each country, Japan and the United States, I have studied four cases of successful cooperation between the government and the private sector. For Japan, I chose shipbuilding because it was the first heavy industry to develop after World War II and because, though less well known than steel and autos, it was far more successful. It also represented government-business cooperation at its maximum. Next I chose machine tools, both because Japanese machine tools are now poised to dominate the world and because they are now so critical for shaping the future of manufacturing around the world. In addition, I wanted a sector that succeeded in spite of low government priority. Third, I chose the closing of the coal mines in Kyushu, because it is by far the largest case of regional decline Japan has yet experienced. And finally I chose computers and telecommunications, because of Japan's recent efforts to gain world supremacy in this critical field and because I wanted a sector to illustrate how Japan copes with new problems of research and development. All four Japanese efforts were designed to increase international competitiveness. .

To respond to the Japanese challenge, both public and private sectors in America need to reach out in new directions, and I therefore wanted to look at a range of cases where America achieved great success in major innovative projects. There are many such examples. I might have chosen TVA, synthetic rubber or other industries in World War II, the interstate highway program, aerospace, nuclear energy, or many parts of the defense industry. I chose NASA because it is the classic case of government and business working together to achieve a clear national target. I chose agriculture because it is the best example we have of close government-private cooperation to sell more goods in world markets. I chose private housing after World War II because it illustrates how our government can pick winners and provide special financial help. Finally, because many initiatives in reviving American industry will be taken by states, I wanted one example of how local business and government leaders broke new ground in advancing their particular areas and I chose one outstanding example, the Research Triangle of North Carolina. None of these efforts was designed to increase international competitiveness, for, until now, this has not been considered necessary.

In the final chapter, I present my own conclusions as to what America needs to do to make a comeback. In the eight case studies, four Japanese and four American, I have tried not to anticipate my conclusion but to report as objectively as I know how the main factors that accounted, respectively, for Japanese and American success.

Part Two

SUCCESS, JAPANESE STYLE

2

Shipbuilding: High-Priority Basic Industry

No story better illustrates the readiness of Japanese businessmen, engineers, academics, and government officials to work together than does that of shipbuilding after World War II. No story better illustrates their thoroughness in developing a global strategy to take advantage of opportunities and their determination to achieve global dominance. And no story better illustrates how excessive confidence and unrestrained expansion can lead to new problems when the world market declines and new competitors appear.

By the mid-1970s, only thirty years after World War II, Japanese steel-production costs were the world's standard because Japan's steel industry was acknowledged as the world's most efficient. Japan was producing steel of unexcelled quality, in the world's most modern plants, in the greatest quantity in the free world. By 1980, only thirty-five years after defeat, Japan was producing more automobiles than the United States. Its small cars were priced so low that American carmakers could not come close to matching them. Without import barriers in foreign countries, Japan would be producing and exporting far more steel and cars.

Yet both these achievements pale by comparison with the Japanese record in shipbuilding. In 1949, the Allied Occupation gave permission for the Japanese to revive shipbuilding, and seven years later, in 1956, Japan became the world's largest producer of ships. Since the mid-1960s, Japan has been producing each year about as much shipping tonnage as the rest of the world combined. Between the mid-1960s and the early 1980s the number-two position in shipbuilding passed from Britain to Sweden to West Germany to Korea, but during that time rarely did the number-two shipbuilder produce as much as one-fifth of the shipping tonnage that Japan produced.

One can argue that the Japanese experience in shipbuilding before and during World War II paved the way for the postwar development, but the achievements of the 1930s and 1940s are not in the same league as the achievements of the 1960s and 1970s. In 1919 Japan produced a record 611,000 tons of ships, and despite the buildup prior to World War II it did not surpass this until 1943. In 1944, its peak year of wartime production, Japan produced 470,000 displacement tons of naval ships and 1,580,000 tons of commercial ships. By 1965 Japan was producing twice as much tonnage each year as it had produced in all of World War II, and in the mid-1970s it produced more shipping tonnage each year than all the tonnage it produced from the late nineteenth century, when it began building modern ships, through the end of World War II. Beginning in 1967, Japan began producing more commercial shipping tonnage each year than the entire world had produced in any year prior to 1957. Furthermore, as Japan began expanding shipbuilding in the late 1940s, it had no exporting experience to draw on. Until 1945, except for a brief and unusual period in World War I when the United States, short of ships, and Japan, short of steel, made an unusual arrangement for Japan to produce ships for the United States, Japan never sold ships abroad until 1947.

1. PREPARING FOR REVIVAL

At the end of World War II, Japan's potential for shipbuilding could hardly have been greater. As a small island country with few resources, Japan needed fishing boats as a matter of survival, ferryboats for coastal transportation, and merchant ships for international trade. Yet it suffered from an acute shortage of ships. By the end of the war virtually all of Japan's ships had been destroyed. Japan had begun World War II with more than 6 million tons of merchant shipping, and it ended the war with approximately 1.2 million tons, less than half of it serviceable. According to the American Strategic Bombing Survey of Japan, during World War II the United States destroyed approximately 8.6 million tons of Japanese merchant ships and 1.9 million tons of naval vessels, about three times as much tonnage as Japan was able to build during the same period. The United States, in contrast, with a highly successful shipbuilding program and modest wartime damage, entered the postwar period with far more cargo ships (Liberty ships) and T-2 tankers than it needed.

Japan's docks were in remarkably good repair. A few shipyards near Kobe and Yokohama had suffered during the war, but the largest shipyards, concentrated along the Inland Sea west of Osaka and in Nagasaki prefecture, where deep coastal waters are relatively protected by land barriers from the stormy open sea, were virtually untouched. Even the shipyards at Hiroshima and Nagasaki remained basically intact. Japanese shipyards, being partly under water, were much more difficult targets than were ships. Besides, Allied planners had decided they would need Japanese docks and ports for the postwar occupation. The Strike Mission, assessing damage after World War II, estimated that Japan had approximately eighty shipbuilding yards capable of producing ships of 100 tons or more, thirteen of which could produce ships of more than 20,000 tons. The Strike Mission estimated the combined facilities could easily produce 800,000 gross tons of new ships a year, which, while inadequate for what Japan was to build by the late 1960s, was ample for Japan's shipbuilding production through the mid-1950s.

In 1945, thanks to its prewar and wartime shipbuilding programs, Japan also had the skilled manpower needed to build large modern ships. In Britain, which developed modern shipbuilding in the nineteenth century, shipbuilding skills were largely passed on by an apprenticeship system. To catch up, Japan, like France, made shipbuilding a high-level science and developed an elite university course, giving top engineers a strong theoretical base as well as high prestige. As shipbuilding became more complex in the 1950s and 1960s, Britain's apprentice-trained technicians had difficulty staying on the technical cutting edge, while graduates of Japan's leading shipbuilding programs in faculties of engineering gave Japan a high level of sophisticated leadership. Unlike France, which then chose not to expand an elite training program that produced about twenty shipbuilding engineers a year, Japan had been producing about a hundred a year in the 1930s and 1940s and continued to produce such numbers after World War II.

Because the construction of warships required higher levels of technology than that of merchant shipping, the Japanese navy had developed shipbuilding training programs rivaling those of the best civilian institutions. After 1942, when the Japanese navy took over the administration of all shipbuilding, including merchant shipbuilding, naval engineers had ready access to civilian shipbuilding technology. Although the quality of shipbuilding workers greatly deteriorated with the manpower shortages of World War II and the frantic efforts to replace the unexpectedly large destruction of ships through bombing, after the war, with the return of demobilized servicemen, shipbuilders had no shortage of skilled and unskilled workers.

Despite all these strengths and great potential demand, at the end of World War II no foreigners and few Japanese imagined that Japanese shipbuilding would soon dominate the world. In the late 1930s, Japan had generally ranked third or fourth among the shipbuilders of the world. In 1940, Japan produced one-fourth as much shipping tonnage as Britain, which had dominated world shipbuilding for over a century. In 1950, after modest revival, Japan again produced about one-fourth as much shipping tonnage as Britain. Within Japan, demand was virtually zero because shipping and fishing companies had no funds with which to purchase ships.

Shipbuilding is highly dependent on other industries, such as machine tools, engines, quality steel, and sophisticated electronic and communication equipment, and in all these fields postwar Japan was in a state of disaster. American officials sent to inspect the Japanese shipyards were amazed that ships could be built at all with the tools available. Japan appeared to lack the capital to build modern plants. The country was not then even considering building modern steel plants, the first of which was not completed until 1957. The shipbuilding engineers from various companies who began meeting in 1946 and 1947 to discuss common technical problems even had problems getting rail tickets to hold their meetings, to say nothing of locating modern equipment.

At the beginning of the war, the great battleships *Yamato* and *Musashi* had been state-of-the-art, but during World War II Japanese shipbuilding technology fell behind that of the United States and Western Europe. Under pressure to turn out tonnage faster and conserve materials, Japan was forced to lower the quality of basic design and to standardize its ships. Twelve types of ships, including four types of tankers and four types of transport vessels, became standard, and technology was therefore stalemated. With labor shortages, time pressures, and poor quality of materials, the quality of workmanship also deteriorated.

The Allied Occupation (1945–52) also limited shipbuilding potential. To eliminate the possibility that Japan might make war again, Occupation authorities initially wanted to eliminate anything, including significant shipbuilding capacity, that might contribute to rearming. In November 1945 the Pauley Report advised that Japan be allowed to produce only 150,000 gross tons of ships per year (less than one-tenth of peak wartime production) and that much of Japan's shipbuilding capacity be used for reparations.

These harsh plans were gradually softened. Initially Japan was allowed to produce small fishing and local shoreline transport vessels. In 1947 it was permitted to produce whaling ships to increase the availability of proteins in view of widespread malnutrition. Because whaling ships had to travel to distant seas and needed substantial engines, Japan could again produce real oceangoing ships. By 1949, when Japan began to be viewed as America's Asian ally against the rising Communist threat of China and Russia, and especially after the Korean War broke out in 1950, Japan was allowed a moderate expansion of shipbuilding. It was then in a position to lay the foundations for rapid growth.

Foreigners had underestimated two crucial factors that proved crucial to Japan's success: determination and national leadership. The determination came above all from an acute sense of vulnerability to cutoffs of international trade. This sense of crisis, despite foreign views to the contrary, was new. Only a century earlier, it will be recalled, U.S. President Millard Fillmore had sent a letter through Commodore Perry urging Japan to open its ports to trade. In the early twentieth century Japan not only had enough energy supplies to meet its needs but it actually exported coal, and once Japan acquired colonies the colonies supplied needed resources. The new sense of crisis began only on the eve of World War II with the fear of losing access to oil, and it was heightened at war's end by the loss of colonies and the return of 6 million soldiers and civilians from overseas. From 1944 to 1947, as a result of American bombing of Japanese shipping, not only did supply shortages strangle industry but food shortages caused widespread malnutrition. For the generation that had experienced these short-ages, the need to produce competitive exports and ships to carry them and the imports they could then buy required no explanation.

Japan's postwar industrial strategy gave priority to basic industries that could be building blocks for national growth: coal, electric power, construction, trans-portation, steel, ships. For exports, the country's leaders realized they would need to rely temporarily on handicrafts, textiles, and other small-scale industries in which Japan enjoyed the advantage of cheap labor, but they calculated that the need for imports could not be met by light industry alone. However, although many light industries might develop with little or no government assistance, heavy industry required government support. For some industries, therefore, the question was not whether they would receive assistance but when. Many Japanese doubted that Japan could ever become competitive in steel and autos, and at best that would be decades away. In one heavy industry, however, the Japanese saw the potential to become competitive within a decade: shipbuilding. It received high government priority.

2. THE FRAMEWORK FOR REVIVAL: THE SHIPS BUREAU AND THE COMPANIES

The government unit guiding shipbuilding development after World War II was not a bureau in the more famous Ministry of International Trade and Industry (MITI) but the Ships Bureau (Senpaku Kyoku) of the Ministry of Transportation. The Ships Bureau became the great nerve center for planning the revival and advance of Japanese shipbuilding. Ships Bureau bureaucrats were among the brightest graduates of shipbuilding engineering courses, mostly from Tokyo University but with a few from the shipbuilding programs at Kyushu and Osaka universities. However, their success depended less on their brilliance than on their readiness to draw on personal relationships from university and wartime days to get the best possible inside information and achieve the highest level of cooperation in mobilizing resources for the nation as a whole.

The Japanese government had initially played a major direct role in shipbuilding, beginning in 1853, when it responded immediately to the arrival of Commodore Perry and his black ships by lifting its ban on building large ships and establishing its own shipworks in Uraga, Tokyo Bay. The navy especially had played an important role in shipbuilding. But after World War II shipbuilding was done entirely by private companies, with the government playing only a supporting and facilitating role.

It took several years after World War II for the shipbuilding companies to get reorganized, and when they did the government concentrated its efforts on helping the ten biggest and strongest. Although hampered by lack of capital and physical plant and by restraints from the Occupation, these ten companies had people with critical know-how and they could hire experienced workers as demand increased. By the end of the Occupation, as the golden age was about to begin, the top ten shipbuilders in order of size were: Mitsubishi Shipbuilding, Kawasaki Heavy Industries, Hitachi, New Mitsubishi Heavy Industries, Harima Docks, Mitsui, Mitsubishi Japan Heavy Industries, Uraga (Sumitomo), Nippon Kokan, and Ishikawajima.

Mitsubishi Heavy Industries, the General Motors of Japanese shipbuilding, had its beginnings in 1857 when Dutch engineers helped build a forge in Nagasaki to repair foreign ships. The forge became a shipyard in 1871, and in 1884 it was leased to Yataro Iwasaki, who bought it three years later and used it as the centerpiece of his new company, Mitsubishi. Mitsubishi Heavy Industries soon became the preeminent shipbuilder. In the fall of 1945, amid the rubble of World War II, only one company in Japan announced examinations for new employees: Mitsubishi Heavy Industries. It took five new employees in shipbuilding, and the entire graduating class in shipbuilding at Tokyo University sat for the examination. As Japanese servicemen and civilians came back from overseas beginning in late 1945, all those who had been employees of Mitsubishi Heavy Industries were formally reaccepted into the company. Most of them had to be released temporarily because there was no work for them, but the hope was expressed that as the company revived it would gradually welcome them back.

The Allied Occupation originally intended to be very severe with the zaibatsu (Japan's largest prewar financial combines, of which Mitsubishi was one) but by 1950, when Mitsubishi was split up, Japan had become an ally and Occupation trustbusters were less severe. Mitsubishi Heavy Industries was divided into three companies, one in eastern Japan centered in Yokohama, one in the west centered in Nagasaki, and one in the middle centered in Kobe. Although the three were not to reunite until June 1964, they cooperated in personnel and technology, so division was not a great handicap. Like General Motors in its heyday, Mitsubishi Heavy Industries so dominated its sector that it could afford to be generous and did not use its clout to destroy competition. By its statesmanship, Mitsubishi maintained broad public support for the government measures it benefited from.

As in the case of New Japan Steel, which took a similar approach, its participation in shipbuilding associations and other cooperative ventures virtually ensured their success. Japan's famous cooperation among private companies and between sectors and the government does not work as smoothly as foreigners imagine, but in shipbuilding the power and enlightened self-interest of Mitsubishi leaders, along with substantial government support, made for easy government-business relations in shipbuilding.

The other powerful shipbuilding firms belonging to zaibatsu (later to be called "groups") were Mitsui, with facilities near Okayama, and Sumitomo, which had taken over the old Uraga works near Tokyo. These companies would soon be surpassed, however, by Hitachi and two other companies, Ishikawajima and Harima, which were to merge in 1960 to take over the old naval base at Kure and become the number-two shipbuilder.

Other companies also made good use of former naval yards. Aside from the submarine-building facilities at Osaka, which were closed, and Yokosuka, which passed to the U.S. Navy for ship repair, all naval bases were used by Japanese companies. Hitachi Shipbuilding Company, which grew out of the Osaka Ironworks, established in 1881, and which already had a major shipyard at Hiroshima, acquired the naval shipbuilding facilities in Maizuru, on the back side of the main island of Honshu. A new company, Sasebo Heavy Industries, was formed in 1947 to take over the large naval shipyard at Sasebo, Nagasaki prefecture. The naval facilities at Kobe were taken over by Kawasaki Shipyard, a part of Kawasaki Heavy Industries, long located in the Kobe area.

Hakodote Dock Company, located on the northern island of Hokkaido, maintained facilities that began with late Meiji (1868–1911) government efforts to develop that island. Nippon Kokan, a steel company as well as a shipbuilding company, had docks in the coastal areas east of the Izu peninsula.

3. BEGINNING TO REVIVE

The first new orders for ships that came in 1947 were for small wooden vessels to be used for ferryboat transportation and fishing, not what shipbuilders consider ships. Rather, the first real activity at shipyards began with scrapping or finishing ships already begun before the end of the war. Some Occupation officials initially proposed that the warships remaining after the war simply be sunk, just as the great battleship *Tosa* had been used for target practice and sunk in 1922 after the Washington Naval Conference. Eventually, Occupation authorities allowed them to be scrapped, and a good part of shipyard activity in the late 1940s consisted of tearing down the warships and other outdated and damaged vessels. At the war's end, some 122 steel merchant ships had been under construction, and after two years the Occupation granted permission for their completion. Some work was postponed for years because of shortages of materials. Meanwhile, shipbuilding companies turned to producing pots and pans, small engines, and other small implements to keep some of their people occupied and to make use of the scrap metal from the dismantled ships. It was to be years before shipbuilding workers employed in World War II could find work in shipbuilding again.

As hopeless as things then seemed, even in 1945 leading shipbuilding engineers began to meet to discuss how to prepare for technological modernization. A senior professor at Tokyo University asked a young faculty member, Masao Yoshiki, to organize a small group of leading young engineers in various firms to begin drawing up plans for technological modernization. A dedicated and deeply patriotic engineer with little patience for financial and other considerations, Yoshiki had long believed that shipbuilding faculty ought to be involved in actual shipbuilding activities. He had visited all the commercial shipbuilding sites during World War II.

Under the sponsorship of the Society of Naval Architects, Yoshiki began in December 1945 to consult broadly to select members and set the framework for the select task force of ten engineers that began meeting formally in December 1946. Their average age was under forty, but they were already responsible for engineering modernization at the leading shipbuilding companies and they were to become leaders of their companies. Seven of the ten were former Yoshiki students at Tokyo University, and the other three were from Kyushu and Osaka universities. Their common university and wartime backgrounds provided a basis for personal cooperation. When they first assembled, Yoshiki explained that, although they now worked in private companies, they must continue as they had in wartime to share information or else Japanese shipbuilding could never be revived.

As much as these eager young engineers wanted to deal with technological issues related to building large modern ships, the crucial issues that occupied their time during the first several years centered on how to make do with less than adequate materials. They could not, for example, find enough animal fat to use in the launching of ships and finally, on the basis of a Swedish patent, they hit on the use of small rolling balls. At their meetings, depending on which company had the appropriate facilities, individuals were assigned to explore certain technical problems. When a problem was solved, members in other companies knew about it the next day. Gradually this group took the lead in making key advances in the technology of welding, photomarking, and eventually "block" (modular) construction, so critical for postwar shipbuilding modernization. In 1982, Yoshiki, by then head of Japan's space agency, was received in an audience by the Emperor and awarded the Order of Culture for his contributions to shipbuilding.

4. PLANNED SHIPBUILDING: EXPANDING SHIPPING AND SHIPBUILDING

Aside from shortages of materials, the key problem for government planners was finding someone with the capital to buy the ships. After the war no private firms had the capital to create effective demand to take the place of the navy, which had purchased all the ships built since 1942. In May 1947 the Ministry of Transportation, responsible both for shipbuilding and shipping, implemented a scheme known as "Planned Shipbuilding" by which a government Shipping Corporation (Senpaku Kodan) ordered and bought ships and then leased them to shipping companies. As the shipping companies generated profits they paid for the leases and the corporation used these funds to order more ships.

Shipping companies hoping to lease a ship applied to the Shipping Corporation, which, with guidance from the Ships Bureau of the Ministry of Transportation, selected company proposals on the basis of which companies had the resources to make best use of the proposed ships. Once the corporation announced a decision to buy ships, shipbuilding companies submitted bids to produce them.

In the fall of 1947, with Occupation permission, the Shipping Corporation accepted its first bids from shipbuilding companies for twenty-three ships averaging about one ton each. The Shipping Corporation and the Reconstruction Finance Bank (a government bank formed to finance key development projects) supplied 70 percent of the funds needed to purchase the ships. Other government sources provided some 22 percent, and private banks supplied the remaining 8 percent. In a second plan, in late 1947, the Shipping Corporation placed orders for some twenty-eight ships averaging about two tons each, and by this time private banks had sufficiently revived that they could cover 23 percent of the financing. By the fourth plan, in late 1948, when the Shipping Corporation ordered some sixteen ships averaging about three tons each, 70 percent of the funds came from private sources.

Within a decade these early orders would seem minuscule. In the five years from the end of the war through 1950 Japan produced scarcely half a million tons of steel shipping, scarcely 3 percent of annual production in the mid-1970s.

Beginning in 1948, as inflation came under control and shipping companies became strong enough to repay loans, a new source of funds was tapped to provide loans to shipping companies, replacing the Shipping Corporation and its leases. When food and other supplies donated from America were sold to the Japanese public, the proceeds went as "counterpart funds" to Japan's Reconstruction Finance Bank, which in turn used them for public purposes. Counterpart funds supplied about half of the money for Planned Shipbuilding loans until the end of the Occupation in 1952. Decisions on what ships were built were made by the Ships Bureau on the advice of an outside advisory committee (Shin Zosenpaku Kenzo Shisakai) that became a repository of information about each shipbuilding company's history, capital, and capacity.

The Ships Bureau reviewed the requests of shipping companies for new ships twice a year, decided which ships would be built, and then placed the orders with the shipbuilding companies. Although the bureau required precise information on costs, it did not necessarily give shipbuilding orders to the lowest bidders. Rather, it apportioned the orders in such a way as to encourage some specialization among the shipbuilding companies and to provide balanced work for a number of the strongest ones. Its goal was less to save money than to create the strongest possible shipping and shipbuilding companies.

In 1951, when the Japan Development Bank was founded to supply capital at proprietary rates for Japan's infrastructure and its expanding industry, it immediately turned its attention to shipbuilding. The bank was in a sense a revival of the Reconstruction Finance Bank, which had stopped making new loans in 1949 following the Joseph Dodge mission to control inflation.

The Development Bank thus began as the Occupation was drawing to a close, and under the bold leadership of Ataru Koybayashi it focused clearly on long-term industrial development, with matching funds from private industry. Beginning with the ninth shipbuilding plan in 1953, as counterpart funds dried up, the Development Bank provided the loans for the Planned Shipbuilding program, and this system continues to the present day.

In the early years of Planned Shipbuilding, with so much money flowing from the government and so little flowing from private sources, it is not surprising that politicians were accused of meddling in the award of shipbuilding contracts. Indeed, in a famous 1954 scandal, officials determined that Eisaku Sato, minister of transportation, had used political influence, but his role was judged sufficiently modest that it did not prevent him from becoming prime minister. What is remarkable is not that there was such a case but how little political influence there was. Since standards and criteria were publicly discussed and arrived at, decided upon collectively by government bureaucrats who had a strong sense of elitist pride in their work, and monitored by an outside committee, it was difficult for politicians to wield influence unless the choice was between companies of approximately equal merit.

Over the years the amount of funds going to Planned Shipbuilding has increased slightly, but private financing has increased so much more that the program's relative role has declined. Indeed, its role is no longer to provide essential capital but to provide balance and predictability in a highly volatile market. From 1947 through 1980, through Planned Shipbuilding, Japanese shipbuilders built 1,153 ships weighing 35 million gross tons. For this program, the

Development Bank lent some 1,750 billion yen* to private companies, and private banks extended loans of 840 billion. Reasonable men have argued that, once shipbuilding was flourishing, Planned Shipbuilding was no longer necessary. But with the volatile market after the oil shock of 1973, even the most independent-minded shipping and shipbuilding companies acknowledged that government control through Planned Shipbuilding was necessary to provide a modicum of order to a troubled market. And no reasonable man has doubted that Planned Shipbuilding played an indispensable role in the early postwar years.

5. MODERNIZING AND PROMOTING EXPORTS

Many Westerners search for cultural explanations for Japan's success, but the history of Japanese shipbuilding since the end of the nineteenth century is rather the story of great flexibility in developing and implementing fundamentally new approaches. In the early 1890s, as the Sino-Japanese War approached, Japan was so concerned about war and so far from being able to produce viable warships that it used its scarce resources to buy warships from Britain. In 1896, after the war, it began to build modern ships in earnest. Despite tremendous efforts, it could not produce enough to meet its goals and continued to buy ships from abroad until World War II. Except for the brief period at the end of World War I, however, Japan was not able to export ships until 1947.

In 1947, no sooner had Planned Shipbuilding started than Japanese began to explore selling ships to other countries. The American market was hopeless because America had so many war-surplus ships, and even in Europe Japan had to compete for sales with America's surplus. Japan then had only small wooden ships to offer, for which the most hopeful prospects were the Scandinavian countries, which had funds and needed more fishing boats than they could produce. A bright and personable young Mitsui Shipbuilding official named Isamu Yamashita received permission from the Occupation authorities as early as 1947, being awarded passport #625, to travel to Denmark. He had studied diesel engines in Denmark in 1938 and 1939 and had established good relations within the Danish shipbuilding community. (In fact, three Danes had gone to Japan during World War II, two of them remaining through the end of the war to help Japan develop submarine engines.) Yamashita returned with detailed specifications for the first Danish order, a small fishing boat. Yamashita later became

---

* From 1949 until 1971, the yen-dollar exchange rate was fixed at 360 yen to the dollar. After the exchange rate floated, the value of the dollar decreased to 281 yen in 1973, rose to 306 yen in 1975, dropped below 180 yen in 1978, and thereafter rose, sometimes to as high as 280 yen, but generally remaining in the range of 220 to 250 yen to the dollar through early 1985.

chairman of Mitsui Shipbuilding, vice-chairman of the powerful business organization Keidanren, and one of the four Japanese members of the United States–
Japan Wisemen's Group.

Japanese also succeeded in getting orders for fishing boats from Norway and
the Soviet Union. Export sales began at extremely modest levels: a total of
22,000 tons for the years 1949 and 1950 combined.

Despite early promising beginnings and Occupation permission to expand, in
1950 the Japanese shipbuilding industry was glum. In 1949 the yen-dollar exchange rate had been set at 360 yen per dollar, and shipbuilders thought the yen
was overvalued. In September 1949, Britain had devalued the pound by about
30 percent, making the world's largest shipbuilder more competitive. In the
meantime, the cost of steel in Japan had gone up from 18,500 yen per ton in
August 1949 to 29,000 yen in January 1950. Japanese labor unions, then very
militant, were concerned that shipbuilding "rationalization" meant cutting personnel and were therefore determined to resist cuts.

In mid-1950 things suddenly began looking up with the start of the Korean
War. Now viewed as an ally rather than a former enemy, Japan was suddenly
allowed to let its ships travel as far as the United States, and new orders for ship
parts and repair came from U.S. ships docked in Sasebo and Nagasaki, near
Korea. With the increased demand for shipping created by the war, Japan received foreign orders for some 44,000 tons in 1951 and even more in 1952.
Considering their low expectations, Japanese shipbuilders were overjoyed.

In 1953, after the Korean War, the outlook of Japan's shipbuilding industry
again turned glum as orders lagged and builders had trouble matching the costs
of the British and other European shipbuilders. By 1954, however, orders began
turning up; production reached 133,000 tons that year and 452,000 tons the
next. Twenty years later those sales would seem minuscule, but at the time they
appeared gigantic.

The Japanese shipbuilders' new success in 1954 was in large measure a result
of technological modernization begun during the Korean War. With the new
opportunities created by the ability of Japanese ships to travel abroad and new
repair orders, Japanese companies tried to modernize as best they could. Because
their knowledge and capital were limited, the Ministry of Transportation in 1950
asked the Shipbuilding Rationalization Deliberation Council to develop a comprehensive and concerted program for shipbuilding modernization.

Until the end of World War II, the usual way to build a ship was to lay the
keel, rivet the ribs to it, and then rivet steel plates onto the ribs. Almost all work
was done in the dock after the keel was laid. Riveting was the most time-
consuming task, accounting for a third of the total labor in shipbuilding. With
the exception of a special complex technology developed by Kawasaki, it was not
possible to seal riveted ships to carry liquids.

After the war a new technology imported from America eliminated the ribs. Thereafter, once the keel had been laid, large steel modules or "assembly units" (known in Japan as "blocks"), eventually weighing up to 400 tons, could be brought into place and welded together without attaching steel plates to ribs by riveting. In an adjacent factory, outfitting (electricity, pipes, etc.) could be preassembled and incorporated into the blocks, which were moved by huge cranes to the dock. Step-by-step improvements in welding, steel, and productivity led to the increasingly larger blocks, revolutionizing Japanese shipbuilding in the 1950s and 1960s.

The new technology required much larger cranes than Japanese shipyards had ever seen, but above all it required new advances in welding and steelmaking, both of which involve complex technologies. Welding had been used as early as 1920 by Mitsubishi, but in 1935 a destroyer had sunk because of welding problems, and therefore, except for the Kure Naval Shipyard, Japan had essentially abandoned welding until the 1950s. Sophisticated welding instruments had been widely used for making American Liberty ships in World War II, but they were not generally available in Japan during or immediately after the war. Even U.S. Liberty ships had split apart at the welding seams in the early part of the war until it was discovered that the "rimmed steel" then used was inadequate to take the welds and the United States developed higher quality "killed steel."

Advances in welding, welding instruments, and steel could not be achieved in a single leap. Welding is delicate and must be tested with a wide range of alloys under wide ranges of temperature. The fear that the breaking apart of one ship, from one Japanese company, could wreck their export plans constantly haunted Japanese shipbuilders, leading to great care in testing every possible combination of welds and steel. They established standards for carbon steel higher than those accepted in the United States and Britain. Of course they sent study missions to learn what they could from America about welding and steel, but the learning was a slow process and they continued for years to import key tools and instruments from abroad. By the mid-1950s they were using their own welding instruments, but once alloys could be used with some assurance they introduced automatic welding ("union melt"), permitting long seams to be welded at once, and again began by using welding equipment from the United States. In major shipbuilding companies, welding was used for about 20 to 30 percent of the work by 1948, 50 percent by 1950, 90 percent by 1958, and 100 percent after 1965.

Since the Meiji period, Japanese shipbuilding companies had worked closely with steel companies to develop steel of appropriate quality. In 1934, to eliminate Japan's dependence on U.S. steel, the Ministry of Communications (backed by the Japanese navy) established a research and inspection center at Yawata, next to a large steel mill, to ensure that appropriate quality steel was available for shipbuilding. In 1950, faced with an acute shortage of resources for steelmaking, Japan closed most of its steel plants, concentrating production at the same mill in Yawata. Because Yawata was located on the northern coast of Kyushu, it could conveniently supply the shipbuilding yards in Nagasaki and the Inland Sea. At the time, there were still no ships to bring iron ore and coal to Japan in quantity, and because materials were so scarce the standard steel formula used at Yawata in the early 1950s included a considerable amount of scrap steel, available from former warships. When steel is reused it loses some of its tensile strength and is less suitable for welding. New research centers, sponsored by the steel and ship-building industries, therefore worked under great pressure to develop new alloys. By the late 1950s Japan was beginning to use its own "killed steel," and by the early 1960s Japanese engineers were convinced that their research on welding and steel had put their shipbuilding technology ahead of that of the United States.

Japanese engine technology had also lagged behind in World War II. In 1950, not yet able to produce their own engines, Japanese began importing large diesel engines from major foreign companies—B&W in Denmark, Mannesman in Germany, and Fulzer in Switzerland. In 1953 they began to invest heavily in turbine engine development, but they continued to develop diesel engines as well.

Shipbuilding modernization proved very expensive, and Ships Bureau officials were constantly trying to devise new fund-raising schemes. The most unusual and successful scheme drew on gambling proceeds from motorboat racing. Motorboat-race betting began in 1950, and in the following year, thanks to Ryoichi Sasak-awa, a law allocating these proceeds for shipbuilding passed the Diet. Sasakawa, a colorful strong-minded ultraconservative politician linked in the popular press with Japan's underworld, had been a Diet member in World War II and had enjoyed close relations with Japan's key political leaders. In 1949 when he fin-ished a prison term for wartime collaboration, he sought a new cause and found it in motorboat racing, which he proceeded to organize.

In 1951 Sasakawa founded the Japan Shipbuilding Promotion Association (reorganized in 1962 as the Japan Shipbuilding Industry Foundation) to admin-ister the betting proceeds, and thereafter he headed the organization for three decades. Although proceeds from motorboat racing were modest at first, they turned out to be extraordinarily lucrative. In the early 1980s, in appreciation for American help in the early postwar period, Sasakawa donated $50 million to found the United States–Japan Foundation, with Angier Biddle Duke as presi-dent, but his main focus was shipbuilding. In 1962, the Japan Shipbuilding Industry Foundation gave only 556 million yen to shipbuilding, but in its first twenty years, 1962–81, its contributions for ship-related purposes totaled some 377 billion yen. In 1981, for example, it gave 58.5 billion yen, mostly as loans for various shipbuilding rationalization projects. Rich as it is, the foundation is quite strict about the use of its funds: They cannot be used to purchase property or buildings, only equipment directly related to shipbuilding. Among foundation executives are former officials from the Ships Bureau, who ensure close coordination of their mutual efforts to help Japanese shipbuilding.

Because of the national priority for shipbuilding, not only the Japan Development Bank but other government banks were poised to do their share. In 1951 the Export Bank (founded in 1950 and renamed the Export-Import Bank in 1952) devoted 38 percent of its loans to assist the export of ships; in 1952 the figure reached 63 percent, and it remained above 40 percent until the early 1970s.

Japanese banks, like German banks, maintain close and long-lasting connections with private companies. For investment decisions they want all the inside information that sheds light on long-term company strength, especially the talent of key officials and their capacity to work together. Bank officials carefully analyzed publicly available data on the shipbuilding companies, but they also used connections to get reliable inside information. At banks like the Industrial Bank of Japan, superb research departments helped make decisions about which shipbuilding firms to invest in.

Modernization required not only funding but a broad overview of where shipbuilding should move and a framework for getting the cooperation to make this possible. Although Ships Bureau officials remained the key coordinators, they used prestigious leaders and academic experts to deliberate key issues and come up with recommendations that all competing companies would have to acknowledge as legitimate for strengthening shipbuilding in the nation as a whole. They had two such prestigious committees, the Shipbuilding Technology Deliberative Council, concerned primarily with technology, and the Shipping and Shipbuilding Rationalization Council. Both began work in 1950 and both commissioned research reports, translated foreign monographs, and published their own reports on major issues confronting the industry. These groups were very helpful in focusing on the key issues and in building a consensus for what needed to be done. At the same time groups of company executives, engineers, and lower level staff people constantly met under a variety of auspices or on their own to find areas of common interest. As companies expanded and became more competitive, they could not maintain the level of cooperation that the small group of engineers under Yoshiki had achieved in 1946, but they continued to find far more opportunities to share common research, marketing, and other information than is common in American industrial groups, and Ships Bureau leaders were constantly trying to strengthen these bonds of cooperation to develop programs of common interest.

Contributing to this cooperative framework are a number of research organizations linked with the Ships Bureau of the ministry, with private firms, or with both. One research organization directly under the Ministry of Transportation, with a staff that includes some 200 engineers and scientists, is the Ship Research Institute. The institute conducts some research projects of its own, but its principal aim is to monitor foreign research so as to give better policy guidance to the ministry. Another key organization, the Shipbuilding Research Center, is an association of private firms to support applied research of more immediate commercial utility. The Shipbuilding Research Association of Japan was established in 1952 to provide a forum on shipbuilding matters that involve broader public issues.

Although these organizations were helpful, the real work was done by the private shipbuilding companies themselves, and they have been ferociously competitive. Until retrenchment in the mid-1970s, they competed to build the largest and most modern facilities, reinvesting income whenever possible. In 1950 the eleven largest shipbuilding companies had 57.6 billion yen of borrowed capital and only 7.0 billion of their own capital, a ratio of eight to one. By 1956, the ratio was four to one, and in the meantime these eleven companies had increased their own capital some tenfold. From 1950 to 1955 they spent a total of about 20 billion yen for new facilities. Almost a third of this went for engine development, a fifth for hull assembly facilities, another fifth for transport facilities such as cranes, and the rest for improvement of docks and expansion of electric power sources.

The introduction of automatic welding, block construction, and large cranes, along with the virtual elimination of riveting, greatly speeded ship production regardless of size. Although measures are not precisely comparable because large ships permit greater efficiency per ton, still the progress is striking. In 1950, in major shipyards, it took an average of 136 worker hours per gross ton (a measure based on space for cargo) of ship built; in 1954 it took 98 hours, and in 1958 62 hours, worker output more than doubling in eight years. In August 1957, *Birtschaft Dienst* magazine could report that for a freighter of 10,000 deadweight tons (a measure of weight of cargo that could be carried), the time required from the laying of the keel until the ship was delivered was 281 days in Britain, 182 days in Sweden, 165 days in Germany, and 164 days in Japan. By then Japan had already closed the technological gap.

The terrible shortages of materials forced the Japanese to find ways to conserve materials and get tight inventory control. In 1957, on the basis of goods needed for ships launched that year, Britain had enough goods on hand to last for 3.7 years, Germany 4.0 years, Sweden 5.3 years, the United States 5.7 years, and Japan 1.8 years. Japanese creativity in inventory control would receive belated world acclaim some twenty-five years later.

All this—finding sources of capital, introducing new technologies, modernizing equipment, developing new efficiencies, and getting special help from government banks—was not enough for Japanese companies to remain price-competitive in the critical period after the Korean War. At this strategic juncture national awareness and determination made the critical difference.

One of the biggest stumbling blocks to success was the cost of steel since MITI tried to protect its "baby," the steel industry, just as the Ministry of Transportation tried to protect its "baby," the shipbuilding industry. At the end of the Korean War, a ton of rolled plate steel cost 44,000 yen in Japan and 30,500 yen in Britain. Lower labor costs in Japanese shipyards did not fully compensate for the higher cost of steel. Therefore the Development Bank stepped in to subsidize steel going to shipbuilding companies, reducing its price some 11 percent, and the Export-Import Bank lowered the interest it charged to shipbuilding companies from 4.5 to 4 percent.

Even this was not then enough for Japanese ships to match the price of British ships. At the beginning of 1954, therefore, a "links" system, used in the Sino-Japanese War of 1895, was revived. Shipbuilding companies were given special licenses to import raw sugar, which was in short supply in Japan. Shipbuilders paid low prices for the sugar, which they sold in Japan for a substantial gain. From late 1953 through March 1954, this links system provided, in effect, a subsidy of 10 billion yen, virtually all for shipbuilders. Their profits allowed shipbuilders to reduce the export prices of some forty-two ships weighing a total of some 855,000 tons by at least 5 percent. The links system continued through March 1955.

Even this was not enough to meet the export competition. Prices for ships to be exported were then set substantially lower than prices for ships going to Japanese shipping companies. From mid-1953 through 1955 the price of ships sold for export dropped to below $120 per ton, while those for Japanese shipping companies under Planned Shipbuilding averaged closer to $150 dollars per ton. In short, determined Japanese leaders used every conceivable resource at their disposal to meet price competition at this strategic juncture, and their success began to pay off handsomely after 1955.

6. OVERTAKING BRITAIN WITH THE GREEK CONNECTION

Having prepared their strategies, Japanese shipbuilders were ready to take advantage of opportunities that came their way. Already at the beginning of the 1950s, energy specialists began to suspect that oil would remain a cheap fuel and would be in great demand as industry around the world recovered from World War II. Owners of tanker fleets had the potential for making millions. It was Greek shipowners who had the funds and the confidence to act speedily. Operating tramps, ships without long-term contracts, they were always ready to place an order with a new company that built seaworthy ships at lower prices. They had no special relationships with Japanese companies at the beginning, but they found their initial purchases satisfactory. Most Japanese companies prefer to do business with trusted long-term partners, but by 1955 they were sufficiently confident of the Greek shipowners' intentions that expanding capacity did not even seem risky. By then Japanese economic planners were as confident as the Greeks about the growing need for oil and for tankers. In 1955, led by Greek shippers, the boom in tanker demand began. The Japanese knew what they had to do to compete with British prices and they were determined to do it.

British shipbuilding production had remained fairly steady through the early 1950s. Every year between 1949 and 1957, Britain produced between 1.2 and 1.5 million gross tons of ships. Japan, which produced .15 million tons in 1949, produced .43 in 1954, .83 in 1955, and 1.75 in 1956, when it overtook Britain as the world's leading shipbuilder. The next year Japan produced 2.40 million tons, almost twice as much as Britain. Although Japan's surpassing Britain was little heralded outside the shipbuilding industry, this turning point was perhaps as critical for Britain as the loss of its colonies, for Britain had dominated shipbuilding for almost a century and was not to be a serious contender afterward. It was perhaps just as critical for Japan, which was to dominate shipbuilding from then on and extend the lead to other areas of international trade. Britain, scarcely aware of the shipbuilding battle with Japan, had gone about business as usual. Meanwhile Japan had regarded the shipbuilding battle with Britain as a strategic opportunity and had mobilized accordingly.

It was perhaps inevitable that as shipbuilding became more complex and required higher levels of engineering, Japan, which treated shipbuilding as an advanced science, would overtake Britain, which treated shipbuilding more like a large-scale handicraft industry. It was perhaps inevitable too that a country as determined as Japan, with more information collected on foreign markets, more capital channeled to industrial development, greater continuous attention to technological modernization, and greater readiness of capital and labor to cooperate for the national good, would overtake a country less preoccupied with international competition. But the advantage that won the day with the Greeks over the British was not price, quality, or technology but the ability to promise rapid delivery and meet deadlines.

British shipbuilding companies, like companies elsewhere concerned about downturns in the economy, had substantial backlogs and were unprepared to expand rapidly to meet demand. Moreover, they had as many as twenty different unions and considerable labor unrest, and it was not always clear if the British shipbuilding companies would even be able to meet the lengthy deadlines for delivery that they themselves had set. Japanese shipbuilders had plenty of labor unrest when shipbuilding companies were cutting back on workers before and after the Korean War. They had often cracked down on militant unions and formed second unions with more friendly workers when they deemed it necessary. But in the mid-1950s, foresighted Japanese managers spent countless hours in informal heart-to-heart discussions with workers to gain their trust and positive cooperation to take advantage of new opportunities for their mutual benefit. Shipping companies, and especially those trying to take advantage of the tramp trade, required fast predictable deliveries. The Japanese met the Greek demands and the British did not. It was as simple as that.

Japanese companies were able to expand production at unprecedented rates and meet fast schedules not only because of their rapid modernization and the reserve of laborers from World War II but also because of their flexible use of temporary workers and subcontractors. Productivity increases came so fast in Japan in the early 1950s that shipbuilding companies rapidly expanded production without adding more regular employees. The top twenty-four shipyards in Japan in 1952 had 71,812 regular workers, and in 1957 they had 70,353. Company strategy was to keep a small regular work force, maintaining flexibility for upswings and downturns by hiring temporary workers when necessary and increasing the amount of goods supplied by subcontractors.

In 1955 and 1956 the Japanese shipbuilders did this on such a grand scale that they called it "human wave" tactics. Some subcontractors were even brought en masse into the shipyards to work alongside regular workers. In 1952 these same twenty-four major shipyards had 25,470 temporary and subcontracted employees, constituting some 26 percent of their workers. After the Korean War in 1954, this dropped to 15 percent, but by 1956 it rose to 41 percent and by 1957 to over 43 percent. In short, from 1954 to 1957 the shipbuilders increased their work force by roughly 50 percent without increasing the number of permanent employees, thus beating the British in the race against time.

7. EXTENDING THE LEAD

Japan expanded its share of the shipbuilding market just when international demand grew, setting a pattern that was to be repeated in other industries. But with the 1956 Suez crisis, demand leveled off. The world produced 8 million tons of ships in 1957 and 8 million tons in 1962. During this period Japan failed to take away England's old customers, but its share of the world market remained firm at 25 percent.

Because the domestic Japanese economy grew rapidly during this lull in world shipbuilding, Japanese shipbuilding companies diversified into other areas. Most large shipbuilding companies had long been diversified; without existing suppliers they had had to develop their own engines, cranes, scaffolding, and equipment needed on ships, and skills thus acquired could be used for nonmaritime purposes. In 1958, 46 percent of the business of Japan's top shipbuilding companies was unrelated to ships, and by 1960 this figure had climbed to 67 percent.

The Transportation Ministry took advantage of the lull in shipbuilding growth to scrap 730,000 tons of old and low-quality ships left over from the war and prewar days, just as it had scrapped ships in the 1930s. This greatly upgraded the modernity of Japan's merchant fleet as well as stimulating some shipbuilding demand.

In 1957, because Japanese shipbuilding companies had consolidated at a new high plateau, they required less special government help than in the period just after the Korean War. In 1957 the Development Bank ended special privileges for shipbuilders, including preferential interest rates. Until 1957 steel prices to shipbuilders had remained fairly stable, but then, despite valiant efforts of the Transportation Ministry to keep down steel prices to shipbuilders, prices rose, for the companies could no longer claim special need. Beginning in 1957, however, the new steel plants begun in the early 1950s began to come on stream so that by 1962, when shipbuilding took a new upturn, Japanese steel was cost-competitive. The continued modernization of Japanese steel plants and their production of high quality steel in the most efficient plants in the world was to give Japanese shipbuilders an additional advantage against competitors by the mid-1960s.

As they diversified during the 1957–62 lull, Japanese shipbuilders continued to upgrade their technology and their efficiency. In 1962, when world shipbuilding demand began to pick up again, the Japanese were ready, and again they moved to take advantage of the expanding market. European countries complained of dumping, but when Japanese representatives explained the scale and modernity of their new facilities, Europeans were taken by surprise and dropped their complaints. Such was the gap Japan had created since it had overtaken Britain six years earlier, and such was foreign ignorance of Japan's progress.

It was difficult to make sudden leaps in the size of ships because each new upgrading required new testing, new equipment, and new adjustments in the building process. Most growth was continuous, but the jump from the usual 30,000- or 40,000-ton ship to the mammoth supertanker represented a fundamental breakthrough. It was not the Greeks but a maverick Japanese oil company owner, Sazo Idemitsu, who had the imagination and the urge to get an edge over competitors, and in 1956 at the beginning of the Suez crisis Idemitsu turned to Hisashi Shinto, then chief engineer at National Bulk Carrier.

As a young naval architect, Shinto had taken part in building the giant battleship *Yamato* at the Kure Naval Shipyard, which National Bulk Carrier had taken over. Shinto was able to tell Idemitsu not only that the berth in which the *Yamato* was built was still intact but that many of the plans, still available, could be adapted for a tanker and many of the same workmen used. This reduced development costs and hence the price of the ship. Idemitsu therefore ordered the first supertanker, 114,000 deadweight tons (dwt) displacement. It was completed in 1959, precisely the same length as the *Yamato*.

Idemitsu had done some shrewd calculations before he ordered the ship. Until the Suez crisis, a 30,000-ton tanker leaving the Persian Gulf had a shorter route to Europe, via the Suez Canal than to Japan. However, the trip around Africa to Europe was longer than that from the Middle East to Japan, and a supertanker could not pass through the canal. Even with Suez reopened, a supertanker could carry oil from the Middle East to Japan more cheaply than a smaller tanker could carry oil to Europe through Suez. Because Middle Eastern oil was then cheaper than U.S. oil, the bottom line was that, with the supertanker, Japan would have the lowest energy costs of any industrialized country. It was a great coup for Japan, but the immediate success was achieved by Idemitsu and Shinto, not the bureaucrats.

Idemitsu again took the world lead, ordering the *Nissho Maru*, a 132,000-dwt tanker, completed in 1962, and then the 210,000-dwt tanker *Idemitsu Maru*, completed in 1966, again by Shinto working at Kure, now taken over by Ishika-wajima-Harima (IHI). Many shippers feared that a ship of 200,000 tons might crack, so it took another year of waiting before others were willing to try. Then came the age of the big ships.

When supertankers first appeared they were called "very large" (200,000 dwt or above), but they were soon superseded by another generation of still larger ones, then called "ultralarge" (300,000 dwt or above). New world records continued in 1968 with the 326,000-dwt tanker *Universe Ireland*, in 1971 with the 377,000-dwt *Nissei Maru*, and in 1972 with the 483,000-dwt *Globtik Tokyo*. With new analysis of wave resistance and structural dynamics, later generations of mammoth tankers became more spherical and cylindrical at the front end, fatter, and deeper, providing more enclosed space and faster speed.

It was the mammoth tanker and the expansion of shipyard facilities to produce them that raised Japan to unassailable domination of world shipbuilding in the mid-1960s. Beginning with Mitsui's new shipyard in Chiba in 1960, most other major companies followed quickly with new shipyards capable of producing supertankers. From 1956 to 1965 Japanese production of small ships (from 4,000 to 20,000 gross tons) increased 1.2 times, that of larger ships (above 20,000 tons) eight times, and that of large tankers thirteen times. In the second period of great increase in world demand for ships, in the mid-1960s, Japan's share of world shipbuilding increased from 25 percent (in 1962) to 50 percent (in 1966), a market share Japan roughly retained until the mid-1980s.

Hisashi Shinto became the best known of the engineers who revolutionized shipbuilding. He had learned a great deal from Dan Ludwig of National Bulk Carrier, which had leased the former naval base at Kure until 1960. There Ludwig had introduced modern shipbuilding techniques pioneered with American Liberty ships in World War II. Shinto had served as Ludwig's chief engineer and learned not only about modern American shipbuilding but about world shipbuilding markets. But that was only the beginning. After IHI took over the shipyard, Shinto continued to make creative new advances. A central part of shipbuilding had long been "mould loft development," the precise measuring out of the model to full scale, based on blueprints, and a mocking-up by highly skilled craftsmen of where the parts should be placed. Shinto eliminated this process by training higher quality people to do the original design with such precise specifications for final mock-up that it became mechanical, eliminating the need for skilled craftsmen and their laborious "mould loft development."

Shinto also conceived ways of developing stronger steel with a new formula of manganese and silicon, of building still larger blocks to speed assembly, of simplifying construction by finding ways to make more parts with the same standards, and of expanding and automating preassembly, thus greatly reducing the amount of time required once the keel had been laid. The great innovations were not, as some Americans imagine, precise engineering adaptations but whole new systems of production. So innovative was IHI under Shinto that his company basically caught up in sales with Mitsubishi and observers came in droves to see his new techniques.

The first visit of a worshiper to a Shinto religious shrine after the New Year is called *Shinto natsu moode,* and in the shipbuilding business the term became a pun to describe the first worshipful visit to see what Hisashi Shinto had wrought at IHI. But Shinto was not alone. Creative engineers at Mitsubishi and elsewhere were constantly pushing new advances, and new successes in one company were still (though less quickly than in the late 1940s) passed on. From 1958 until 1965 large Japanese shipbuilding companies cut the average number of working hours per one gross ton of ship from forty-six to nineteen.

Some of the greatest advances in the 1960s and 1970s were in electronics. The report to the Transportation Ministry in February 1960 from the Ship Technology Council advocated an increase in automatic controls, including the introduction of an automated rudder. With new advances, all ship controls could be combined in a single room and in 1961, for example, on the new ship *Kinkasan,* a system of remote control was developed so the ship could be guided from the bridge.

As the boom continued in the mid-1960s, aggressive Hong Kong magnates like Y. K. Pao and C. Y. Tung displaced the Greeks as the world's leading shipowners and, like the Greeks, they purchased primarily from the Japanese. More specialized ships for transporting raw materials and commodities like iron ore, coal, bauxite, pulp, and grain and products like autos replaced more general ships. The Japanese made all these, but they particularly excelled in supertankers.

From 1972 through 1975, Japan turned out thirteen tankers a year of 100,000 to 150,000 dwt and repaired eight to ten. The very largest tankers were produced by Japan alone. Moreover, in sizes that other countries could produce, Japanese companies enjoyed an estimated 20 percent cost advantage over their nearest foreign competitors. During the boom years 1962 to 1977, Japanese shipbuilding was extraordinarily profitable.

8. ADJUSTING TO RECESSION

In many respects the Japanese had been lucky. World trade had expanded during the period more than even they had anticipated, and their trade had grown with it. They had not been alone in predicting growth, but they had focused on it more precisely and moved with greater boldness. Bureaucrats had been resourceful in creating the awareness, the framework and the mood, and companies had moved with confidence and vigor. Success had brought new capital for investment, new confidence, and ever bolder schemes. If the Japanese made a mistake, it was that they were so heady from two decades of extraordinary success that they were not adequately cautious about possible downturns. Many leaders in the Japanese shipbuilding industry had expected demand for ships to level off at some point, but they were not prepared for the full consequences of the oil shock of 1973. The earlier "Nixon shock," which floated the yen-dollar exchange rate in 1971, had cost shipbuilders dearly. Orders had mostly been in dollars, and when the dollar value dropped from 360 yen to 308 yen, the payments they received bought 15 percent less in Japan. But this was minor compared to the problems of the mid-1970s, as world demand for ships all but disappeared.

The Japanese were still investing in vaster, more modern facilities—they still had a three-year backlog for large and ultralarge tankers—when the oil shock hit. As older facilities, located near cities, reached their limits, new facilities were built some distance away. At that time no foreign competitors were in the same class as the top seven Japanese companies, each of which could build ships of over half a million tons. These companies were confident that the cost of entry for other countries was so high as to assure their monopoly on big ships. Three companies—Hitachi at Ariake, IHI at Chita, and Mitsubishi at Koyagi—had just completed docks to build 1 million-ton tankers, for which they were beginning negotiations. In Koyagi, for example, in addition to a mammoth factory, the largest dock was a kilometer long and wider than the length of an American football field. Two cranes, each 125 meters wide, were together capable of lifting 600 tons.

Expansion always involved some risks, but for twenty years Japanese shipbuilders had taken risks and been handsomely rewarded. When the first oil shock hit in 1973, it was by no means clear that the world shipbuilding industry would undergo a prolonged slump. After the Suez crisis demand had leveled off, but within four or five years it had risen again. Even in mid-1974, when there were some 250 million tons of tankers available in the world, the Japanese Association of Shipbuilders was still estimating that the world would need 450 million tons by 1980 and they were ready to fill the gap. After mid-1974, however, orders for new ships fell precipitously. During 1973, Japanese shipbuilders had received new orders for tankers totaling 18 million tons, but during the last nine months of 1974 new orders totaled only 1 million tons.

By 1975, Japanese shipbuilders knew they were in trouble, for in one year operating capacity had dropped from almost 100 percent to 80 percent. By 1976 they had only a year of back orders and the world was producing some 300 million tons. During that year projections for world demand in 1980 were reduced from 450 million tons to 240 million tons. The crisis had a number of dimensions:

1. *The companies had just granted enormous wage increases.* After the 1973 oil shocks, the Japanese government stimulated the economy to keep up the growth rate, causing the worst inflation since 1949. Until 1973, Japanese shipbuilding had been more successful than steel and other Japanese industries in keeping down wage increases. The tacit formula for wage agreements that had kept peace in Japanese industry required that wages go up annually with profits and cost of living. In the spring of 1974, with inflation rampant, shipbuilding executives agreed to a 30 percent wage increase. To hedge against rising costs, shipbuilders tried to get purchasers to agree to contracts with escalator clauses to cover cost increases between time of contract and delivery, but competition among ship-builders was intense and they failed.

2. *Big-company facilities were not appropriate to the new demand.* The superiority of large companies was in supertankers, for which they had built appropriate facilities. However, with the cutback in oil from major Middle East suppliers, supertankers could no longer expect to be loaded at a single Middle Eastern port. Users diversified their sources of supply, and new users, like China and the United States, lacked supertanker facilities. Demand for small tankers grew at the expense of supertankers, the area of greatest Japanese strength.

3. *Small and middle-sized companies were crowded out by large companies.* As large companies began to produce smaller tankers and bulk carriers to make ends meet, they cut into the business of companies that specialized in such vessels. With fewer financial resources and less diversification, these smaller companies were particularly squeezed and turned to politicians for help.

4. *The effort to stimulate demand by cutting prices precipitated strong reactions*

from European shipbuilders. In the past, Europeans had lost market share but their absolute sales had remained remarkably steady, for Japanese exports had risen at a time of rising international demand. Now, with a depressed world market, the Japanese were cutting into sales of European ships. Although European shipbuilders and their respective governments had previously complained about Japanese dumping, European customers had continued to buy Japanese ships. The Japanese had never had import quotas on ships, but in the early 1950s, when foreign ships were more competitive, Japanese purchasers simply had not purchased foreign ships. Now European purchasers were threatening to do the same.

5. *Many shipbuilders were located in communities without other industries, and the effects of their contraction on employment were devastating.* Not only small companies but large ones like Sasebo, which had inherited naval shipyards but had had difficulty in adapting to commercial markets, were in trouble, and their communities were also seriously affected.

6. *Above all, Japanese shipbuilding companies had far more capacity than the world could absorb.*

Individual firms tried to deal with these problems as best they could. They again diversified and further reduced use of temporary personnel and subcontractors. They cut prices to stimulate demand, especially among Hong Kong shipowners, who by then had surpassed the Greeks in daring as well as size and were not averse to buying extra ships at bargain prices. Large companies built smaller tankers, specialized bulk carriers, and cargo ships, for which demand was still strong, thereby invading the niches of smaller specialized companies. Without some kind of agreement it was likely that smaller companies would quickly be eliminated and that no company would remain healthy.

Companies were not eager for government intervention because at best it made their lives more complicated, but it was a classic case of a depressed sector feeling it had no choice. There was no question about the government's capacity to enforce an agreement if the companies could reach a consensus. Although it was almost pro forma, the Ministry of Transportation had insisted on keeping the requirement that each shipbuilding company apply for and receive permission before building a ship. And the ministry could also offer financial incentives for cooperation.

Even though everyone acknowledged a crisis, it was difficult to agree on a solution, especially while estimates of the severity of the crisis kept changing. People had disagreed about estimates of future demand during the entire postwar period, and as long as there was hope for an upturn, companies were not about to consent to scrap facilities or even curtail output. Considering their past successes in betting on growth, it is surprising that the companies accepted predictions of declining demand as rapidly as they eventually did. Even when they agreed on the severity of the crisis, the differences among companies, especially small and large ones, made any consensus on a solution of their problem difficult.

As the crisis deepened, shipbuilding companies could agree on the desirability of the government's buying up shipbuilding facilities to take them out of service, but since the oil crisis, the Japanese government had gone into deficit financing to stimulate the economy, and Finance Ministry officials insisted on solutions that did not impose a financial burden on the government.

The conflict of interests between Japanese shipping companies and shipbuilders did not pose a serious problem when demand was strong, but the problem became acute in recession. The shipping industry immediately felt the effects of the glut in world shipping and wanted shipbuilders to reduce their output right away, a view that shipbuilders, needless to say, did not share.

For years after the 1973 oil crisis, discussions between these different interest groups went on continuously or, as some said, endlessly. The urgency declined in the early 1980s as conditions stabilized, but discussions again intensified in the mid-1980s as overcapacity again became acute. Two settlements were agreed to and implemented in 1976 and 1978, respectively.

In June 1976, on the basis of the first years of negotiation, the Shipping and Shipbuilding Rationalization Council made its recommendations. Because it was not then clear that the recession was permanent, the Ministry of Transportation did not then get an agreement to reduce capacity but it did set guidelines for cutting production: By April 1977, companies would reduce production to 70 percent of their 1974 peak, by April 1979 to 63 percent. The ministry sought a mechanism that was simple and easily enforceable, left initiatives with the companies, encouraged efficiency, and was more generous to the smaller, more troubled companies. The mechanism it hit on was simply to set man-hour ceilings. The seven largest companies, those with capacities for 1 million gross tons a year or more, were to cut their man-hours to 83 percent of peak beginning in April 1978, and to 55 percent in April 1979. The seventeen companies with capacities between 100,000 and 1 million tons were to reduce to 70 percent in 1978, and to 66 percent in 1979. The fourteen companies with capacities below 100,000 tons were to reduce to 75 percent in 1978, to 60 percent in 1979. They also agreed to the request of the Cooperative Association of Japanese Shipbuilders, which represents the small and middle-sized companies, that large companies not produce two or more ships in the same docks at the same time during the years 1977, 1978, and 1979, thus decreasing their inroads into the markets of small companies.

By 1976, of course, companies were already cutting personnel. In 1975 the thirty-five major shipyards had 184,000 permanent employees, 90,000 nonpermanent employees, and 90,000 workers in subcontractors' firms, a total of

360,000. This fell to 240,000 by 1982. Of course, the cuts were heaviest among temporary personnel and subcontractors, but by 1978 and 1979 even many permanent employees had to be released. In Japan "permanent employment" commonly represents not a legal contract but a sense of responsibility of management to do everything it can, including going in the red, to avoid discharging regular employees. In a crunch, workers can be discharged, but executives who do not first go to extraordinary lengths to retain them are shunned by friends as well as workers.

Conditions varied widely among the companies. Nippon Kokan, one of the seven largest, was primarily a steel company, with only about 12 percent of its products in shipbuilding, and many workers could be transferred to other parts of the company. Hitachi, the third-ranking shipbuilding company, with only 19 percent of workers nonpermanent, had much greater difficulty adjusting its personnel. Hakodate Dock Company and Sasebo, which were not highly competitive companies, were in particular trouble. Since most shipbuilding activities were localized in certain ports and because of the tight in-group feeling in Japanese companies, transfer of personnel was not easy. Even within groups, a company was reluctant to take middle-aged employees from affiliated companies, and once-proud and profitable shipbuilding companies were in the embarrassing position of having to plead with other companies in their Group for special help.

After 1976 the crisis was exacerbated by the steady appreciation of the yen. In 1976 Japanese ship prices were still 30 to 40 percent lower than Europe's, but the price advantage eroded quickly as the yen increased in value from over 300 to the dollar in 1976 to 290 in the spring of 1977, 240 in the fall of 1977, and 180 in the fall of 1978. In these two years Japan's share of the world's new orders declined from 50 percent to 43 percent. But a bigger problem was the continued decline in world demand with little hope of an upturn. As order backlogs disappeared, Japanese ship production fell from 16 million tons in 1976 to less than 12 million tons in 1978 and to 5 million tons in 1979. The situation had so deteriorated by 1978 that even the shipbuilding companies had to acknowledge that shipbuilding was not undergoing a temporary decline but had become a structurally depressed industry. They acknowledged that to avoid a total collapse of many companies and the ensuing social chaos they would have to work out an agreement that reduced basic capacity while leaving companies as competitive as possible in pursuing the world's orders for ships.

With shipbuilding very much in mind, the Diet in May 1978 passed a new version of the Structurally Depressed Industry Law. Shipbuilding companies accordingly filed a joint application for relief to the Ministry of Transportation, which announced in November 1978 a program that provided for:

1. *Special purchase of vessels by the Japanese government for its Self-Defense Forces and other government uses.* This program continued through fiscal 1981 and provided for construction of 300,000 gross tons in fiscal 1978, 1.6 million tons in 1979, and 1.8 million tons in 1980 and again in 1981.

2. *A Recession Cartel to reduce shipbuilding capacity and curtail operations.* To cope with the objection of Japan's Fair Trade Commission that administrative guidance to restrain capacity violated antitrust regulations, the Recession Cartel was formally organized in August 1979 and continued through March 1982. Capacity was cut an average of about 35 percent, with the largest cuts, as before, by the large diversified companies.

3. *Encouragement of the merger of smaller firms.* Firms that combined were allowed to distribute reductions in capacity and operation as they wished. Hence, a successful medium-sized company that took over two failing companies might keep its own facilities while drastically reducing the facilities of the failing companies, presumably making some use of their equipment and personnel. One effect was to enable three medium-sized companies—the Kurushima Dockyard (which absorbed Sasebo), Tsuneishi, and Imabari Shipbuilding—to make enough acquisitions to become major companies. Another effect was to preserve companies with the best facilities, as they combined with failing companies and took responsibility for disposing of failing company assets.

4. *Purchase by a new government-supported purchasing agency of land and facilities taken out of operation.* During fiscal 1978 and 1979, each shipbuilder contributed .1 percent of the value of new shipbuilding contracts for sizable ships for this purpose and slightly more in fiscal 1980. The government provided some additional funds to subsidize the process of taking land and facilities out of service. By 1980, some nine shipyards had been purchased through this agency, to be converted to other uses and then sold.

5. *A new scrap-and-build program.* For four years, beginning in fiscal 1979, the government paid shipbuilding companies to scrap some 4 million tons of outdated shipping, thus making Japan's merchant fleet still more modern.

6. *Indirect financial aids from the government to shipbuilding companies.* These included deferral of loan repayments, long-term low-interest loans to facilitate diversification to other lines of business, and special tax privileges, such as tax exemption on profits from sale of facilities and reduction of the fixed-asset tax on suspended facilities.

7. *Administrative guidance on some sales of ships so as to distribute orders to companies especially in trouble.*

The period 1975-80 was disastrous for Japanese shipbuilders. In 1980, with demand for small tankers, bulk carriers, and freighters beginning to increase slightly, their operation rate rose to 51 percent of the 1973–75 peak period from

39 percent the year before, and it continued to rise slightly in 1981. The industry was leaner than a few years earlier, but it still had excess capacity, especially for supertankers. Executives considered their remaining work forces still larger than needed. They continued to release temporary workers and subcontractors, to cut wages of regular workers, and to offer special inducements for early retirement.

As accustomed as Japanese shipbuilders were to expanding rapidly, their ability to reduce capacity while maintaining competitiveness and minimizing social disruption is almost as remarkable as their twenty-year record of growth. The framework for cooperation among firms and between them and the government proved as suitable for managing decline as for managing growth. By 1980, while still bloated with excess personnel and operating at only 50 percent of the capacity of 1973–75, most Japanese shipbuilding companies were in the black and competitive in the world market.

Compared to the golden days of the early 1970s, the outlook for Japanese shipbuilders remains bleak. They have, however, shown creative adaptation in new areas. Kawasaki built a pulp factory on a barge and towed it to the Amazon River, where it was parked and put into production. Hitachi built a water-purification plant on a barge and sent it to Saudi Arabia. Japanese lumber-mill ships purchase logs in Alaska, process them while en route to the state of Washington, and sell finished lumber there at prices lower than for local logs. Fishing boats that double as canning factories have been produced. Ships for ocean exploration, first built for the Okinawan Expo in 1975, have proved highly successful.

Japanese shipbuilders confidently expect that, as the length of Japanese vacations increases and the postretirement population grows, the market for pleasure vessels will blossom. But the low world demand for ships and the complaints of other countries about Japanese dumping make likely further bankruptcies and mergers. Japan's greatest worry is the unexpectedly rapid rise of Korean shipbuilding. At its peak, Japan turned out roughly 100 university graduates in shipbuilding engineering each year, but Korea in the early 1980s was graduating 400 a year while occupying 50 percent of the forty-odd student slots in MIT's shipbuilding course. Given Korean determination and low wages, no matter what the Japanese do, their world market share may slightly erode. By contrast, consider Japan's shipbuilding troubles: a 40- to 50-percent share of the world's market in a basic industry, companies operating in the black with the world's most modern facilities, and lots of spin-offs of technology and personnel to help other sectors.

9. NATIONAL INTEREST AND GOVERNMENT-BUSINESS RELATIONS

Shipbuilding illustrates what Japanese government and business can do together in a high-priority sector. Like steel and electric power, shipbuilding was considered worthy of special help at every stage, not only for that industry's sake but for its contribution to the economy as a whole. It therefore attracted continuing support from the entire economic bureaucracy, especially from its ever-attentive protector, the Ministry of Transportation. It also enjoyed the backing of the Diet, above all of members from shipbuilding communities, regardless of party.

Drawing on their century-long modernization efforts, Japanese government officials have been far more successful than those of socialist countries in developing a fruitful framework for working with a priority private sector. Their goal, to make Japanese shipbuilding the most competitive in world markets, was unequivocal and never changed, but the techniques and programs were flexible and had less to do with traditional Japanese culture than with what was judged best for adapting to new conditions. The government did give substantial subsidies, but, more important, bureaucrats persisted in trying to understand the big picture. They concentrated on the key strategic points, and they were resourceful in providing the environment that enabled companies to peform at their best.

Government officials were less the commanders than the coaches, constantly pushing the companies to greater efforts, creating a mood of greater urgency, calling attention to the severity of new challenges, providing the forum for companies to work together. They helped create a wide variety of formal and informal associations to bring firms into dialogue with each other.

Although bureaucrats had the power and the determination to make decisions when necessary, they were constrained by the views and interests of the shipbuilding companies, large and small, and of the labor unions. When no other choice was available, ministry officials would come down on the side of certain interests as opposed to others. Nonetheless, they exerted themselves to help find solutions in the interests of all.

Solutions were achieved not through some mystical consensus-making procedure but through (1) agreement that final decisions must be good for the sector as a whole and enhance competitiveness with foreign countries, (2) frank exchange of views among key interest groups, and (3) the power and commitment of association leaders and government officials to make decisions stick. What was called "government policy" was often little more than the enunciation of programs worked out by the shipbuilders themselves. The Ships Bureau of the Ministry of Transportation prodded and goaded the industry, but it succeeded only because it acted on decisions laboriously arrived at by the sector as a whole.

Unlike European countries, which provided direct subsidies and sometimes socialized their basic industries in the post–World War II period, Japan's basic industries remained private and fiercely competitive on world markets. Even when the government awarded contracts by planned shipbuilding, it was because companies had shown themselves to be competitive, and companies of all sizes knew that they had to struggle to keep modern, to keep costs low and quality high. Even when minimum prices were enforced, companies competed intensely in quality, delivery time, and productivity, preparing meanwhile for the next round of competition. Bureaucrats understood that the best solutions were those that gave companies adequate leeway to make whatever adjustments were required while keeping government support to a minimum.

Because shipbuilding was the first modern basic industry in Japan, it helped to drive the development of steel before and after World War II. The machinery used in shipbuilding and on ships helped propel the machinery industry. The development of modern engines for ships paved the way for the production of generators and power plants.

Shipbuilding was a training ground for the development of technology and of organizational frameworks for new sectors like automobiles and airplanes. It produced business leaders like Toshio Doko, who was to go on to head Japan's most powerful business community organization, Keidanren, and the major committee to examine government operations in the 1980s, the Administrative Reform Committee. It helped train government leaders like Eisaku Sato, a shipbuilding official in the Ministry of Transportation who served as prime minister longer than any other in postwar Japan.

In the United States, acting on the recommendations of various commissions that examined American shipbuilding and found its manpower costs noncompetitive, the government after World War II decided that it was not in the national interest to continue to subsidize the industry. Rather, a small shipbuilding sector would continue to produce warships and serve as a nucleus in case of national emergency. This may have been the correct policy at the time, but new problems arose. The government continued subsidizing shipbuilding for national defense purposes but American shipbuilding productivity fell far behind. In addition, America allowed the same fate to befall other heavy industrial sectors until, by the mid-1980s, it could no longer export enough goods to import the energy resources and consumer goods it wanted.

3

Machine Tools and Robots: Auxiliary Industry

After World War II, the Japanese assigned the machine-tool industry low priority. Indeed, early postwar industrial strategy kept the machine-tool industry farther back than it would have been had only market forces been operating. As the sector revived, however, government policy provided an environment and critical assistance that helped it to modernize, to achieve economies of scale, and eventually, by the mid-1980s, to dominate the world market. The experience of the Japanese machine-tool industry illustrates how the framework of government-business cooperation helped even a sector of low priority, and provided the base for strategic support when new opportunities enabled this sector to drive the "second industrial revolution."

The postwar machine-tool industry in Japan was in many ways strikingly similar to its counterparts around the world. Machine-tool companies everywhere make the small number of "mother machines" that in turn produce other machines, permitting other manufacturers to achieve what the machine-tool industry cannot: mass production. In Japan as elsewhere the industry was small and fragmented into hundreds of firms. In the early 1980s the United States and Japan, the world's largest machine-tool producers, each produced less than $5 billion worth of machine tools a year, and the entire world was producing only $30 billion worth a year.

Manufacturing firms around the world want rugged, dependable machine tools, and often they want them tailored to their particular needs. They have tended therefore to develop close relationships with reliable machine-tool makers or the dealers who sell their products. Because machine tools commonly last ten to twenty years and manufacturing firms often look to their old suppliers when they need replacements, small, reliable, long-lived family or familistic firms are characteristic of the industry. Not only in Japan but around the world, in Britain, Germany and in American cities like Cincinnati, Milwaukee, and Cleveland where German toolmakers settled, machine-tool firms tend to be familistic if not actually family-run.

In Japan as elsewhere, machine-tool workers and even managers have been artisans. Most low-level machine-tool workers in the early postwar period had received only elementary school educations, and even the higher level workers were products of the prewar five-year technical secondary schools. Machine-tool building in Japan, as elsewhere, was never elevated to a university specialty, although second and third generation family owners generally receive university training in business or engineering.

In all market economies, manufacturers want machine tools quickly when an economy is on the upswing, and few want any when it is on the downswing. Machine-tool companies must learn to manage these drastic cycles, especially in recent years when they have come rapidly. The trick is for companies to find ways in downswings to stay solvent and keep skilled workers occupied or otherwise available so when upswings come they can move into production quickly enough to satisfy impatient customers and take advantage of new market opportunities. One of the best techniques to prepare for downswings is accumulating backlogs of orders in boom times, but in the late 1970s long American backlogs were to give Japanese makers a major opportunity for global market entry. With a world strategy, the Japanese in the 1970s gave greater value to meeting demands of foreign markets than they did to meeting demands of their own.

In one critical way Japanese machine-tool makers differed from their foreign counterparts. They enjoyed close links with subcontractors, with the manufacturers, and with trade associations. At critical junctures these links proved enormously beneficial.

Like Japanese shipbuilders, Japanese machine-tool makers rely on subcontractors to help cope with market swings. This is easy because machine-tool makers and customers are both concentrated in major metropolitan areas. In the 1970s, 60 to 70 percent of Japan's general machinery, electrical machinery, and transport equipment was still produced in three large metropolitan areas (Tokyo, Osaka, and Nagoya). In 1973, 86 percent of the nation's machine tools were produced in those areas (48 percent in metropolitan Tokyo, 20 percent in the Nagoya area, and 18 percent in the Osaka area). Machine-tool makers that serve specialized manufacturers like the agricultural machinery industry in Niigata, the weaving industry in Kanazawa, and the papermaking machinery industry in Toyama have more difficulty in finding parts makers during upswings. But for the vast majority of Japanese machine-tool builders in the three metropolitan areas, the ready availability of nearby subcontractors is a great advantage in handling cycles.

In a sector composed of small firms, the connection of specialized machine-tool makers to large manufacturers has been highly advantageous. This has been particularly so for the machine-tool companies established by manufacturers to meet their own needs. Historically, many large Japanese firms—entering new areas, finding no Japanese machine-tool makers capable of meeting their needs, and anxious to get appropriate machine tools quickly—started their own tool-making departments. In the 1930s, for example, when Japan began to produce trucks and autos, Toyota developed its own machine-tool workshop. In 1937, as business expanded, Toyota built a new automobile factory in Koromo, since renamed Toyota City, a few miles away from the old plant. The machine-tool workshop remained on the original site and in 1941 became Toyota Koki, a semi-independent subsidiary producing machine tools. While Toyota Koki does not produce machine tools for Toyota's major rival, Nissan, it does get economies of scale by producing for many other auto companies, Japanese and foreign. Toshiba and Hitachi, large machinery producers, also established their own machine-tool subsidiaries. Other leading companies like Komatsu (construction equipment), Yanmar (diesel engines), YKK (zippers), Seiko and Citizen (watches), and Mitsubishi Heavy Industries (shipbuilding) followed the same strategy.

Over the years, as these subsidiaries grew, they generally increased sales to other companies and acquired a measure of independence, but in management style they have remained more like large corporations than small familistic firms. While permitted and even encouraged under certain circumstances to sell products to competitors of their parent companies to achieve economies of scale and acquire new experience, they know that keeping their parent companies satisfied is the key to their success. In return, as long as they perform well, they not only have semiprotected markets but access to new technology and capital for modernization. The close link between tool makers and large firms was to prove especially helpful with the coming of electronic controls as it enabled Japanese firms to move in this area with great speed.

1. IMPORTING MACHINE TOOLS

Modern Japanese machine-tool companies were started in the 1890s to serve newly developing industry, but they could not modernize fast enough to meet the demand for state-of-the-art machine tools. Until the eve of World War II, therefore, large numbers of tools, especially those needed for specialized and sophisticated tasks, were imported. In 1939, for example, Japan imported machine tools worth an estimated 157 million yen, then a very substantial sum. Just as American machine-tool firms got their start in the Revolutionary War and then supplied tools for America's emerging textile industry early in the nineteenth century, so Japanese machine-tool firms received their first big boost during Japan's first modern war, the Sino-Japanese War of 1895, and then supplied tools for Japan's expanding textile industry early in the twentieth century.

Nonetheless, the Japanese machine-tool industry remained much smaller than those of the leading industrial powers until the 1930s when it expanded to serve rapidly growing war industries. In 1931 an estimated 1,920 employees producing some 3.9 million yen worth of tools constituted the entire Japanese machine-tool industry. By 1944 some 103,000 employees produced some 723 million yen worth of machine tools. In 1937 there were some 295,000 machine tools in use in Japan, and the eight years from 1937 through 1944 the industry produced an average of 57,000 tools a year. At the end of the war Japan had some 600,000 used machine tools, far more than could be used in the early postwar years before industrial activity revived.

After World War II, Japanese leaders tried hard to persuade Occupation officials to eliminate or at least reduce their demands for Japanese reparations to war-damaged countries. Nonetheless, some 40,000 of these used machine tools were shipped to China and Southeast Asia to assist their industrial revival. Japanese leaders also tried to persuade the Occupation not to destroy "war-related" machine tools. When the Occupation decided in 1948 that no more machine tools would be used for reparations and that, aside from modest scrapping of dilapidated stock, machine tools would not be destroyed, most Japanese leaders were enormously relieved. Machine-tool makers looking forward to revival, however, realized their problem. The availability of so many inexpensive used machines dampened demand for new machines. Eliminating reparations may have been good for the nation but not for them. Unlike the shipbuilding industry, which got off to a vigorous start replacing ships sunk in the war, the machine-tool industry remained moribund until the mid-1950s.

During rapid modernization in the 1950s the key question was how best to use the limited supply of capital, especially the very limited amount of foreign exchange, to benefit the economy as a whole. Japan was technologically far behind. The first postwar American delegations to inspect the machine-tool industry were amazed that Japan had been able to sustain a war effort with such antiquated tools.

To catch up in the postwar period, Japanese industrial leaders endeavored to import a few foreign machine tools as models and then, through purchase of patents, licensing, or reverse engineering, to produce them locally. For simple, widely used machines and in high-priority areas, this was achieved within a few years, but with complex machine tools and in low-priority areas the process took decades.

Because Japan was so far behind in machine tools, because catching up would be terribly time-consuming, and because in the short run a small number of the most modern foreign machine tools could help Japan immediately to produce very modern machinery, it made sense strategically to import the most modern foreign machine tools. In the early years after World War II, bureaucrats monitored imports of foreign machines so carefully that each required approval, but advanced machine tools for Japan's most modern sectors were generally granted prompt approval.

In 1951 a young technician, Soichiro Honda, who three years earlier had started a company then worth $3,000, went abroad to visit factories and observe motorcycle races. An avid motorcycle racer himself, he was convinced that to get the attention of the world he would have to produce motorcycles capable of winning international races. When he saw how far ahead foreign motorcycles were compared to anything he could produce, he was aghast. While still abroad, he urgently contacted Mitsubishi Bank, which found him very promising and agreed immediately to lend him some $1.25 million to buy modern machine tools. He then went on a buying binge.

When these machine tools began arriving in Japan, Honda's subordinates were bewildered, and even Honda himself was not sure how all the tools would be used. But he and his assistants began tinkering to adapt and even improve the machine tools to make machines that would in turn make better motorcycles. He continued buying the most modern machine tools he could find anywhere in the world. He could not hope to acquire enough money to buy all the foreign machinery he wanted for his factory, but with a shrewd investment in the most modern foreign machine tools he could produce machinery as modern as any in the world and in turn use this for producing motorcycles.

Before the end of the 1950s his company had become the largest motorcycle company in the world, and his motorcycles were winning international races. It was later discovered that many of the same machine tools used for making motorcycle machinery could be used for making machinery for automobiles, but when he started producing automobiles Honda continued to get the most up-to-date machine tools anywhere in the world.

This strategy of getting the most up-to-date machine tools was a great boon to many modernizing Japanese industries, but in the short run it did not help the Japanese machine-tool industry. Since large Japanese companies were buying many of their most modern machines abroad, the Japanese machine-tool industry had trouble acquiring the orders and the support needed to become a modern sector competitive with the West's. In 1955 Japan produced only about $10 million worth of machine tools and imported about $11 million worth. Even in 1960, fifteen years after the war, when Japan was trying hard to produce the most widely used standard machine tools and was already producing some $150 million worth, it still imported $55 million worth of the most modern and complex foreign machine tools.

2. DEVELOPING INSTITUTIONS FOR GROWTH

In the early 1950s, Japanese machine-tool companies recovered very slowly, but from 1955 to 1960 machine-tool makers could scarcely keep up with the growing demand. Driven by the rapid expansion of manufacturing industries, which required new machine tools, machine-tool companies grew from almost nothing to producers of usable standard tools worldwide. As the companies began to revive, so did the organizations that were to furnish them links with outside developments in technology, markets, and strategy, links that later reports analyzing the failure of the American machine-tool industry were to acknowledge as sadly lacking in America.

Ministry of International Trade and Industry (MITI)

The prewar Commerce and Industry Ministry was reorganized in the late 1940s with a new name, Ministry of International Trade and Industry (MITI), reflecting its new commitment to international trade. Japan had accepted a role for government in guiding modernization since the late nineteenth century, but the scope, sophistication, and variety of the government's approaches have expanded greatly since World War II. The approaches are less a result of tradition than of careful analysis of new conditions and rapid adaptation.

Although their methods of operation have evolved, the 500 to 600 elite MITI officials have worked to formulate and guide the implementation of an industrial strategy in line with Japan's national interest. They aim to see the big picture of changing world economic trends, determine the basic course of action needed to improve Japan's future comparative advantage, and mobilize each sector to make its maximum contribution to the whole.

They have gradually fashioned their role as that of a coach of Japanese industry who gets others to help devise the plays. They do everything to build the strongest possible team, letting everyone know how he fits in with everyone else, creating the mood of excitement that breeds a cooperative spirit, but letting team members call the plays and do the playing. MITI bureaucrats don't do research themselves, but they aim to keep informed on relevant research around the world and to promote special studies where information is lacking. They evaluate national policy not only for how well it promotes favorable macroeconomic trends but for how well it promotes the health of the nation's firms and the welfare of society. The various sections of MITI are responsible for corresponding sectors of industry and commerce, but the interests of these sectors are balanced at the highest levels in the ministry and officials rotate among sections so as always to keep in mind MITI's overall mission.

Because their statutory authority and budget are sharply limited, officials have no choice but to work with others in formulating and implementing policy. MITI does not have as much independent power as many MITI officials would like, nor as much as many foreigners believe. MITI officials are constrained by all those with whom they must cooperate.

They are constrained by business associations that can be as passionate in defending their interests as businesses elsewhere and as resentful of outside interference. Although they may see representatives of major firms in a sector, MITI officials generally talk to representatives of the industry associations and to academics, journalists, and politicians concerned with the sector as a whole. To make the most of their influence and to facilitate communication with these industry associations, they use a minuscule amount of money to help the associations with organizational expenses and place former officials on their staffs. Associations, needing to keep MITI's goodwill, accept the funds and former officials. As needed, MITI officials encourage the creation of other outside associations and organizations to extend their leverage without diminishing their control or the intimacy of their inner circle.

MITI officials do not give loans themselves and must persuade the Development Bank, the Export-Import Bank, and other public and commercial banks of the wisdom of the loans they recommend. They cannot decide on tax incentives by themselves but must persuade officials in the Tax Bureau of the Finance Ministry, which considers MITI's requests in the light of overall national tax policy.

MITI officials are constrained by public opinion in general, but they try to create a public mood and prepare the public for dealing with issues that involve the national interest. Representatives of the general public, consumer, labor, and other groups sit on deliberative councils to review their major policies. MITI is also constrained by powerful politicians who sometimes represent particular local interests more effectively than MITI considers good for the economy as a whole.

MITI officials have power to grant licenses and patents and to determine which firms will participate in which projects, but the real power of MITI rests on the quality of its information, the care it takes in consulting with outsiders, the persuasiveness of its arguments, and the will to use its persuasiveness to favor those firms that cooperate. MITI officials have not always proved correct in their projections, but their thoroughness and the close consultation with business sectors spreads the burden of error, and like private business leaders they can change their estimates as new information becomes available.

Business leaders generally follow MITI's advice. They know that its officials are willing to exercise their authority when challenged and, more importantly, they know that MITI's advice represents more than bureaucrats' views; it represents the distillation of broad consultation. Companies know that MITI's advice, once formulated, has great influence with banks, politicians, other parts of the bureaucracy, and other industrial and commercial sectors as well, and they are rarely willing to challenge it.

Agency of Industrial Science and Technology (AIST)

AIST is a semi-independent organization under MITI with the mission of promoting technology useful to Japanese commerce and industry. It monitors scientific and technical developments throughout the world and consults closely with Japanese businessmen, academics, and other knowledgeable people to identify technology that is likely to be important for the nation's businesses. Through consultation with Japanese companies it tries to develop a rough timetable for technologies that are likely to be of optimal use and to encourage necessary patent and licensing arrangements or sponsor research that will make available the needed technology in a timely fashion. It has its own research staff, but although it does develop some base technology its goal is less to perform research than to maintain the capacity to evaluate and manage technological developments.

AIST evolved from a prewar institution similar to the U.S. National Bureau of Standards, but in Japan's century-long effort to catch up with the West, leaders set and used standards not only to promote uniformity but to encourage and measure progress. In the government reorganization of 1948, the twelve research institutes that had previously served corresponding national ministries to guide technological development in their respective areas were combined within AIST to provide easy coordination of all commercially relevant science and technology. Since then four more research institutes have been added to AIST.

Other organizations in Japan are also concerned with science and technology. The Science and Technology Agency deals with new areas that require major ongoing efforts like space and atomic energy. Universities under the Ministry of Education promote basic research, but they have modest budgets for large-scale research projects compared to that of AIST, and universities play a much smaller research role than in the United States. Companies themselves can deal with short-range research of obvious commercial utility. But AIST is the most important because its role—finding technology and science to assist the competitiveness of Japanese business—has the highest priority.

Since AIST's success is so easily defined by the usefulness of results to Japanese industry, the sense of responsibility, the social pressure, and the sense of urgency are much greater than in American basic research. AIST officials responsible for developing projects are embarrassed if a multiyear project achieves its results sooner than expected, but they are more embarrassed if the project does not achieve significant advances within the time frame originally announced. Until the 1970s when most projects were catching up with advanced work abroad, the time frame was more predictable, but as they move to the frontiers of technology Japanese planners are confronted with greater uncertainty. Nonetheless, officials are willing to take calculated risks when advisers, politicians, and concerned businesses understand and share responsibility.

The leading officials in AIST are part of MITI's elite engineering and technical corps, about equal in number to MITI's regular (administrative) elite. About twenty-five such young people, graduates in science and engineering from Japan's best universities, enter MITI each year to become administrators in science and technology. They are rotated between MITI proper, where they are concerned with broad issues of science and technology policy, and AIST, where they are concerned with the selection and administration of research projects. In addition to these technical administrators, professional researchers and lower level technical staff are recruited directly into AIST and the sixteen labs under it. In all, about 4,000 people work in AIST and the research labs under it.

Of AIST's labs, seven are spread throughout Japan to assist industry in various regions, but the other nine were brought together in the 1970s in the newly developed science city of Tsukuba, north of Tokyo. These nine labs try to remain on top of basic developments in their respective fields, but to maintain easy control they do not ordinarily take in external fellows. Large projects involving substantial company personnel are organized in a wide variety of special outside facilities, often designed for a specific project. On some projects, AIST may assign companies to develop certain technologies or prototypes within their own company facilities.

Although a number of the sixteen AIST laboratories, such as the Industrial Research Institute and the Electrotechnical Laboratory, conduct research related to the machinery and the machine-tool industry, by far the most important laboratory for the machinery industry is the Mechanical Engineering Laboratory, which by the late 1970s had stabilized with a staff of some 300 people, about 220 of them professionals. Among the topics they have investigated are numerical control machinery, machining centers, and flexible manufacturing systems. They carry on research on modern composite materials used in manufacturing, on computer-aided design, on robot engineering, on machining technology, and on the accuracy and reliability of machine tools. They do not ordinarily have day-to-day contact with the companies, but they are part of the network that funnels information, informally as well as by written papers, to machine-tool associations and to the individual machine-tool builders.

Japan Society for the Promotion of Machine Industry (JSPMI)

In the early postwar period, when Japan suffered from an acute shortage of capital and officials explored all possible sources of funds to finance rehabilitation and modernization, local governments and a number of ministries devised a system to use the proceeds of racing for public purposes. Just as the Ministry of Transportation was allowed to use boat-racing proceeds for shipbuilding, so MITI was able to set guidelines for the use of the proceeds from bicycle and motorbike racing to promote the machinery industry, of which machine tools was one small part.

At first, most of the money was used for rehabilitation of local communities, and then for the bicycle and the motorbike industries, but then, as these revived and racing income expanded, more was used for the machinery industry in general. Associations that administer these funds are officially private, but MITI officials consult closely. From the view of participants, the private nature of these associations had the virtues of shielding them from Diet debate and, later, after foreigners criticized Japanese subsidies, of making foreign scrutiny difficult.

By the early 1980s, with the growth of betting, racing funds were able to provide some 10 billion yen a year for the promotion of the machinery industry, more than 4 billion for export promotion, and more than 8 billion to help promote rationalization of various machinery industries. Only about 100 million yen a year went directly to help support the Japan Machine Tool Builders' Association, but a much larger amount was used to support the machinery industry, and a thriving machinery industry of course drives demand for machine tools.

There are two auxiliary research institutes under JSPMI, the Economic Research Institute and the Technical Research Institute. Because they are sponsored jointly by JSPMI and private industry, they are oriented much more toward immediate concerns of private industry than is AIST. The Economic Research Institute is a small institute that does not engage in basic research but aims to provide information about the current state of the economy, tailored to the needs of the machinery industry.

The Technical Research Institute was founded in 1959 and in the early 1980s had a budget of about 6 billion yen per year, mostly from racing funds, and about one-quarter from member fees and services. The institute's lab is small compared with AIST's Mechanical Engineering Laboratory but it does carry on small-scale projects and has, for example, helped develop in cooperation with Shin Nippon Koki and FANUC a five-axis machining center.

The main function of JSPMI, however, is not research but exchange of information. Since the late 1960s, JSPMI has had its own large building near Tokyo Tower, housing the offices of more than seventy associations connected with the machinery industry. It provides libraries, meeting sites, and other services to bring together businessmen, bureaucrats, and others interested in the development of machinery. Every day there are literally dozens of seminars and public meetings for the exchange of information, but information is ordinarily for members only.

Japan Machine Tool Builders' Association (JMTBA) and Japan Metal Forming Machine Builders' Association (JMFA)

These two associations, one for metal cutting (including turning, boring, drilling, planing, milling, and grinding) and the other for metal forming (including pressing, bending, and shearing) are in their American counterparts combined into a single association, the National Machine Tool Builders' Association. Yet the functions of the associations in Japan and America are in many ways similar. In both countries they provide information for members, lobby on behalf of the industry, and prepare for trade fairs. But there are two crucial differences. Japanese associations are not constrained from working together by fear of antitrust actions and they are more closely linked to a strong outside network, to MITI and JSPMI. These differences bring to Japanese firms better worldwide technological and marketing information and involve the associations in a much more active search for ways to upgrade the sector as a whole.

By helping MITI formulate strategy on behalf of the whole sector, the Japanese associations consider issues and hammer out agreements that their American counterparts do not. The link with government policy makes for a stronger association, for top leaders of Japan's machine-tool firms consider these issues critical to their success. It is not so much that the Japanese associations receive major outside funding, although they receive some and are housed in the JSPMI building. It is that the continuous liaison with a strong supportive outside network, now reinforced by location in the same JSPMI building as other machinery-related associations and by association officers who were formerly MITI officials, immeasurably strengthens Japanese associations and, indirectly, Japanese firms.

America's National Machine Tool Builders' Association has about 300 to 350 member companies, about 85 percent of machine-tool companies. In Japan, as in most countries, the metal-cutting sector is three to four times as large as the metal-forming sector, but Japan has so many small metal-forming companies that the two associations have approximately the same number of members. When JMTBA was founded in 1951 companies were very small. Many rustic family companies doubted that the association would be useful, and only forty companies joined. Gradually, virtually all major companies saw the benefit of membership, and by 1982, JMTBA had 113 member companies, accounting for some 85 percent of total metal-cutting machine-tool production in Japan. In 1982, JMFA had some 117 member companies.

These associations by themselves do not guarantee company success, but their role in the network provides better information to Japanese companies about outside competition, marketing opportunities, and technologies. The firms run with the ball, but small, rustic, familistic, artisan firms are nonetheless taking part in well-informed discussions of global marketing strategies, something much harder for their American counterparts. These discussions encourage firms to devise common programs of research, development, and division of labor that their foreign counterparts do not. It took three decades for the value of this network to be fully felt in international markets.

3. SUBSTITUTING DOMESTIC PRODUCTION FOR FOREIGN

Although Japan still imported substantial numbers of foreign machine tools through the 1960s, even in the early 1950s promoters of the Japanese machine-tool industry, like promoters of other sectors, were using the magic word *kokusanka* (substitute domestic production for foreign). In 1951, as the Occupation was drawing to a close, the newly established Industrial Production Technology Council, reporting directly to the MITI minister, proposed ways to promote *kokusanka* in machine tools: replace old machines with new ones and general-use machines with specialty-use ones, speed semiautomation, and "rationalize" production. "Rationalization" became a key word for two decades, including everything that cut expenses and increased efficiency: introducing new manufacturing technology, reducing costs of supply, reorganizing to cut work time, and specializing to get economies of scale.

In time, as industries became competitive, rationalization was the key to a global marketing strategy, but in machine tools, far behind world levels, the purpose for decades was primarily defensive. Machine-tool makers concentrated on producing ordinary tools in great demand, and machinery makers bought domestic machines as they became available. No Japanese and few foreigners could disagree with the policy, and even foreigners who disagreed were silent, for they could not then conceive a future threat in their own markets.

In the early years, the machine-tool makers, especially small, independent ones, did not work well with MITI. They received little government aid, and they believed MITI was not doing enough to keep out foreign machine tools. As rustic, self-made artisans, they were not comfortable with elite bureaucrats who favored the "basic industries." Even when MITI began funneling aid to machine-tool makers, priority went to the bigger companies like Makino and Ikegai or to subsidiaries of major firms like Hitachi, Toshiba, Fujitsu, and Citizen, where MITI expected aid to have a bigger impact. The small, struggling, independent machine-tool makers hardly looked with favor on a policy that strengthened their largest competitors. The small, independent firms of JMTBA even fought strenuously to prevent an ex-MITI bureaucrat from being sent as a staff person to their association, and it was not until the 1970s that MITI finally succeeded in getting its former officials firmly entrenched in JMTBA.

Yet MITI bureaucrats wanted to help all Japanese industry, including, when consistent with their overall goals, the machine-tool industry. Much of what they did for machine tools they did either indirectly or for industry in general. The decision to scrap old machinery and replace it with new machinery of course helped create demand for new machine tools. The investment of racing proceeds in the machinery industry (reaching over 20 billion yen a year by the late 1970s) also indirectly increased demand. Similarly, the effort to stimulate the economy and to give tax exemptions on new investments in plant and equipment all indirectly helped the machine-tool sector. But in addition, the following measures were specifically intended to promote the domestic machine-tool industry:

1. *Strategic use of foreign exchange controls and assessment of import duties.* Until 1962 Japanese importers were required to get permission on a case-by-case basis to obtain foreign exchange to buy foreign machine tools. If a Japanese machine tool was available to perform the needed function, even if it was not as high quality as the foreign tool, the would-be importer was advised to buy a domestic brand. Duties and controls were also applied strategically. For example, in the 1970s, when Japanese planners saw numerically controlled machine tools as the wave of the future, foreign tools with numerical controls (NC) were assessed much higher duties. Not until 1983 did threats of foreign protectionism force a change.

2. *Subsidies for experimental production of advanced tools.* Beginning in 1953, MITI developed a three-year plan for the experimental production of Japanese machine tools with the goal of reducing the import of foreign tools. Individual companies interested in developing important new machine tools could apply for grants. In 1953, twenty companies were awarded grants totaling 100 million yen. In 1954, nineteen companies were awarded 95 million yen, and in 1955 seventeen companies were awarded 90 million yen. Similar strategic programs have continued since that time. For example, when machining centers loomed as important in the late 1960s, these were supported by MITI and JSPMI subsidies and displayed for the first time in 1970 at the Japan International Machine Tool Fair, the first event in what was to become a major export campaign.

3. *Analysis of foreign machine tools.* In addition to the sending abroad of a number of delegations to study foreign machine-tool developments, especially in the 1950s, in 1956 a research laboratory was established with a grant of 16 million yen to study imported machine tools. Funding for such programs was begun even

before the center was established. For example, in 1955 a grant of 25 million yen was made to study foreign machine tools. In 1967, as NC was becoming more important, 485 million yen were allocated for the purchase and study of several American NC machines, although not all the funds were eventually used for this purpose. Foreign machine-tool makers, seeing new Japanese tools very similar to their own, understandably felt that their technology was being stolen with Japanese government encouragement, but Japanese makers hoped to use the understanding of foreign technology to develop machines that were even better than foreign machines and sufficiently different so as not to be liable for international patent violations.

4. *Release of technology developed at government labs.* The Mechanical Engineering Laboratory (MEL) at AIST developed advanced machines and made available the technology either to Japanese firms in general or to certain firms especially able to make use of it. For example, an early numerically controlled jig borer known as JIDIC, developed in 1959, was made available for commercial development. Although machine-tool companies tend to have almost no direct contact with MEL and, when accused by foreigners of receiving subsidies, play down its importance, Japanese toolmakers do receive prompt though usually indirect information about new MEL technology.

5. *Rationalization programs.* For major new industrial programs, MITI commonly formulates and the Diet enacts a law granting authority to MITI to work out tax, financial, and other measures to implement the law. In 1956, the Diet passed the Extraordinary Measures Law for the Promotion of the Machinery Industry (the Kishinho) to be effective for five years. The law was renewed in 1961 and 1966 with some revisions and continued until 1971, when it was replaced by a new law combining the electronics and machinery industries. The law provided the base for the early rationalization programs for machinery, and machine tools were one of the eighteen areas included within machinery.

Given the small amount of funds available from the government for the development of machine tools, the best hope for rapid modernization was in pooling the resources of several firms and increasing specialization. Because of the intense competition among small firms, no one worried about the dangers of monopoly. Though many companies agreed that specialization was in their interest, precise plans were difficult to achieve because ambitious firms were reluctant to accept restraints, especially when the market was looking up. Particularly in the 1960s, MITI used the foreign pressure for trade liberalization, and the danger of huge foreign companies invading Japanese markets, to create a mood where associations could more easily achieve agreements between firms for specialization in product development and manufacture in order to give them economies of scale and assurance for undertaking major investments.

Although the sectoral association works out the plans, the association itself has little power over members other than moral suasion and must rely on MITI to enunciate the program and to enforce the sanctions to make it work. MITI has a number of meaningful sanctions. It can license new factories and products and determine when products do not meet standards. It can establish standards that assist the easy substitutability of parts between companies and products, making it easier to achieve economies of scale. It can provide limited amounts of funds for certain projects.

By assigning certain projects high priority, MITI can help obtain low-cost loans from government banks and special tax incentives from the Ministry of Finance. Furthermore, commercial banks recognize that such projects have lower risks and are therefore eager to fund them at low rates of interest. MITI did not hesitate to use these levers of power to push the sector forward and to make things difficult for firms that were less than cooperative. Thus even though machine tools had low priority within MITI, as long as the sector did not interfere with other national priorities strategic assistance played an important role.

The 1957 machine-tool rationalization program set 1960 quality and performance targets for lathes and milling, boring, drilling, grinding, and other machines. Some twenty-two companies were organized into a "rationalization cartel" to increase specialization and upgrade products, with a 1.8 billion yen Japan Development Bank loan. The industry considered the funds inadequate to reach the ambitious goal of achieving new machines of international quality, but for an industry still moribund in 1957 the program made an enormous difference.

Agreements among companies for specialization of manufacture were much easier to achieve when growth in demand leveled off and cutthroat competition threatened to destroy the industry. The first such year was 1960, and JMTBA members then reached agreement that companies produce tools only within broad areas of specialization. MITI enforced the agreement through product approval required of all new machines. Usually MITI gave approval automatically, but it withheld it for products outside a company's specialty. The biggest recession in machine tools since the revival in the mid-1950s occurred in 1965, when cutthroat competition forced fifteen members of JMTBA and even more nonmember companies into bankruptcy.

In that year, with strong MITI support, some forty-four leading companies organized themselves into ten groups to share information and increase specialization. The Number One Group, with 16 percent of the market, included Hitachi Seiki, Ikegai, Toyota Koki, Kashifuji, and Hamai Sangyo. A Tokyo group with some 10 percent of the market included Toshiba, Mitsui, and Makino. A Central Group, with some 11 percent of the market, included Okuma, Osaka, and Shin Nippon Koki. Other groups were the Automatic Group, Standard Group, Osaka Group, Kansai Group, Eastern Japan Group, Eastern Lathe Group, and Automated Machine Group. Members visited one another's factories for observation and held discussions of common problems. Within a year or two, the second golden age of machine growth made genuine cooperation more difficult. Some specialization and sharing of information continued, but many groups became largely social.

In 1968, with the cooperation of JMTBA, MITI tried a new way to increase specialization. An agreement was reached so that by 1971 companies could manufacture products only if they had 5 percent or more of the total market or if the product constituted 20 percent or more of the firm's output.

The efforts by companies to control ruinous competition and by MITI to promote sharing of resources and increased scale to meet foreign competition were not always successful, but they did have a cumulative impact. Specific agreements whereby, for example, Yamazaki would market a certain CNC lathe in western Japan and Ikegai would market it in eastern Japan were not common, but constant discussion about specialization did undoubtedly influence companies thinking about new products. Even companies that complained about MITI's efforts were sometimes quietly grateful to be protected against ruinous competition and to have an assurance that big new investments would pay off. The efforts worked because enough companies felt it was in their interest and MITI had the power to enforce the companies' agreements.

6. *Proprietary funding to counterbalance low-cost foreign credit.* Foreign companies are sometimes accused of not trying in Japanese markets, but many foreign machine-tool companies worked hard to enter the Japanese market and in the early 1960s they offered very favorable credit terms. Japanese users found these terms so attractive that MITI worked out an arrangement with the Industrial Bank of Japan and the Long Term Credit Bank whereby some 3.2 billion yen were made available to purchasers of domestic machine tools to reduce the cost and lengthen the time for repaying credit.

These programs, combined with the vigorous activity of the individual companies, brought quick results. By 1959, two years after the first rationalization program began, the *American Machinist* reported from the 1959 Tokyo International Trade Fair that "Japanese machines for the first time appear to merit recognition and to be competitive with machines of the most advanced industrial nations." This was not true for all types of machines, but it was accurate for an increasing number of them.

In the late 1950s, when Japanese companies had trouble meeting the explosive demand for machine tools, it was hard to keep down foreign imports, but the leveling off of demand in the early and mid-1960s made it easy to reduce dependence on imports. From 1960 to 1962, Japan imported more than 40 billion yen worth of tools per year, over 30 percent of its domestic machine-tool consumption, but in 1963 imports dropped 50 percent, and in 1965 they dropped 50 percent again. Once Japanese companies could produce acceptable machines of a given type, imports of that type of machine basically ended, even if foreign machines were competitive in quality and price. This combination of improved domestic machine tools beginning in the late 1950s and the leveling off of overall demand for machine tools in the early and mid-1960s thus made it possible for Japanese makers to increase rapidly their share of the domestic market.

By the time capital was liberalized in 1970, allowing foreign countries to form joint ventures (not wholly owned subsidiaries), Japanese companies could make most standard products. Still a number of leading foreign companies quickly formed joint ventures, generally to produce in Japan machines with which foreigners still had a technological advantage. Unfortunately for foreign companies, 1971 and 1972 were not terribly good for machine tools, and 1975 and 1976 were equally bad. By the mid-1970s many foreign companies were complaining that Japanese partners were not adequately pushing the machines in their joint ventures and that Japanese partners had taken their technology without giving adequate return. Japanese companies were complaining that American partners did not understand or adapt to the Japanese market.

Virtually all the joint arrangements for development of the Japanese market were dissolved, or they continued to exist in little more than name only, as Japanese partners began producing tools similar to those that had been made in the joint ventures. The dissolution was to end the serious threat of foreign market penetration for more advanced machines as it had ended foreign market penetration of the most popular items in the mid-1960s.

4. FAILING IN FOREIGN MARKETS

In 1962, when the shortage of foreign currency led Japan to promote exports wherever feasible, MITI set a goal of exporting 20 percent of new machine tools by 1970. By then, with the growth of demand for increased capital investment in railroads, the electric industry, heavy industry, and above all the auto industry, old wartime machine tools in Japan had been replaced by new tools. By 1963, according to MITI's survey of machines, there were some 673,000 cutting tools and some 223,000 forming tools in use in Japan; 40 percent were less than five years old. The value of machine-tool production had increased from 7 billion yen per year in 1956 to 82 billion yen per year in 1961. With this rapid growth, some machine-tool companies were developing economies of scale and, with the completion of the first rationalization plan in 1960, approaching international levels of quality. Unlike shipbuilders, machine-tool builders had not made rapid productivity gains but met growing demand largely by adding workers. When demand leveled off in 1960 and in 1965–66, they were eager to cooperate with

MITI's export push, for they much preferred searching for new markets to laying off workers.

Within months of MITI's setting these goals, forty-six Japanese machine-tool companies interested in exporting formed the Japan Machine Tool Trade Association. Before the year was over several machinery associations together sponsored Japan's first International Machine Tool Fair, through which they hoped to attract numbers of foreigners who might become purchasers of their machine tools. Within a year the new association opened display rooms in Chicago, Dusseldorf, and São Paulo, the most promising sites for foreign sales.

For export, the Japanese machine-tool makers offered medium-sized and small standard milling, drilling, turning, and grinding machines. Foreign visitors to Japanese fairs found these machines reasonable in price, but they did not sell well in the United States. For one thing, Japanese companies could not always take their most advanced products abroad because of licensing arrangements with foreign companies that prohibited that. More important, American companies whose manufacturing work could be interrupted if a tool broke down insisted on rapid service. When they bought a machine tool, they wanted it to be able to take abuse and last twenty years, and they wanted service within twenty-four hours. Japanese machines tended to be less rugged, and the small scale of their companies made it almost impossible to offer this kind of service to foreign customers.

Also, because the Japanese toolmakers were too small to have their own specialized staffs abroad, to establish an American presence most Japanese machine-tool builders worked through Japanese trading companies. These trading companies had many products they sold in much larger quantities than machine tools, and they did not give the attention to machine tools that they gave to products with greater volume. Furthermore, despite progress in Japanese machine tooling, it was the judgment of most American specialists that Japanese machines were not yet up to international levels.

The nature of the American machine-tool sales outlet made it particularly difficult to penetrate the American market. The machine-tool sales outlet expects to provide service and tends to have close relationships with its customers. It ordinarily carries only a single company's machine for a given size and type of machine. The best dealers in the United States already had machine tools from the best American manufacturers for most major standard items and were thus not really looking for machines from new companies. At best, Japanese machine tools were placed with lower quality distributors or even with distributors of used machine tools.

Despite these difficulties, some Japanese makers began to get a toehold in the American market by 1966 or 1967. However, no sooner had exports begun to rise than the Japanese market began to pick up so rapidly that firms were kept busy keeping up with orders at home. With the economy booming, skilled labor was scarce. Machine-tool companies were less attractive to workers than larger, more modern companies that were also seeking employees. Even subcontractors were hard to find. It was essential to keep their Japanese users happy, and thus in the boom of 1967 most machine-tool companies concentrated primarily on the domestic market, with the striking exception of an ambitious company that was to become Japan's biggest machine-tool producer in the 1980s, Yamazaki.

Yamazaki Tekko had not been one of the major Japanese machine-tool builders before the 1960s. In the early 1960s the five major machine-tool builders were Toyoda Koki, Toshiba, Hitachi Seiki, Ikegai (the oldest Japanese machine-tool company, founded in 1889), and Okuma. The elder Yamazaki had begun as a maker of pots and pans in Nagoya in 1919 with one apprentice, but he soon turned to making machines to make tatami mats, giving his firm the name Yamazaki Tekko in 1923. He first made machine tools in 1927 to meet the needs of his own factory. The company grew slowly, and in World War II Yamazaki became a subcontractor for the Nakajima Aircraft Factory, which produced Zero fighters.

Returning to pots and pans and the like after the war, the father was joined by his eldest son, Teriyuki, who had just returned from university study. In 1947, they opened a shop to repair and sell used machine tools no longer needed for war factories, including some foreign machine tools that had been imported in the 1930s. They rebuilt several hundred machines, including some first-class foreign lathes, before they turned to making new lathes in 1958. As part of the first machine-tool rationalization plan, they received a government grant of 50 million yen to purchase and analyze six foreign machine tools. They considered the experience of analyzing all aspects of the foreign machines extraordinarily useful in raising their technical level.

Two younger sons also joined the business, and in 1961 the father retired, passing the leadership to his three sons. The business had grown slowly, for the father had refused to borrow money, expanding only as the company's capital accumulated. The ambitious sons, buoyed by the enormous growth that began in the late 1950s (they reached 100 workers in 1959, 250 in 1961), immediately assumed a sizable debt to build a new factory, which opened with considerable fanfare in October 1961. Within months, machine-tool demand fell off sharply. This was followed by five bad years for the Japanese machine-tool industry. For some years the sons feared that their father's opposition to assuming debts had been correct.

In 1962, with a new factory and a large debt, the three brothers felt they had no choice but to push for new markets as rapidly as they could. Among other things, they packed machine tools in trucks and drove around the country trying to attract buyers. Although none of them had ever been abroad, they had experience with foreign machines and were determined to try their best at exporting, which the Japanese government and JMTBA were just then pushing. They had made their first overseas sale, a lathe, to Indonesia in 1961.

In the spring of 1962 the company took two models to Chicago, where they attracted the interest of Simon Morey, chairman of Morey Machinery, a specialty trading company. Morey came to visit the Yamazaki plant, and Teriyuki, eldest of the brothers and the company's president, made his first trip to the United States. Morey proposed to buy 200 lathes at $2,500 a lathe, 30 percent lower than the price for which it sold in Japan. It was to retail in the United States for $5,000 with a great many technical adaptations for the American market and under a Morey brand name, Hercules Ajax.

As unattractive as Yamazaki found the terms, the prospect of selling 200 machines to the American market was impossible to pass up. When the first thirty lathes were completed, Morey came to Japan to inspect the machines and found them unsatisfactory. It was a bitter blow to the Yamazaki brothers, but before the end of the next year they had machines that satisfied Morey. Later the brothers were to express thanks for being forced to raise their standards to meet the quality demands of the American market. In early 1963, a younger brother lead a team of Yamazaki employees on a two-month tour of Europe and America that included all sizable producers of lathes.

Closely studying techniques in Eastern Europe, Russia, and elsewhere, and adding some ingenuity of their own, the Yamazakis devised some techniques for producing larger numbers of small standard automatic lathes, developing economies of scale and competitive prices. By 1968, they were producing more engine lathes than any other Japanese company. By 1970, with a new factory, they could produce 470 lathes a month at peak times, becoming the world's largest lathe producer in value, second only to Britain's Colchester in numbers.

Yamazaki had gone into debt for the first time in 1961 to build a new factory. From then on expanding production required continued financing. Because machine-tool companies are small and subject to cyclical demand, and because banks in an era of capital shortage have so many other places to put their money, Yamazaki, like many other Japanese machine-tool companies, turned to a major general trading company, Marubeni. Marubeni handled the sales of some of the products both abroad and in Japan, but beginning with the serious downturn in 1965 the relationship with Marubeni ran into difficulties. In that time of pinch, Marubeni asked Yamazaki to produce far fewer machines. Yamazaki preferred to send out caravans of its employees to push sales or to make extra efforts in foreign markets. Yamazaki had similar divergences with Marubeni during the recession of 1971, but it still needed Marubeni's financial help. In 1973, a strong financial year, Yamazaki paid off Marubeni and terminated their relationship.

Yamazaki was also unhappy with Morey, who tried no harder than Marubeni to push Yamazaki products in periods of downswing and made its products indistinguishable from those of other Japanese makers by putting the same brand name (Hercules Ajax) on all of them. In 1968, at a time when most Japanese makers were turning to their home market, the Yamazaki brothers decided to open an office on Long Island and do their own marketing and service. American operations remained in the red for five years. In 1974, after two profitable years, they opened an American factory, getting a lead on other Japanese toolmakers. They believed that having their own factory would give American customers confidence in their service commitment and help expand sales. They had found that New York was not the optimum place in the United States for machine tools and located their factory in Florence, Kentucky, near the airport for Cincinnati, the heartland of the American machine-tool industry. Customers who flew to Cincinnati to look for machine tools could easily stop in to see their wares, and there they could easily find skilled workers. American machine-tool companies hardly noticed their coming, for their operations were small and most had never even heard of Yamazaki.

Yamazaki's commitment to America and its success in finding a way to produce a large-selling standard item—small automatic lathes—proved especially advantageous in 1975 and 1976, when the Japanese market dipped sharply but American demand remained strong. By 1976, some 62 percent of the Japanese company's sales were overseas, mostly in America.

Yamazaki was among the first firms to commit itself to numerical controls (NC), gaining an early lead. The brothers opened a technical development center for NC in 1966 and made their first NC lathe in 1968. They made two critical licensing arrangements, with Burgmaster (a subsidiary of Houdaille) for machining centers, and with American Tool Works for large NC lathes. They participated in the Japanese national System T project in 1970, providing two lathes among the twenty machine tools in the system. In 1971, some 10 percent of their products had NC and by 1973 more than 40 percent. By 1977 they had developed a system that went beyond the machining center, permitting more comprehensive manufacturing, which they named a "machining system."

In 1981 Yamazaki opened a new flexible manufacturing system (FMS) with eight machining centers for a small-parts line and ten on a large-parts line. A team of twenty engineers had spent six months designing the system and nine months writing the software. In 1982, it displayed at the Chicago Trade Fair a new flexible manufacturing system and then installed it at the Kentucky factory, the first FMS system in the United States for making machine tools. In 1983 it opened a new FMS facility in Japan that was widely regarded as the most advanced flexible manufacturing system in the world. These systems required an investment estimated at more than $50 million. Rival companies were convinced that Yamazaki had to assume a substantial debt, although Yamazaki reported it was debt-free.

The Yamazaki story illustrates the rugged entrepreneurial spirit that is very much alive in Japan. Yamazaki does not have close relations with the Japanese government, but without a small government grant it could not have mastered up-to-date foreign machines when it did. Without government efforts in 1962 to provide information and assistance for exporting, it is doubtful that Yamazaki would have gone abroad. Participation as an NC lathe maker in the System T project gave them national recognition for that specialty as well as invaluable technical experience. The government role, minor in financial significance, was therefore indispensable at certain strategic points.

Other Japanese companies were not nearly as successful in the American market. MITI's goal of exporting 20 percent of machine-tool production by 1970 was not met. Despite the success of other Japanese products in the American market, the total value of machine-tool exports from Japan to all countries in 1970 was less than 22 billion yen, about 9 percent of the value of machine-tool production (240 billion yen) and only 60 percent of the value of machine-tool imports. Domestic demand had absorbed these companies' attention during the boom years 1968–70, and the growth of the domestic market had pulled in a considerable quantity of foreign machine tools.

5. DEVELOPING NUMERICAL CONTROLS (NC)

Ask a Japanese familiar with the machine-tool industry why Japanese machine tools began to do so well in the late 1970s and the answer is likely to be: FANUC. The story of FANUC is inseparable from that of its dedicated president, Dr. Seiuemon Inaba, who has driven the Japanese development of NC machines. A compact, scholarly looking engineer-executive born in 1925, he hails from Ibaragi prefecture and has a strong Tohoku accent. Japanese find his rustic yet dedicated manner charismatic. He studied precision instruments during World War II to prepare for munitions research, graduating in 1946 from the Engineering Faculty at Tokyo University. Through Hanzo Omi, a Fujitsu official from his native prefecture, he was invited to join Fujitsu in 1946. In the same entry class was Toshio Ikeda, a brilliant mathematician who was to play a central role in Japan's computer development.

In 1955, Inaba was assigned by Omi to lead a small research group working on a topic considered important for the future, although still ill-defined: electrical controls for machines. Talented and determined, one of the few mechanical engineers in a company filled with electrical engineers, Inaba seemed a logical choice to head the team. The term "mechatronics," the linking of mechanical and electrical engineering, was to become popular in Japan, and its rapid exploitation is central to Japanese industrial successes in cameras, watches, and consumer electronics. In practice, it has meant the replacement of mechanical by electrical and then electronic functions.

In a ten-minute speech he gives to incoming employees annually, Inaba tells them that they are to forget whether they were trained in mechanical or electrical engineering and work together. When he began his work on NC, Inaba could tap into work that had started in 1953 at AIST's Mechanical Engineering Laboratory, at the Tokyo Institute of Technology, and at Tokyo University's Engineering Faculty. All this work had been stimulated by the news in 1952 that the Servomechanisms Laboratory at the Massachusetts Institute of Technology had developed a milling machine that could contour, that is, control the movement of the cutter on three dimensions. When Inaba and his small group began their work at the end of 1955, the MIT report on this research became their bible.

The research by Inaba took on sharper focus in March 1956 because of a request by Tsunezo Makino, then chairman of JMBTA and president of Makino Milling Machine, one of Japan's leading machine-tool companies. The previous fall, as part of the Japanese business community's exploration of export markets, a delegation that included Makino had been sent to India. In a meeting with an Indian machine-tool leader, Makino was asked whether Japan could make machines with NC. The Indian regarded NC as a sign of how advanced a machine-tool industry was, and Makino was distressed that Japan had none. Fortunately, he had attended the Machine Tool Show in Chicago a few months earlier and had seen a machine tool with NC. Makino replied that, while Japan did not yet have NC, his questioner should come to Osaka International Trade Fair in the spring of 1958 to see what the Japanese had accomplished.

Determined to meet his own deadline, Makino now made the rounds of government offices, but without success. Officials then regarded NC development as too uncertain to compete for funds with projects they considered more predictable and more urgent. Nor were the universities or the Mechanical Engineering Laboratory prepared to work on the project. Makino concluded that Inaba's group at Fujitsu was the most promising. Inaba and his group immediately seized the opportunity to produce an NC machine for Makino.

On December 25, 1956, Inaba and his group announced their first success in using NC to move a machine. They had used a primitive Sanyo motor, substituting parametrons for the 2,000-odd vacuum tubes used in the MIT machine (though parametrons later turned out to be far inferior to transistors), and they linked this to a Wiedemann punch press imported from the United States. Directed by NC, this simple machine punched holes in a small metal plate. Primitive as it was, it was the first NC machine announced in Japan and was a cause for celebration.

To the Inaba group, development of NC was not a task but a cause. By March 1958, in time to demonstrate at the Osaka Fair, they had put together an NC milling machine of sorts, though it was not yet commercially viable. By November of that year they had assembled the first NC machine tool that was actually used. It was a machine tool financed by Mitsubishi Heavy Industries' Nagoya Aircraft Factory in collaboration with Hitachi Seiki.

Fujitsu was not the only place that was beginning to produce NC. The Tokyo Institute of Technology research lab had produced an NC lathe in early 1957, and the Mechanical Engineering Lab had produced an NC jig borer in early 1959. Toshiba, Yaskawa, Mitsubishi, and Okuma also worked on NC, but it was Fujitsu with its leading position in computer technology combined with Inaba's indefatigable group that was beginning to take the lead. Fujitsu consolidated the lead with two new Inaba inventions in 1959 and 1960.

In 1959, assisted by newly licensed foreign technology, Inaba developed an electrohydraulic pulse motor. He used a tape with holes to pass electric signals (pulses) to the motor, releasing oil, and this controlled the slides, in turn moving the tool. The MIT machine had used closed-loop NC, which could not only command the machine to move but monitor the results. Inaba found no way to make a closed-loop system reliable. A stickler for reliability, he decided to use the less sophisticated but reliable open-loop system. America had more complex NC systems in use at the time, but Inaba's goal, like that of Japan's machine-tool builders, was to find an inexpensive, reliable way to make standard products in substantial numbers. By then the transistor was coming on stream to replace the parametron. The combination of transistors, the open-loop NC system, and the electrohydraulic pulse motor made possible a simple, inexpensive, commercially viable product.

Some thought it wise for Fujitsu to build machine tools, but Inaba and his group decided that if they did this they would be seen as a competitor by the machine-tool companies. If they wanted to get volume, it was wiser to cooperate with any number of machine-tool companies and to become specialists in NC.

With this new technology and the tie-ups with machine-tool companies, Inaba's section in 1965 emerged in the black for the first time, nine years after they began. Inaba was duly thankful to his superiors at Fujitsu, to Makino, to Mitsubishi Heavy Industries, Fuji Heavy Industries, and Japanese government officials who had helped in various projects to share the developmental costs. Their trust in him had weighed heavily on his mind until his efforts began to pay for themselves.

Beginning in 1966 and 1967, Fujitsu began a modest commercial expansion in NC, and by 1968 it had begun to make inroads into markets in the United States and Europe. From a section of Fujitsu, Fujitsu FANUC (Fujitsu Automatic Numerical Control) became an independent subsidiary in 1972. In 1982, deciding that "Fujitsu" in the title was redundant, Inaba shortened the company name to FANUC. Although Japanese continue to use the English term NC, in the mid-1970s, as the devices began incorporating minicomputers and later microcomputers into controls, making possible shorter and simpler programs, Americans began using the term CNC (computer numerical control). Whichever, FANUC became for machine control specialists what Xerox was to xerography.

A new round of technological developments in motors and microprocessors created opportunities for great market expansion of CNC in the mid-1970s. Inaba had been closely identified with the electrohydraulic pulse motor, and no one expected him to give it up soon. But it was messy, complaints had increased, and when costs of closed-loop DC motors began to come down quickly, he was afraid that if he did not change by mid-1974 he would begin to lose market share. Unknown to the outside, at the beginning of 1974 he had told his engineers to try to come up with a DC servomotor by May 31. If they could not, he would have no choice but to license a motor elsewhere.

On May 31, when the deadline arrived, his engineers had come up with a DC servomotor, but it proved unsatisfactory on account of noise. On that day, having investigated other possible technology in the meantime, Inaba wired a small Wisconsin company, Gettys Manufacturing Company, that he was coming immediately, and on June 3, in Wisconsin, he signed an agreement with Gettys to license the production of DC servomotors for a period of ten years. It shocked the industry that a company so proud of its own technology should give up its renowned product so easily, but Inaba was unsentimental. Someone else had superior technology and it made sense to license the Gettys motor—until seven years later, when FANUC replaced it with its own motors of similar design. Within two months after licensing, Fujitsu had ironed out the kinks in production, and although few would have thought it possible to move with such speed, it had a system on display at the International Machine Tool Fair in November. The replacement of the hydraulic system by a closed-loop electric system made the machine cleaner, more reliable, and more predictable.

In the mid-1970s, microprocessor technology made possible smaller control units with greater reliability, more capability, and lower costs. In the late 1960s, Inaba's NC for a lathe with transistor technology required 300 print boards. With new integrated circuits, he could replace this with five boards by the mid-1970s and in 1981 he was using one large print board. By the mid-1970s, advances in reliability and reductions in price had been sufficient for a rapid take-off in sales. Numbers are small compared to consumer products, but the 12,000 CNC produced in three years from 1975 through 1977 equaled the number FANUC had produced in the nineteen years from 1956 through 1974. By 1980 FANUC was producing 20,000 a year.

In the early 1970s, while FANUC was collaborating with Fujitsu in developing state-of-the-art large-scale IC (integrated circuits) for use in CNC, General Electric, whose Mark Century Control had dominated the world NC market in the late 1960s, fell behind. The division responsible for NC would later be criticized for complacency. GE divisions give purchasing priority to GE-produced equipment, and other divisions of GE made it the world's largest consumer of NC. Besides, higher management, aware that the demand for higher-priced CNC tools was not firm, lacked FANUC's continuous single-minded devotion to developing CNC. When GE woke up to FANUC's advances with new microprocessor technology, it rushed to market new equipment. Machine-tool companies later complained that this new equipment was unreliable and cost them dearly, for customers held them responsible for the total product, including NC, while Japanese competitors using reliable FANUC controls were invading their markets. Thus did FANUC's CNC overtake GE just as the market began to take off.

Meanwhile, by 1970 some developing countries like Taiwan had begun to produce high-quality machine tools with skilled manpower at much lower wage rates than Japan. MITI projected that by the end of the 1970s its machine-tool industry would be in trouble if it did not stay ahead with technological advances, and NC was the key to this strategy. Furthermore, if Japanese companies specialized in certain machines, all with FANUC controls, they could get scale economies and reliability, build up experience in the domestic market, and expand exports. With luck Japan might overtake the United States and Germany, then the world's two leading machine-tool makers.

To speed this process, the new basic law for machinery, the Kidenho (Extraordinary Measures Law for Promotion of Specific Electronic Industries and Specific Machinery Industries) of 1971, combined for the first time electronics and machinery, providing for a new rationalization program for machine tools using CNC. As in the 1957 rationalization plan, MITI set performance and quality standards to be met in 1977 by Japanese machine-tool makers for a variety of machines like lathes and drilling, boring, grinding, and milling machines. It stipulated that, by 1977, 50 percent of machines produced by Japanese machine-tool makers be CNC machines. Although Japanese machine-tool makers who wanted to develop new types of ordinary machines had difficulty getting government approval, getting approval for developing tools with CNC was no problem. As before, MITI encouraged companies to specialize in different machines so as to develop economies of scale and provided tax incentives for purchases of CNC machine tools. When capital liberalization was introduced in 1970 and foreigners could invest in machine tools in Japan, machines with CNC were excluded from the liberalization. Foreign CNC machine tools were categorized as computers and subjected to higher duties. It was a familiar story: strategic protection and encouragement for an area identified as critically important for the future.

The new CNC developments in Japan created excitement as Japanese companies raced against each other and against foreign companies to see who could incorporate CNC in the highest proportion of their tools. Foreigners scarcely knew there was a war going on, but at each machine-tool fair Japanese manufacturers and reporters for trade journals were busy calculating for each company and for each nation the proportion of new machine tools of each category that had CNC. At each successive fair, they happily reported that Japan was gaining. By the mid-1970s Japan was pulling even with the United States and by 1978 Japan was ahead, with 31 percent of its machine tools possessing NC compared to 28 percent for the United States. MITI's goal of 50 percent NC by 1977 proved too optimistic, but progress was rapid. In 1981, at the European Machine Tool Fair in Hanover, of the 1,000 CNC-driven machine tools displayed, 50 percent used controls made solely by FANUC, and another 30 percent had controls made by FANUC in a joint venture with Siemens. FANUC had by then captured 50 percent of the world's market for CNC.

No one doubts that this success would have been impossible without twenty-five years of persistence by Inaba's engineers. Yet Inaba's success would not have been possible without the Japanese government and many people like Makino who were looking out for the sector as a whole. Without the government labs, the development funds from the National Railways, and other national projects, the technical developments could not have taken place in such timely fashion. Without ready acceptance of the cartel-like arrangement whereby FANUC made products for virtually all companies, which in turn specialized in certain tools, they could not have achieved economies of scale. Without MITI's and JMBTA's constant efforts to promote awareness of the importance of the link between machinery and electronic controls and their search for means to speed the process, it would not have been possible to achieve the timely link between CNC and machine tools that was to provide the critical edge for Japanese dominance of the world machine-tool industry.

6. EXPANDING EXPORTS

By the late 1970s, as the Japanese reached advanced world levels in machining, not only did they enjoy a competitive edge in CNC machine tools but CNC tools opened a wider portion of the world machine-tool market, especially the large American market, for easy penetration. The machine-tool market is commonly divided into the commodity market of standardized machines and the "tailor-made" market of machines produced to meet a customer's particular needs. By the late 1970s, within the commodity market, a customer buying a machine and expecting it to last fifteen or more years generally acknowledged that CNC machine tools, being the wave of the future, were the wise purchase.

The tailor-made market required close relations between the customer and the user, and in America the domestic producer had enjoyed a decided advantage over the Japanese exporter. CNC, however, gave a tool much more capability and versatility, enabling a commodity machine tool to perform many functions previously requiring tailor-made tools. Because CNC commodity tools could get economies of scale that tailor-made machines could not, they could be sold at substantially lower prices. Thus when CNC became available, the commodity tools expanded partly at the expense of tailor-made ones, giving the Japanese exporter new opportunities.

The relatively slow years 1975–76, in both Japan and the United States, did not see an increase in Japanese share in the American market. But when the American market began to spurt in the late 1970s, American firms fell behind in meeting demand. In 1979, U.S. machine-tool companies had a backlog of about $5.6 billion worth of orders that would take about sixteen months to fill. Overly occupied with meeting their own orders and wanting to keep good relations with their customers, American firms were willing to cede the less profitable small end of the scale to the Japanese. The Japanese, who in their own home market had tended to run six months to a year behind by then, considered their home market in effect protected and gave priority in delivery time to foreign orders.

As in shipbuilding in 1955 and in many other sectors, it was the combination of expanding market and superior delivery times that gave the Japanese a critical edge. By 1979 they had acquired a better reputation for quality, and their low cost of capital, combined with a strategy of selling bare machines while maintaining ample supplies of accessories ready for fast service, enabled them to meet American service demands. By the late 1970s Japanese firms had also achieved significant cost advantages. During 1975 and 1976 the recession forced radical cuts in personnel. Even larger firms like Okuma and Ikegai were in danger of bankruptcy. As production resumed, the companies tried to raise production by introducing far more computer controls and reorganizing work without increasing their work forces. They were therefore far leaner but could even expand exports in the late 1970s when the value of the yen reached its peak. In 1971 Japan exported approximately $10 million worth of machine tools to the United States. By 1980 Japan was exporting $600 million worth of machine tools to the United States and had captured 40 percent of the American market for CNC tools of all kinds. In the early 1980s, as the yen declined in value, American firms were to find the Japanese cost advantage overwhelming.

The biggest-selling item was the CNC lathe. The Japanese companies had correctly identified lathes as a fast-growing market. Machine tools cannot yet be mass produced, but in lathes the Japanese had achieved significant advantages of scale. By the time CNC lathes began to level off in the early 1980s the Japanese were ready with another attractive market entry, the machining center. Developed in the United States, the machining center was first produced in Japan in 1966. Its flexibility in allowing one large CNC machine with rotating tools to perform on prismatic parts a wide variety of functions previously performed by many machines enabled the market to absorb more of a given model and producers to develop greater economies of scale.

With technological advances, spearheaded mostly in the United States, the number of tools that could be stored and rotated into use by CNC in a single machining center increased, separate racks of tools could be loaded in and out, and damaged or worn tools could be replaced automatically. After 1960 the Japanese had identified the machining center as important for the future, and Japanese companies rushed to make licensing arrangements with leading American producers. AIST's Mechanical Engineering Lab organized a development team and, with the cooperation of FANUC, Hitachi Seiki, Makino, and others, was by 1970 producing its own machining centers. By 1972 Japanese machine-tool builders were producing some 300 a year, although it took a decade before they began to dominate the world market.

With their low costs, Japanese toolmakers maintained their share of the American market in the severe recession of the early 1980s. Some estimated that Japanese in their enthusiasm had by 1982 close to a year's supply of machines warehoused in the United States, poised for a pickup in demand. The recession as always was difficult for American firms, but the low prices offered by the Japanese competition seemed below the break-even point for American firms. Some questioned whether Japanese firms were overextended and might be in trouble again as they had been in 1965 and 1975. In any case, many American machine-tool companies, some dating back for generations, confronting recession and low-priced foreign competition, were threatened with extinction.

Why was Japan so successful?

1. *Quality products at lower prices.* Japanese firms do have access to lower-cost capital. While Japanese machine-tool makers may not pay workers much less than their American counterparts do, they use subcontractors who not only provide a cushion for economic cycles but perform labor-intensive tasks at significantly lower costs. Some have estimated that as much as one-fourth to one-fifth of the work of toolmaking in Japan is subcontracted, reducing costs and allowing the machine-tool company to concentrate its efforts on a smaller number of tasks.

Japanese toolmakers also cut costs by not "rounding out a line" (producing a complete range of products) but producing only those products that are in significant demand. Specialization of products among firms gives a firm greater economies of scale. In the past, Japanese gained price advantage partly by producing simpler, less rugged machines with fewer add-ons. They sometimes sacrificed speed for steadiness and low cost. But now they have such a cost advantage from other sources that they are beginning to produce more rugged machines capable of greater speed.

The most significant drop in costs for Japanese toolmakers came from productivity increases since the 1973 oil shock. In 1972 the United States had about 77,000 workers in the machine-tool industry while Japan had about 55,000. By 1982 the United States had decreased the number of workers almost one-sixth to 65,000 while the Japanese decreased them by more than one-third to 34,000. During the same time, the value of Japanese production increased more rapidly than America's. The United States lacks detailed studies, such as those it has for the auto industry, comparing the efficiencies of Japanese machine-tool companies and its own, but observers of both countries acknowledge that Japanese machine-tool firms have found it easier to recruit electronics engineers than have their Western counterparts.

Japanese productivity gains came from improvements at virtually all stages of designing and engineering, but in recent years the greater availability of electronic engineers in Japanese machine-tool companies have been particularly important. These engineers have developed and adapted new manufacturing software systems that improve control of materials handling and scheduling, maximize "up time," (the amount of time the machines are actually running), extend the amount of time machines can be left untended, and group their machines so several tasks can be performed by a single operator. Because Japanese engineers who design products spend more time on the production line, their designs are often better adapted to the production process. Although no precise quantifiable studies are available, careful observers of machine-tool workers in both countries acknowledge that Japanese workers spend less time in casual conversation and in coffee breaks and other rest periods than do their American counterparts. By the 1970s, when Japanese machine-tool makers caught up in quality they were therefore able to pass on these quality goods at lower prices.

2. *National receptivity to new technology.* Although many small Japanese "job shops" still use simple old tools, once Japanese firms have the financial resources they replace old tools and machinery much more rapidly than their American counterparts do. The *American Machinist* reported (March 1977) that in 1973 in Japanese metalworking plants with 100 or more workers, 59 percent of the metal-cutting machines were less than ten years old as were 65 percent of metal-forming machines. Only 31 percent of American machine tools were less than ten years old. The low cost of capital, high depreciation write-offs, and other special programs encourage the purchase of machinery, but the competitive mood, the constant awareness that competitors are moving rapidly to modernize, causes

the Japanese to introduce up-to-date tools even before careful analysis shows they will be cost-effective.

3. *Global strategic thinking.* Because the American market has been until recently much larger than that of any other country, small American firms like machine-tool builders have overwhelmingly oriented their strategies to the domestic market. Since the 1950s the Japanese have been observing world markets, carefully comparing their skills and products, especially with those of Germany and the United States, the largest and most advanced machine-tool builders. While American demand for machine tools remained high during the early and late 1970s, American machine-tool companies enjoyed high profits and felt no great pressure to develop new products and higher levels of efficiency. Until the late 1970s, when the Department of Commerce, because of requests from the National Machine Tool Builders' Association, began getting better statistics on Japanese machine-tool exports to the United States, American machine-tool companies were not even able to monitor accurately the exports of their competition.

Although initially the Japanese had difficulty getting their products sold by reputable American firms, Japanese company names gradually became known and earned respect. Despite information about Japanese machine tools in trade magazines, recognition of Japanese products tended to lag behind reality. When Yamazaki first moved to the Cincinnati area its presence was virtually unnoticed by its American competition, but by the beginning of the 1980s it had become the firm to watch. In the *American Machinist* poll of brand preferences, the name FANUC was hardly recognized in the United States among users as late as 1978, but in 1980 it rose to thirteenth and, in an unprecedented rise, to second in 1982. As Japanese names became better known, better American distributors were willing to handle their products. In a period of great demand there is always a temptation, for Japanese as well as American machine-tool makers, to find shortcuts, to avoid the extra fees paid to a distributor, and sell directly to the buyer. For American distributors thus pushed aside in a time of big demand, nothing was more logical than to replace the American product with a Japanese one. Japanese firms patiently waited, poised to take advantage of opportunities.

4. *Superior links to outside systems.* The links to MITI, to AIST's Mechanical Engineering Lab, and to JSPMI provide superior information to Japanese firms for monitoring foreign markets and foreign and domestic competition. Perhaps more important than all these specific measures is the general climate of concern for the sector as a whole generated by the government and sectoral associations. The flow of detailed information among Japanese companies through common forums, publications, and foreign study contributes to this general climate and helps firms adapt to the international marketplace with greater precision and less risk.

5. *Strategic protectionism and cartelization.* At critical stages the Japanese government and the JMTBA made it difficult or impossible for competitive foreign products to enter Japan, and also assisted in the specialization of products permitting economies of scale.

7. DEVELOPING ROBOTS

In 1967 Joe Engleberger, founder of Unimation, went to Japan to lecture on robotics. When he lectured in the United States he attracted at most a few dozen listeners, but in Japan he attracted audiences of up to 600. In 1968 he signed a licensing agreement with Kawasaki, and by 1969 Kawasaki was producing Japan's first robots. While initially behind the United States, within a decade Japan was leading the world in robot production by a substantial margin.

The robot industry began largely outside traditional machine-tool companies, and robots are not ordinarily classed as machine tools because they combine several different operations of machine tools. Yet their development is now thoroughly intertwined with the development of machine tools. The controls FANUC makes for robots are virtually identical to those it makes for other machine tools, and in 1980 over one-fourth of what Japanese classed as robots used CNC. Even machine-tool makers that do not manufacture robots make machine tools that can be used alongside them in flexible manufacturing systems, and many of the leading machine-tool companies now make robots themselves.

Because robots can be developed and produced relatively inexpensively and are considered important future technology, many independent small companies as well as large machine-tool and electrical-equipment manufacturers rushed to produce them. By 1980 some 150 Japanese firms were producing robots. Many of the most successful robot makers (like Hitachi Seiki, Toshiba Kikai, Matsushita, FANUC, and Yaskawa) began by developing robots for internal use and debugging them before selling them to others. Their products cover an extraordinary range, and it was only beginning in 1976 that production was large enough for successful companies to get economies of scale. By Japanese definition, which includes "dumb" robots (pick-and-place robots that load and unload) as well as more sophisticated ones, 76,000 robots were in operation by the end of 1980. From 1968 through 1975, Japan produced 14,000; in the next five years production reached 60,000; and production continued to grow in the 1980s. Because America keeps statistics only on more sophisticated robots, those that can perform variable sequences, "playback" (in which information can be stored and then recalled), CNC robots, and "intelligent robots" (that can respond to different stimuli), America has no comparable figures, but by American definition at the end of 1980 Japan had some 14,000 robots, the United States 5,000.

Robot use increased rapidly after 1976 for several reasons in addition to Japan's general efforts to absorb new technology. First, with the great advance in microprocessors and their reduction in price, the cost of robots became more competitive with the labor they replaced. The inflation of 1974–75 following the 1973 oil shock was accompanied by very large wage increases, reinforcing this trend. As the rapid Japanese growth rate turned more moderate in the mid-1970s, Japanese companies became more cost conscious and cautious about hiring workers for whom they might have responsibility for more than thirty years. Instead, they hired temporary workers or installed robots. With robots instead of regular workers, they had lower fixed costs and thus lower break-even points in downturns. With growing affluence, Japanese workers continued to work hard, but they were becoming more reluctant to work nights or to perform unpleasant tasks. Demand for robots spurted especially in the auto industry because of the need for retooling after the oil crisis. Auto factories found good use for robots in painting and welding and became the biggest robot customers until 1980, when they were passed by electrical-appliance manufacturers. By then, the reduction in price of robots had enabled large numbers of small and medium-sized enterprises to make use of robots.

Japan could also move fast because of its employment pattern. Japanese unemployment was still under 3 percent in the early 1980s, the economy remained strong, and Japanese firms generally accept very great responsibility for the continued livelihood of their workers. But by the mid-1980s even in Japan some workers were uneasy about their possible replacement by robots, and Japanese employers, with considerable experience in getting labor cooperation for new technology, were sensitive to the issue, discussing it with worker representatives prior to introduction, reassuring workers about jobs, introducing robots first for unpleasant dirty work, and making detailed plans for retraining and reassignment of displaced workers. Most of the firms that introduced robots rapidly were growing companies that could increase production without reducing the number of workers except by attrition or reduced hiring.

As with CNC, MITI regarded robots as helpful to manufacturing in general and as a potentially important export item. By the time Japanese robot manufacturers were producing substantial numbers and had caught up with their natural demand, MITI moved to speed up the natural market forces to get economies of scale. In 1979, MITI encouraged the formation of the Japan Robot Leasing Company (JAROL) so users could lease robots at reasonable rates. The Japan Development Bank provided 60 percent of the capital, large private banks the rest. In addition, the Small Business Finance Corporation in 1980 set aside funds to be used as loans to small businesses to acquire robots. Knowing they had a firm market through JAROL, robot manufacturers did not hesitate to expand capacity.

Until the early 1980s virtually no robots were exported because internal demand was so great. As usual, Japanese waited until the experience curve brought down the price before rapidly expanding exports. It is no secret, however, that planners consider robots a promising area for exports. MITI estimates that 20 percent will be exported by 1990. By that time General Motors, which is forecasting the use of more robots than any other American company, expects, with a new joint venture with FANUC, to have 14,000 installed. Matsushita by the same time expects to have 100,000 installed.

In advanced research in intelligent robots, the United States in the early 1980s still held the lead, but Japan was beginning to give the field very high priority. In 1983 AIST's Electrotechnical Lab launched a seven-year 30 billion yen research program to develop intelligent robots. Some ten major robot, computer, and machinery manufacturers were combined into a joint research association, with roughly half of the funding coming from private sources. In 1983, a new association of academics working on robotics was launched with almost 1,000 members. With this concentration of efforts, there is no reason to believe that Japanese will be less successful in intelligent robots than they were with other robots.

8. LAUNCHING THE SECOND INDUSTRIAL REVOLUTION: FLEXIBLE MANUFACTURING SYSTEMS (FMS)

By the late 1970s Japan's century-long goal of catching up with Western technological levels was basically achieved. During that period it made little sense to invent basic technology, for it was cheaper to borrow than to reinvent, and the Japanese could concentrate on engineering improvements that would give them an edge over foreign competitors. In the 1980s, having already attained world levels, they intend to lead in many areas, or, as more diplomatic spokesmen put it, "make a contribution to world science and technology." Foreigners may take this as a challenge or competitive threat, but proud Japanese leaders, scientists, and engineers, who have been accused of being copiers, have a mission to prove their ability to the world. And "mechatronics," the link between mechanics and electronics, is at the heart of the mission.

AIST's Mechanical Engineering Laboratory is now undertaking many projects relevant to machine tools. Its engineers are conducting research to evaluate the rotating accuracy of the machine-tool spindle in order to improve accuracy in cutting. They are investigating machine-tool bedways, aiming for a configuration of bedways to facilitate machine loading and increase machine accuracy. They are investigating the use of gases as substitutes for bearings, the use of traveling wire electrodischarge machines to cut metal, and the use of optical fibers and laser beams for measurement, transmission, and control. Many private companies have their own central labs in which they are beginning to take up similar research topics. It is difficult to estimate the future impact of research on the frontiers of science, but it is difficult to imagine that any research project will have as much influence on the machine-tool industry, and on the process of manufacturing itself, as the research and development of the flexible manufacturing system complex.

A flexible manufacturing system (FMS) is commonly defined as an assembly of electronically controlled machines to allow the continuous but adjustable flow and processing of components. Electronic controls and new machining make possible the economical production of "small batches" and eventually the virtual elimination of workers on the production line, changes so fundamental as to constitute a second industrial revolution.

The idea of FMS did not originate in Japan, or even in America. A creative Englishman, D. T. N. Williamson, had outlined the basic features of such a system by 1970. His Molins System 24, designed to produce cigarette-making machines for the British company Molins and to run twenty-four hours a day, received some British government support, but when it seemed to require more funds without having a clear financial payoff, the British government pulled out. A number of American companies like Cincinnati Milacron, Warner and Swasey, White-Sundstrand, Cross and Trecker, and Giddings and Lewis have developed or are developing flexible manufacturing systems for companies like Caterpillar, John Deere, and General Electric. But, as with CNC and robots, Japan concentrated its energies more sharply and applied the new technology with greater speed and thoroughness.

FMS requires sophisticated computer software like DNC (direct numerical controls), which, with central controls dedicated to several machines, controls all the machines at once. DNC was pioneered in the United States, but when early efforts did not prove commercially viable, interest waned. In the mid-1960s the state-owned Japan National Railway footed the bill for the development of Japan's first DNC program as part of its modern repair facility for the new *Shinkansen* bullet train that had started operating in 1964. With the cooperation of FANUC and Ikegai, it developed and installed System K with three fully automated and four partially automated lathes controlled from a central facility. In 1968 FANUC began the commercial development of DNC, and FANUC, along with Ikegai, Okuma, Toshiba Kikai, Hitachi Seiki, and Makino, started a joint program for DNC with the financial sponsorship of MITI and under the technical leadership of AIST's Mechanical Engineering Lab. Completed in 1970, their product became commercially available as System T. By 1975, the *American*

Machinist could report that DNC was installed in some sixty Japanese companies, substantially more than in any other country.

As with other important new technologies, AIST thoroughly monitored foreign FMS developments from the beginning. In 1973 its Mechanical Engineering Laboratory began a three-year study then called the "unmanned manufacturing system." By then it was already clear that the key components of an FMS system would be machining centers, CNC lathes, robots, CNC, and DNC, and the Japanese government and private companies therefore earmarked these areas for priority development. As usual their study included analysis of foreign developments, technological requirements, and social impact. They expected to launch a large-scale project in the near future but, with the oil shock, energy-related problems seemed more urgent, and national priority in 1974 was therefore given to the "sunshine" (new energy sources) and "moonlight" (energy conservation) projects, thus delaying the start.

In 1973 the study group had been called the MUM (Machines for Unmanned Manufacturing), but after the oil shock, with the slower pace of economic growth and with many employers worried about a possible labor surplus, promoters of the project dropped the term "unmanned" and gave the new rationale, batch production to meet diversified social needs. Later promoters added "lasers," a glamorous new technology that helped attract public support. Although with known technology lasers could cut only thin pieces of metal, they had the revolutionary potential of cutting with great precision, of welding, and even of heating the metal to such levels as to make machines without conventional cutting.

The new project, "flexible manufacturing system complex provided with laser," was begun in 1977, administered by the Mechanical Engineering Laboratory. It had a budget of some 15 billion yen from the government, excluding the salaries of regular employees of government laboratories and contributions made by private industry.

As part of the project, completed in 1983, a research association for FMS (sometimes abbreviated FMC for "Complex") was formed with nine machine-tool companies, seven large electronics manufacturers, four large heavy-machinery companies, and FANUC. Companies were assigned various parts of the project, all to be compatible with one another. The overall system was designed to handle work weighing up to 1,100 pounds in batches of 300 of a given item. Electronic controls were designed for a hierarchy of controls at three levels. Each machine cell can be controlled independently. At the second level of control, computers can direct the whole system (whether it be for machining, assembly, laser processing, inspection, or material handling). A still higher level of control permits direction of the entire production process. As always, such integrated projects hastened standardization and specialization between companies.

While interest in FMS is booming, the extreme complexity of software systems, the need to redesign projects and rethink the entire manufacturing and supply process, the lack of experience of both producers and users, and the high costs mean that even in Japan widespread commercialization will take some years. In the mid-1980s, many companies are beginning by using a cell (or "module") of two or three machines that could later be combined into a larger FMS.

Until 1980 it had been common to transport work in progress by a conveyor belt or other transfer machine, but once Cincinnati Milacron demonstrated automatic carts (with rubber tires, somewhat like large golf carts) in 1980, this became the new rage in Japan.

A robot may be used to pick goods off the cart and place them on the machining center, but the process is sometimes simplified by the use of a pallet, a metal platform that can slide directly between the machining center and the cart, carrying work in progress without a robot. Machining centers have been developed not only with automatic tool changers that can change as many as a hundred tools by electronic command but with separate racks of replacement tools for broken tools that can be substituted automatically and separate drums of even more tools that can be loaded in and out of the machining center. Manufacturers are now trying to develop still more flexible machining centers that change large parts of the machining center for different tasks, thus "metamorphosing" a machining center.

When first introduced in the United States, FMS generally referred to the machining process ("floor to floor"), but it has gradually been expanded to include all materials handling ("door to door"). In some systems, the warehouse is also automated so materials can be brought from the warehouse to the machining areas and to the shipping room automatically by these same unmanned carts. Yamazaki is talking of a "flexible manufacturing management system" that would include "shop loading" (the scheduling of work and assignment to various machines) and analysis of costs by the same computer system.

In mid-1982 the trade journal *Nikkei Mechanical* conducted a survey of twelve different sectors concerning company experience with and attitudes toward FMS. Some 80 percent of the companies polled recorded basic satisfaction with their systems, and on the average reported that the system was able to pay for itself in two to three years. In addition to the 118 Japanese companies that already had a total of 281 systems, these companies, along with 138 others, planned to install an additional 596 within two years of the survey.

The cells and FMS systems have the potential within a few years of radically reducing the number of workers, cutting costs, eliminating model turnover time, and fundamentally changing the manufacturing and supply processes. No one doubts that the Japanese have a substantial lead in this effort and that the government encouragement, linkages between firms, and availability of electronic engineers in manufacturing have given them a critical edge.

When the new emperor ascends the throne in Japan, a new era is said to begin and a new era name is assigned. When Emperor Hirohito ascended the throne in 1925, the name Showa was assigned to his era. So revolutionary is this new technology that in the Japanese popular press, 1980 is known as the first year of the Robot Era, and 1981, the first year of the FMS Era.

4

Kyushu Without Coal Mining: Managing Decline and Regional Renaissance

Mature industrial nations losing major sectors to newly industrializing countries must now learn to cope with adjustments of unprecedented scale. During the Great Depression of the 1930s America developed new institutions and programs for dealing with economic cycles, but we do not yet have a system of assigning responsibility for coping with the decline of entire sectors. Does a firm have a responsibility to inform employees it is closing so they have time to find new work? What should the firm do for long-time employees when certain labor specialties are no longer needed? Is no one but the employee and his family responsible for the readjustment? Who decides when a problem is serious enough to deserve help from local and national governments? How do we develop a process for coping with these problems? These issues require more careful consideration if we Americans are to maintain the vitality of affected regions and maintain our self-image as a humane nation.

Like America, Japan has found problems of decline to be far more difficult than problems of growth, especially when they affect a whole region. To the dismay of MITI bureaucrats, Japan expends far more effort and money on declining sectors like coal, textiles, and shipbuilding than on many sectors given priority for the future. Yet Japanese bureaucrats have clear responsibility for determining when a sector is so severely and permanently affected as to be considered structurally depressed and for working with government agencies and the firms involved to guide the adjustment process.

By far the largest case of structural adjustment in Japan was caused by the closing of the Kyushu coal mines. It required huge and rapid adjustment by any standards and involved loss of employment on a scale comparable to the loss of American employment in steel and autos in the 1970s and 1980s. The adjustment was painful, and the pain is not over even two decades later. Yet considering the problems involved, Japan's success—in speed of adjustment to market forces, positive cooperation of many groups of people, and maintenance of a healthy society—was as striking in its way as the creation of competitive shipbuilding and machine-tool industries.

1. DEVELOPING THE MINES

Phasing out the coal mines undid almost a century of development. Although coal had been discovered and used in Kyushu at least as early as the eighteenth century, mining really developed in the late nineteenth century to meet the needs of growing industry, as it had in Europe a few decades earlier. In 1873 an Englishman, Edmond Glover, purchased the small island of Takashima off Nagasaki, brought in mining equipment, began pumping water out of old mines, and established the first modern mine. His local partner was Yataro Iwasaki, who founded and developed Mitsubishi. Substantial coal reserves were prospected in four of Kyushu's prefectures (Fukuoka, Nagasaki, Saga, and Kumamoto), and for years around the turn of the century there was a coal rush. Even the other three Kyushu prefectures (Oita, Miyazaki, and Kagoshima) were drawn into the coal economy by supplying workers, and gradually Kyushu regional planning encompassed the entire island. For decades the mines not only supplied Japan's energy needs but produced an equal amount of coal for export.

There was no need for the government to play a major role in developing the coal mines, and initiative was in the hands of the entrepreneur. Speculators came in to buy land, prospect, and develop it. Some owners rented parts of mines to prospectors, and prospectors in turn rented out smaller areas to entrepreneurs.

Of the great independent coal-mine developers, Keiichiro Yasukawa was unique. Not unlike the gold rush in the United States, the coal rush attracted adventurers, and small mine owners were often nouveaux riches who delighted in the accumulation of wealth, its conspicuous display, and the pleasures it bought, and had little regard for long-term investments, to say nothing of social responsibility. Yasukawa, however, had been a samurai of scholarly bent from the Kuroda clan of modern Fukuoka. He used his profits to modernize his mine, bringing in modern electrical equipment (that became the basis of Yaskawa Denki) and other modern machinery. He established a railway and one of the most modern technical schools in Japan. Not unlike the Cabots, Lodges, and Rockefellers, his descendants played major roles in business and cultural activities. His son Daigoro became the preeminent leader of the Kyushu business community after World War II.

When Meiji officials were deciding where to locate the first modern steel plant in 1898, Yasukawa accompanied the mayor of the fishing village of Yawata to Tokyo and persuaded them that Yawata was the ideal location, for it had great potential as a port, coal was nearby, and the main island of Honshu was only a few miles away. Two years later, a steel mill was opened at Yawata, and thus began Japan's golden age of coal and steel. It brought prosperity particularly to the large Chikuho coal fields south of Yawata. At first, horses pulled coal carts to the ships and then it was an hour by ship to Yawata. Within several years railways carried the coal to the ships. Many other industries, including Yaskawa Electric (the "u" was dropped in the name of the electric company at the suggestion of an American who thought it would sound better to Westerners), grew up to serve the steel and coal industries.

In addition to the independent family-owned enterprise, groups of companies linked by a financial holding company, the zaibatsu, began to develop. As the scale grew, zaibatsu mines pioneered in developing a professional managerial class in Japan and in rationalizing procedures to gain efficiency, cut costs, and meet national and international competition. At the center of each zaibatsu was a financial holding company, providing finance and direction to the specialized affiliated firms in coal mining and other areas such as shipbuilding, electricity, and chemicals. As the zaibatsu grew, they acquired the best sites and developed the largest and most modern mines.

Ordinary farmers preferred to go to the colonies rather than work in the coal mines, and the owners therefore had to recruit their laborers from among the poorest farmers and city dwellers and from the tiny outlying islands surrounding Kyushu. Sizable numbers of burakumin, outcasts descended from Tokugawa (1600–1868) criminals and those from such defiled trades as butchery and leathercrafts, were recruited, particularly in the Chikuho area. However, until World War II the zaibatsu made every effort not to hire these outcasts, partly because they feared they might unite and cause labor problems.

During World War II the government took over the mines, but workers were in short supply as were funds and materials to maintain the mines. The government brought in more women and workers from Taiwan and especially from Korea. By 1941 there were 19,000 women and 21,000 Koreans among the 177,000 people working in the Kyushu coal mines. In 1944 there were 38,000 women, 74,000 Koreans, 4,000 Caucasian prisoners of war, and 3,000 Chinese. The big problem was not the number of workers but the shortage of experienced workers and managers.

Koreans were generally used for work inside the mines. In one mine surveyed in February 1945, for example, of 2,300-odd workers, Koreans constituted 63 percent of laborers in the mines and 38 percent of those working outside the mines. As construction and maintenance deteriorated during the war, managers had to use more manpower to mine the same amount of coal. Although Kyushu coal production remained steady at over 30 million tons per year from the beginning of the war through 1943, comprising about 60 percent of national coal production, the number of workers in the mines increased from 178,000 to 240,000. The deterioration of mine equipment and shafts, aside from necessitating the use of more workers, increased the number of accidents. Food was scarce, and inexperienced managers sometimes used harsh measures to maintain discipline. The hostility of the miners, particularly the foreign miners, created an explosive situation. Despite constant surveillance, 44 percent of the Koreans assigned to the Fukuoka mines had escaped by 1942.

The deterioration of mines and the chaos at the war's end led to a crisis in 1945. The Occupation authorities tried to keep the Koreans in the mines after surrender, but the Koreans resisted so strenuously that they were virtually all repatriated between October and December. From 250,000 in April 1945, the number of workers in coal mines dropped to 138,000 by December. Kyushu coal production dropped from 31 million tons in 1943 to 12 million tons in 1945.

Urgent efforts were made to hire returning veterans and workers from recently closed war-related factories. Because there was a severe shortage of jobs, the mining companies were able to recruit people of better background and family status than in the prewar period. In 1933, for example, less than 2 percent of the workers in mines were educated beyond elementary school. At the end of 1948, some 16 percent had gone beyond elementary school, and a much higher proportion had completed elementary school.

Wood had been exhausted during World War II, and foreign currency was not yet available for purchasing energy supplies from outside Japan. Therefore coal was the only fuel, both for personal consumption and industrial use in the late forties. So basic was the "battle for coal production" that billboards in front of Tokyo Station recorded monthly coal production. Coal production became a symbol of the country's revival. The government took an active role in guiding the modernization of the coal mines and providing subsidies.

By 1950, with an adequate work force, government support, and more demand than supply, mine companies of all types—zaibatsu, independent, small subcontractors—and the communities around them were thriving, and miners were again living well.

2. CONFRONTING THE CRISIS

By the early 1950s the remaining coal was difficult to mine, and cheap imported oil was becoming widely available in world markets. This created a crisis in Tokyo and in Kyushu that was to continue for more than a decade. At first, the Japanese struggled to maintain a coal industry that could compete with imported oil. European coal producers, confronted with the same problem, cut back on coal mines, and Japan followed suit. But Japan moved faster and further than European countries, requiring businessmen and officials to address themselves to the consequences of the decline of the mines.

The change was staggering in scope and tempo. In 1955, domestic sources met 76 percent of Japan's energy needs, in 1973 merely 10 percent. In 1955, domestically produced coal met 44.8 percent of Japan's energy needs, in 1973 a mere 0.6 percent. In the same period the proportion of energy needs served by petroleum, virtually all of it imported, jumped from 20.2 percent to 77.6 percent.

There were coal mines in Hokkaido and elsewhere in Japan, but the vast majority of coal production was in Kyushu. Kyushu's mines were mostly small and produced lower grade coal than Hokkaido and were therefore closed down more rapidly. In 1958, 400 coal-mining companies were operating in Kyushu; in 1973 only eight were left. At the end of World War II, 250,000 workers mined coal in Kyushu; in 1958, 163,000; in 1973, 9,000. The nearby communities underwent comparable decline. The city of Omuta had 202,000 people in 1955; twenty years later it had 166,000. In the Chikuho area east of Fukuoka, the population dropped from 250,000 to 160,000. At a time when cities were growing at the expense of rural areas, the city of Kita Kyushu near the Chikuho mines, formerly the fourth largest industrial area in Japan, declined by 40,000. From 1955 until 1970, as the national population increased 15 percent, Kyushu's dropped by 7 percent, from 12.9 million to 12.0 million. During the 1960s all seven of Kyushu's prefectures were among the top ten (of forty-six prefectures) in population loss. In the heart of the coal-mine district, some houses remain boarded up thirty years later, and some villages are desolate. Near Nagasaki the island of Hashima, which had 6,000 residents, was completely deserted, a symbol —like the bald-faced mountains denuded by mining—of the ending of an era. In the mid-1950s Kyushu accounted for about 10 percent of Japan's GNP; a decade later it accounted for less than 6 percent.

The effort to manage and later surmount the decline had several strikes against it. Before World War II, steel plants had been located in Kyushu to be near the coal mines. With the transition to oil, there was no longer any reason for steel plants to be located in Kyushu, and the new steel plants were built elsewhere, in coastal areas near the large industrial centers that would be their customers.

Japanese industrialists are reluctant to open factories in communities where laborers have been involved in struggle, and the closing of the coal mines had involved bitter labor struggles. Despite government and local inducements, Kiyoshi Ichimura, president of Ricoh Company, refused to establish a factory in Kyushu, though he is a native. The founder of Bridgestone Tires, Shojiro Ishibashi, was a Kyushu native and his main factory was located in Kyushu. He refused, however, to hire former miners.

Local banks played major roles in regional development, but Kyushu banks had such heavy investments in coal and related industries that when the mines failed they were in desperate shape. Although the government found ways to rescue them, they had few funds to invest in new developments, and outside commercial banks were reluctant to move into the Kyushu area. At a time when rapid growth created shortages of capital, bankers found other opportunities far more attractive and less risky than Kyushu.

Firms producing consumer goods were then growing rapidly, but they chose to locate new factories near growing markets, not declining ones. The firms that were enticed to Kyushu tended to be weak and to employ female workers rather than former coal miners.

Kyushu's economy lacked a broad industrial base compared to that of the main island of Honshu. During Japan's 100 years of frantic modernization, there were large gaps between the sectors and regions that modernized quickly and those that remained more primitive. Modern industry, government, and culture were overwhelmingly concentrated on the main island of Honshu. Compared to frontier Hokkaido or backwater Shikoku, Kyushu had a substantial industrial base of steel and shipbuilding not far from its coal mines, but most of the island was very backward compared with Honshu. Until very recently, Kyushu leaders seemed like rustic samurai when they met their more urbane counterparts of Tokyo and Osaka. Kyushu crafts and textiles did not modernize as rapidly as their counterparts in Osaka and Tokyo, and many of the companies in these sectors could not survive when low-priced manufactured products began coming down the Inland Sea from Osaka. Kyushu lacked the depth of experienced entrepreneurial talent of the metropolitan areas of Honshu.

Kyushu's biggest problem, however, was the economic dislocation and return migration caused by the end of Japan's colonization. Located near continental Asia with a long history of foreign contact through Nagasaki, Kyushu had sent a far higher proportion of its citizens abroad than had other parts of Japan. As the farthest south of Japan's major islands, it had sent many emigrants to South American countries, especially Brazil, and to Korea and Taiwan even before 1895.

Beginning with the colonization of Taiwan in 1895, of Korea in 1910, and of Manchuria in 1931, emigration became a flood. Poor farm boys with few skills went as soldiers, small shopkeepers went as businessmen, and graduates of secondary schools and universities went out to be public servants in the colonial bureaucracy, which was larger than European colonial administrations. The process had a circular effect. As the most ambitious youths left for opportunities in the colonies, leadership in Kyushu stagnated, opening up few opportunities for youths at home. In an era when colonization was a sign of national greatness, the colonizers, believing as they were taught that they were bringing modernization, felt no more guilt than the early colonists who had gone abroad from the Western powers.

The defeat in World War II ended emigration and forced emigrants to return home. At first, ships were in short supply, and many soldiers as well as civilians had to wait a year or two. Japanese captured by the Russians had to wait longer, and many died before they could be repatriated. In all, about 6 million Japanese soldiers and civilians returned to Japan in the several years after the war. By the end of repatriation, Kyushu, with one-tenth of Japan's population, received half of the returnees; they constituted about a third of the Kyushu population. Most had been born in Kyushu but many had been away for years, and many others were children and grandchildren of migrants with tenuous ties to the island. In the postwar food shortage, especially in Kyushu areas of marginal existence, they were not always welcomed. In rural areas, before land reform, local farmers had reason to fear that men returning to their villages might be allotted portions of land that was already in short supply.

Furthermore, as in Europe, the economy was upset by the loss of the colonies, and this burden was also felt disproportionately by Kyushu, whose economy had been closely linked with the colonies. Iron ore from Manchuria had supplied Yawata Steel, soybeans from the colonies had been used for chemical fertilizer, cheap sugar from Taiwan had increased consumption, and residents of Nagasaki and Unzen had prospered from the tourists who came from Shanghai. After World War II, Korea and Taiwan were not about to return to the old colonial economic relations with Japan, with the same unfavorable terms of trade, but this was even truer of China, which virtually closed off economic relations with Japan, beginning with the Communist conquest of Manchuria in 1947.

Kyushu's special political role within Japan was also altered by the loss of the colonies. Many Kyushu political leaders had been tied to the colonies as leading ideologues for Japan's "manifest destiny" in Korea, Taiwan, and Manchuria, and they too lost their bases of support.

Yet Kyushu had many strengths. As a separate island it had a natural geographical basis for unity that was not diminished by the many tiny islands that are officially part of Kyushu's prefectures nor by the integration of part of Yamaguchi, at the southern tip of Honshu across the straits from Kyushu, into the Kyushu economy.

Kyushu also had strong regional institutions. *Nishi Nihon Shinbun,* one of Japan's two strongest regional newspapers, serves the entire island. Kyushu University is a major national university and, like American land-grant colleges that played a major role in developing modern agriculture, it had been originally designated to help promote regional industrial development. The island boasts a number of important business organizations, which provide regional leadership. The Kyushu Economic Research Center, formed by a group that had served in the largest research organization in the colonies, Manchurian Railway Corporation, is Japan's strongest regional research center. As in other regions, the regional electric power company and regional banks play major leadership roles in thinking about the region as a whole. The island of Shikoku, for example, lacks an islandwide newspaper, research center, or university to provide comparable leadership. These institutions partially compensate for the lack of an islandwide Kyushu government, and for the fact that, because they are elected to represent prefectural districts, Diet members from Kyushu think far more of their districts than of Kyushu as a whole.

Kyushu also has a certain strength of spirit reinforced by its historical importance in modern Japan. For several centuries, while the rest of Japan was closed, Kyushu residents near Nagasaki provided leadership in dealing with the outside world. Young samurai from Kagoshima at the southern tip of Kyushu, along with those from Choshu, led the Meiji government. In the early twentieth century, business leaders at Yawata Steel made Kyushu the West Virginia and Pittsburgh of Japan.

And beyond Kyushu, the national government also stood strongly behind the effort to help Kyushu make its mines competitive and then to overcome the disastrous economic conditions caused by their closing.

3. STRUGGLING TO KEEP COAL COMPETITIVE

In the late 1940s and early 1950s there was plenty of room for raising efficiency in the mines. In 1946 coal production averaged only five to ten tons per worker per month compared to fifteen to twenty tons in the late 1930s. Government and business leaders, with characteristic energy, undertook to "rationalize" mine production and make it more efficient. But in the mines this was not easy. The harsh punitive relations between management and workers in the later war years had left a reservoir of bitterness. Management had held the power before the war and had not hesitated to use it to prevent unions from forming, especially when patriotism became a cloak for crushing labor unrest in war-related industries. Occupation encouragement of labor movements, the leadership of better educated war returnees, and the dedicated support of postwar intellectuals fueled a fierce labor movement in the mines.

Miners working in dangerous deteriorated shafts did not respond to attempts at persuasion, and relations between management and miners were explosive. "Rationalization," so appealing to management, was viewed by workers as a code word for cutting the work force and by labor unions as a marvelous excuse for selectively cutting labor activists. Unlike workers in ordinary private companies who worried about the health of their companies, miners knew that coal had such high priority that government subsidies would in effect pay for raises. Strikers were protesting against their companies' policies, but they were indirectly striking against the government, demanding that it help improve their working conditions, their safety, and their wages.

Once enough coal was coming, government officials concentrated on efficiency, for Japanese coal mines were then far less efficient than European ones. Labor resistance rendered ordinary consultation ineffective, so the bureaucrats found another way to apply pressure. The government reduced subsidies so companies either passed higher costs on to users or cut costs. Prices of coal were then administered, and the big users of coal (electric power companies, gas companies, railways, and steel companies) fought vigorously against rising coal prices. Bureaucrats could then use this as a lever for restraining price rises, keeping on the pressure for efficiency.

In September 1952 the government lowered coal prices 250 to 350 yen per ton, and the coal companies put pressure on workers. The next month workers went out on a strike that lasted sixty-three days. Although public concern about the threat to stable coal supply led to antistrike measures the following year for "coal and other specified industries," the combination of urgent need for coal, government subsidies, deteriorated mines, and miner resistance to rationalization led to continuing difficulties. It was a far cry from later foreign images of "Japanese consensus-building." Bureaucrats much preferred domestic sources of energy to foreign ones, but to remain competitive in international markets Japan needed energy sources as cheap as any in the world. As cheap oil became available and foreign reserves accumulated, bureaucrats let some oil flow in. At first, many bureaucrats hoped that oil imports would goad the recalcitrant coal industry into greater efforts at rationalization that would make it competitive.

The coal companies made considerable progress in efficiency, but by 1954 they were caught in a financial squeeze, and in the spring of 1955 they appealed to MITI for a reduction in the imports of oil, for help in finding stable customers, and for financial help in rationalization. In August 1955 a MITI-sponsored Diet bill, the Coal Mining Rationalization Special Measures Law, paved the way for a variety of MITI activities. The basic policy, known as "scrap and build," similar to the government's efforts to scrap old ships and machine tools to stimulate construction of new ones, was for the government to help purchase and retire from service inefficient mines and to give financial assistance to modernize the mines with the greatest potential for efficient operations. In October the government established a Coal Mining Facilities Corporation to liquidate the inefficient mines and to help troubled companies give separation pay to departing miners. In October, the Diet passed the Heavy Oil Boiler Control Law, which imposed duties on imported fuel oil and taxed newly installed boilers that used oil. This tax was considered a clever device, for it increased efficiency while making the culprit, imported oil, finance the "scrap and build" program.

After the Suez crisis in 1956, as mine efficiency continued to improve, prospects for coal mines improved considerably. Demand for coal rose, companies were allowed to raise prices, profitability improved, and government officials began projecting that total Japanese coal production would rise from 42 million tons in 1955 to 69 million tons by 1967.

By mid-1958, however, as the flow of cheap oil returned, it became clear that even the vigorous "scrap and build" plan of 1955 would not be enough to make coal competitive with oil as a source of cheap energy. The price of coal was allowed to fall, and the financial losses of coal companies in 1959 were the worst in history. The Coal Industry Rationalization Council delivered its report in 1959, acknowledging that the change from coal to oil was not a temporary problem but indeed a structural, long-term trend.

Nonetheless the Council hoped that production could be stabilized at 50–55 million tons a year, and to achieve this it recommended strengthening the "scrap and build" program and further rationalizing coal mining and distribution. By then, however, the boosters of the coal industry were near desperation, wondering whether coal could ever again be competitive. New rationalization plans were more drastic and required further cutting of workers.

In October 1959, a plan was announced for reducing mine workers by 70,000 over the course of five years. As they began to feel the pinch of new rationalization plans, the workers in Mitsui's Miike mines in Omuta in December 1959 began a strike that was to last a year and a half. It was the longest large strike in Japanese history. Because the government had supported the coal mines in the early postwar period, the miners could not believe that the government would fail to support Japanese coal mining or that powerful Mitsui could really be in trouble. In the meantime, the price of oil dropped from an average in 1958 of about $1.90 a barrel to below $1.50 a barrel by the end of 1960. Coal companies felt the financial squeeze and labor disputes became more bitter, but the belt-tightening was still not enough to make the price of coal competitive.

In 1961 Prime Minister Hayato Ikeda announced plans for doubling national income within a decade. To achieve that goal Japanese industry needed access to the cheapest possible sources of energy. In June 1961 the government announced that oil imports were completely liberalized. Bureaucrats had tried hard to devise methods to make coal competitive, and mine owners, squeezed between price pressures and workers' demands, had tried to introduce new techniques while keeping wages down. In retrospect it is impressive how quickly government leaders achieved policy changes in response to changing world conditions. Continued study of the world situation enabled them to act with great assurance as the Suez crisis was resolved in the late 1950s. Labor-management hostilities slowed productivity increases, but it is unlikely that any known technology and any human effort could then have made Japanese coal prices competitive with that of imported oil. The decision of June 1961 to liberalize oil sealed the fate of the coal industry.

4. PREPARING FOR THE DEMISE OF COAL

Once the decision was made, leaders moved to maintain public support and prepare for adjustments. The solution combined crisis management with a clear vision of long-range strategic national interests. In April 1962, Ikeda was able to ward off a massive coal-mining strike protesting further rationalization plans by announcing that a special committee would examine the coal problem comprehensively. In the meantime he ordered companies to refrain from further rationalization. At the same time, he appointed Hiromi Arisawa, a Tokyo University professor, as head of the Coal Survey Commission.

Arisawa was the perfect choice. An economist who specialized in energy problems, he had played a central role in all major energy deliberations since World War II. Articulate and self-assured, he combined a clear sense of national purpose with a shrewd understanding of politics. And he had credentials that socialists and labor unionists, who had no confidence in the government, found difficult to criticize. As a leftist economist in the 1930s, Arisawa had lost his job at Tokyo University for criticizing the government. He had just made three trips to Europe to examine its energy problem and his informed understanding of the European coal problem bolstered his credentials. His Coal Survey Commission undertook an up-to-date survey in mid-1962, including study visits to major Kyushu mines.

On October 13, 1962, Arisawa's Coal Survey Commission issued its report. Officially, the report still talked about "scrap and build," but the essence of the report was that coal, Japan's major source of energy for almost a century, could not compete with oil, no matter how much coal mines were rationalized. Drastic reduction was required. If consumers so chose, coal production could go as low as 30 million tons by 1967. Only the most efficient mines would remain. A skeleton core of people, up-to-date and skilled workers and managers, would remain, able to expand mining activities in case of a national emergency. Coal mines would be phased out over the course of five years, not because Japan had no coal but because its coal was not price-competitive.

The remaining question was how to gain sufficient support for implementing the policies. Ordinarily such major decisions are reached by consensus, but Arisawa and his commission, along with political and bureaucratic leaders, realized that the issue was too explosive to get consensus. If the commission consulted with coal-mine companies it would lose credibility with the workers. The next best thing to consensus was for Arisawa to issue his commission's bold report and then to go around to various groups, including labor unions, to explain the decision. Politicians waited to act until Arisawa had engaged in patient discussions with all concerned and the worst storms had passed, though it was obvious from the beginning that they would support the commission's recommendations.

In Kyushu the response to Arisawa's report was explosive. For the moment, all of Kyushu was united. The striking workers and the intellectuals—like Itsuro Sakisaka, who had fanned the fires of the great Miike strike—joined the industrialists to oppose the report. Local newspapers charged that it was not a proposal to "scrap and build" but to "scrap," and that the commission had come to Kyushu not to save the coal industry but to destroy it.

But as much as they protested, Kyushu representatives were aware they could not halt the report's implementation. The certainty that the Cabinet would support the report (which it did in November) led them to begin adjusting to the report's recommendations even while the clamor was still strong and long before the Cabinet's decision. Political efforts were made to stretch out the life of the coal mines but with little success. In 1961 there were 315 coal mines in operation in Kyushu; by 1967 there were thirty-seven. In 1961 there were 105,000 employees in Kyushu coal mines; by 1967 there were 37,000. Because only the most efficient mines remained open and they continued to modernize facilities, productivity continued to rise from the prewar levels of twenty tons per person per month, reached again in 1961, to seventy tons by 1973. Drastic work-force reductions did not greatly reduce coal production.

By the early 1970s when national policy was to maintain about 20 million tons of coal production per year, Kyushu began to stabilize production at about 7–8 million tons per year. By then the number of workers in the Kyushu mines had declined to about 8,000. Although the policy was reevaluated after the oil shock in 1973, this amount was not changed. Considerable reserves of Japanese coal remain, but they are not easily accessible. Japanese coal cannot compete with coal imported from Australia and elsewhere, and foreign reserves are sufficient for several hundred years. Therefore, beyond the 20 million tons, Japan will import coal as needed.

The Arisawa report acknowledged that the national government had a responsibility to the people displaced as a result of "the energy revolution." MITI officials felt a special responsibility for looking after the coal industry, since coal had been their responsibility and it had been their decision to let oil flow in freely that had shut down the coal mines. Indeed, leaders at all levels acknowledged that coal miners faced a structural adjustment through no fault of their own. Thus, despite all the struggles, there was considerable agreement on basics: The government had to do what was necessary to make Japan competitive, and those who suffered as a result of that effort required temporary assistance in making the transition.

Therefore in December 1961, even before the Arisawa report, MITI developed a five-year program to assist the coal mines and the region through the transition. At the time, no one anticipated that further five-year transition programs, at different levels of support, would continue to the 1980s.

5. ATTRACTING INDUSTRY

Political and business leaders, both local and national, agreed that the solution to the social as well as economic problems caused by closing the mines was to provide jobs: expand existing industrial plants, attract new ones, and assist miners in finding and being trained for the new jobs. The search was to involve national officials working in Kyushu with local officials, but considerable responsibility was in the hands of the Kyushu business community, which reorganized to deal with the new problems.

Kyushu business leaders had been responding to problems of coal-mining decline since the mid-1950s, but the crisis of 1961 required concerted action. There were a number of business associations, but none had clear responsibility for Kyushu business as a whole. After rounds of discussions, business leaders in Kyushu united to form Kyukeiren (the Kyushu-Yamaguchi Economic Federation), modeled after Keidanren in Tokyo. Daigoro Yasukawa, the preeminent leader of the Kyushu postwar business community, who was active in virtually every major business and civic association, became its activist chairman. Kyukeiren officials combined the big picture with careful analysis of relevant information and energetic pursuit of politicians and bureaucrats who could be of help. The Kyushu Electric Power Company and the Kyushu Economic Research Center provided key staff work. Kyukeiren leaders systematically cultivated private businesses that might build local facilities and worked with government officials to improve the local infrastructure and secure special concessions for new businesses.

Powerful rivalries between MITI and the Construction Ministry made timely coordination almost impossible. Although the Economic Planning Agency's Comprehensive Development Bureau (later to be incorporated into the National Land Agency) began to formulate overall plans for regional development, MITI and the Construction Ministry were responsible for implementation. To cope with the coordination problem, bureaucrats from the two ministries who dealt with these issues were joined in the Coal Mine Area Rehabilitation Corporation in July 1962, and a large office was immediately established in Kyushu.

The Corporation had a broad mandate. It planned and built or repaired the infrastructure of roads, water supply, and other public services. It became, in effect, a public real estate agency for abandoned mine areas—purchasing, developing, and managing them until the properties were sold to private companies or given to local government to use for parks, hospitals, playgrounds, or other public purposes. The success of the corporation in dealing with regional development in mining areas, as well as in generating bureaucratic momentum, later led the government to assign it responsibility for other intensive regional development projects. Its name was changed to Japan's Regional Development Corporation.

No one expected that major enterprises would relocate in mountainous areas with high transportation costs. Some small enterprises did locate there, but the best hope in the mountainous areas was to expand the mining of limestone for the cement industry. Much of the same equipment used in the coal mines could be used, and financial incentives were offered that made it attractive for mining companies to switch to or expand limestone mining. However, the main efforts were concentrated in coastal areas accessible to water transportation and other support facilities. Roads were built from mining communities to these new facilities so most former miners could commute without having to change their residences.

The corporation built industrial parks and began to advertise and recruit companies. It worked with the relevant government agencies to provide the infrastructure as well as the financial incentives that would induce companies to come. It worked with Finance Ministry officials to develop appropriate incentives, with the Development Bank to assure proprietary loans, with Labor Ministry officials to deal with questions of recruitment and retraining. It worked with Kyushu Diet members, who assured necessary political support, and with local officials, who cooperated in providing the infrastructure. It worked with the business community to identify firms that might relocate, sent out staff members to contact firms, and showed them around the various sites. From 1962 to 1982, the corporation built 113 industrial parks across the nation's coal mining districts, seventy-six of them in Kyushu. The Kyushu industrial parks were overwhelmingly in Fukuoka prefecture because the two largest coal-mining areas, Chikuho and Omuta, were there, but others were built in Saga, Nagasaki, and Kumamoto.

Although procedures were of course simpler for companies moving into a park, a variety of incentives was offered to companies locating in other designated areas near the mines.

Through cooperation with the Finance Ministry, the corporation was able to offer a number of financial inducements. It had its own loan program for local industry that employed former miners, and it could offer companies loans of up to 40 percent of relocation costs at interest rates about two percentage points lower even than rates of the Development Bank. Between 1962 and 1978 it lent some 195 billion yen nationally, 103 billion in Kyushu. From 1959 through 1980 the Development Bank provided 794 loans of some 256 billion yen for development projects in Kyushu's coal-mining areas. The Small and Medium-Sized Business Finance Corporation also provided special loans for small businesses, many of which had serviced coal-mining companies, to develop new products and facilities.

To determine which communities deserved how much special assistance, surveys were conducted in coal-mining areas beginning in 1961. In February 1962, 216 communities nationally, of which 144 were in Kyushu, were designated "Section 2" communities to receive special assistance. Of these communities, 105 nationally, sixty-nine in Kyushu, were designated "Section 6" communities—deserving of higher levels of aid because their problems were more severe. This initial determination of need provided a standard framework so large numbers of requests could be handled without having to go through individual determinations of need.

As with the earlier "scrap and build" programs, MITI used an oil import tax to finance the coal industry readjustment. It was cheap oil, after all, that had caused the coal problem, and Japanese industry was well able to bear the modest tax.

The Finance Ministry worked out arrangements, some with the cooperation of local governments, to assist with the tax burden. Some local area taxes and enterprise taxes were reduced or eliminated for companies locating in these areas or for local plants expanding facilities and offering new employment. The depreciation schedule for plants newly located in these areas was faster than for those elsewhere. For companies abandoning old production facilities and building new ones in the coal-mining area, profit taxes on the sale of old property were reduced. To qualify for the special loans and tax privileges, at least 30 percent of the employees had to be former miners or their dependents.

In addition, there was a special program for assistance to local communities where the tax base was destroyed. The Japanese government had long been concerned about regional equity in the offering of educational and other services to the population, and its program of equalizing grants to poorer prefectures had long since reduced regional disparities to levels far lower than those among

American states. But even the usual equalizing grants were not adequate for some of the most drastically affected areas to provide basic community services. In 1962, additional national government financial help was given to 181 of the 216 communities judged to be adversely affected by the decline of the coal mines, and of these 117 were in Kyushu. This enabled these communities to maintain adequate schools, street repair, and other community services. In addition, the national government assisted these communities in paying interest on outstanding community bonds.

Local businessmen give high marks to the officials working in the Coal Mine Rehabilitation Corporation for their efforts to attract industry to the coal-mining areas. Despite the unfavorable conditions—the lack of attraction to consumer industries, including auto companies, of an area in decline, the unattractiveness of poorly educated workers who had been involved in bitter labor struggles—the industrial parks built by the corporation achieved an 85-percent occupancy, virtually the same as the national average.

Despite their valiant efforts, however, the corporation and the business community were not able to attract really large factories in the immediate aftermath of the decline of coal. The growth of industrial establishments in Kyushu lagged considerably behind national rates until the end of the 1960s. The greatest efforts were put into the Chikuho area, the largest and most deeply affected area. In the Omuta area, because Miike Mines continued to operate and because the overall numbers were smaller, the scale of the government program was more modest. In need of industries, these areas were willing to accept factories that other communities shunned for fear of pollution. The Ariake area was able to attract aluminum and chemical factories, though most of these have since been affected by recession. In Nagasaki prefecture, shipbuilding absorbed more workers in the 1960s. It was to be 1972 before Mitsubishi Shipbuilding completed its large expansion in Koyagi and 1973 before Hitachi Shipbuilding opened its large docks at Ariake. This helped greatly at the time but led to new problems in the late 1970s when shipbuilding declined. Recruiting industries is thus a continuing problem despite the great successes of attracting a Nissan truck factory to Kanda in 1975 and a Honda motorcycle factory to Kumamoto in 1976.

6. HELPING THE DISADVANTAGED MAKE THE TRANSITION

Japanese leaders studied the experience of earlier developers in welfare as well as in industrial development and concluded that Western countries that provided substantial payments to the unemployed weakened their incentive to return to work quickly. The Japanese therefore devised a system not only with smaller unemployment payments but with special bonuses to those who returned to work quickly. The mines were closed just as Japan was beginning rapid growth and capital was in short supply. Bureaucrats believed that putting the country's resources into industry, eventually raising everyone's well-being, was better than providing sizable direct welfare payments.

The Labor Ministry used its normal channels to identify new jobs, provide consultation services, and make appropriate placements, but it greatly expanded these services in former coal-mining areas. Special new programs were offered to companies that hired former miners, including financial help during retraining. In order to qualify, companies had to be identified as being in sectors where future economic growth was likely. Thousands of former miners were retrained through these programs.

The clear definition that the area was suffering a structural problem led its young people to move quickly to seek employment elsewhere. Each year during the 1960s, for a week in March shortly after junior and senior high school graduations, a special train from Kagoshima carried the new graduates to seek employment in the Osaka area. Approximately 100,000 people left Kyushu each year during the 1960s, most for the urban areas of Honshu. Kyushu was not alone. Rural areas throughout Japan sent their youth to the cities, but the migration from Kyushu was especially large. In a sense, out-migration from Kyushu was a continuation of the prewar pattern except that cities in Honshu replaced the colonies. Of course the scale of migration to the Tokyo, Osaka, and Nagoya areas in the 1960s would not have been possible without the substantial economic growth of those areas.

Fewer middle-aged people migrated. Most Japanese companies preferred to hire the young, pay them low wages, and provide their training. While young graduates could often get jobs in large corporations, former coal miners, with lower educational levels and considered less pliable by employers, went mostly to small shops engaged in light manufacturing. Even *burakumin* (outcasts), who were generally barred from employment by large companies, were able to obtain employment in small metal-working factories in the industrial belt between Tokyo and Osaka.

Many older people in the coal-mining areas decided that it made sense to remain. Given the devastated real estate market, those with property had difficulty selling it for a decent price and those without it could rent or acquire property far more cheaply than they could elsewhere. Some used the retirement benefits provided through government support to acquire a place to live.

There was, therefore, a massive change in the Kyushu age structure. In 1975, 7.9 percent of the Japanese population was 65 and over. In Chikuho, over 15 percent was over sixty-five, and in the affected areas of Saga, Nagasaki and Ariake, the figures were 19 to 20 percent. The average size of household in Section 6 areas declined from five to three, leaving very few youths to follow the common Japanese pattern of looking after aged parents. In 1955, Tagawa had 100,071 people in 20,923 households, but in 1975 it had 61,464 people in 19,237 households. Other areas were similarly affected, and continuing assistance programs were required for old people more than ten or twenty years after the closing of the mines.

A high proportion of coal miners with families had been housed in long barracklike structures known as *nagaya*. Many continued to live there after mines closed. The rent was extremely modest, but over the years the buildings deteriorated and officials replaced them only slowly. Even in the 1980s they were continuing to repair and replace them.

Japan did not give the problem of pollution serious attention until 1970. When coal mines were being closed in the early 1960s, there was almost no thought given to damage to the surroundings. Gradually it was discovered that rain seeping into abandoned mines often washed out chemicals and other wastes into the surrounding areas causing extensive environmental damage. Since the 1970s, Japan has required potentially polluting companies of all kinds to buy insurance against damage, using the proceeds to pay the costs of restoration, but the coal companies had mostly gone out of business by the mid-1960s when the seriousness of the problem was discovered. The government had no choice but to assume the expense.

To deal with the restoration of the environment the government established an independent Coal Mine Damage Corporation in 1963 and greatly enlarged the scale of its activities after 1968. Environmentalists were originally outraged at the government's tardiness in responding to pollution problems, but in the 1970s most gave the government programs high marks. In the early 1980s, some 300 billion of the 500 billion yen devoted to the various programs in coal-mining areas throughout the country were assigned to water quality and other environmental problems.

Omuta had a particularly difficult time of it because the Miike strike had left a bitter aftermath and because that mine's pollution problem was unusually severe. Some chemical factories in Omuta, and especially Minamata, about seventy miles down the coast, had created such serious problems in the 1960s that even local citizens who were in desperate need of jobs opposed certain industries locating in their community. In the late 1970s, the mood in Omuta began to change. Groups of community leaders now have an extensive program for attracting new industry. In front of Omuta city hall there stands a sign: "Bring Business to Omuta So One of Your Children Can Stay and Look After You."

7. DECENTRALIZING THE NATIONAL INDUSTRIAL BASE: OITA

In the late 1960s a new effort resulting from national decentralization began to have an impact in Kyushu. As a fresh start, it was easier to manage and contributed more significantly to Kyushu's prosperity than did the earlier efforts at revival. It began as decentralization of heavy industry, and then took a new turn as Kyushu began moving to a postindustrial phase. Like the earlier efforts, it involved close relations between national and local government and the business community.

The earlier efforts at revival had been a reaction not only to the decline of coal mining but also to the concentration of Japan's national resources in a 300-mile-long metropolitan belt running from greater Tokyo west through greater Osaka. This concentration of resources resulted both from natural economic forces and from government policies. Even before World War II, government and business headquarters, factories, convenient transport facilities, and trained personnel were concentrated in this area. During the 1950s and early 1960s, when funds were still limited, government leaders wanted to place investments where they would have the greatest impact on national growth, and this almost inevitably led to the 300-mile metropolitan belt. Construction Ministry officials, confronted with estimates of population usage, concentrated new roads and highways there, and government and private railways also built there. Waterways, electric power, and port facilities were first rebuilt there. For similar reasons, companies built not only headquarters but their major factories in this same 300-mile metropolitan zone. With this concentration of national resources in this area, Kyushu's efforts at revival ran counter to the dominant trends and therefore required special measures.

Prime Minister Ikeda reversed the trend toward centralization in 1961, for it was clear that his plan to double the national income and triple national industrial production could not be accomplished in the metropolitan areas alone. Major new investment was needed in other regions as well, and this idea was embodied in the first National Comprehensive Development Plan of 1962. One region targeted was Kyushu's Oita prefecture, where the governor and his supporters had long been requesting central government help for development.

During the 1960s and 1970s the idea of decentralization gained momentum. Thoughtful bureaucrats concerned about increasing inequalities between new centers of wealth and remote areas left behind lent their support. Citizens who were disenchanted with long commutes and cramped housing in the metropolitan areas supported it. After 1970 the burst of attention to pollution brought to a head growing dissatisfaction with noise levels, car exhausts, and industrial waste in the metropolitan belt.

Regional politicians naturally jumped on the bandwagon of decentralization as a way to get more national government help for their localities. Their influence grew as a regional reaction to the expenditures lavished on Tokyo for the Olympics in 1964 and on Osaka for the Exposition of 1970. The growing opposition to centralization was strengthened by a peculiar turn in party politics. The party in power, the Liberal Democratic Party, had a strong rural base. In the late 1960s and the early 1970s, because opposition leaders from the "progressive parties" had been elected mayors of many major cities in the metropolitan belt, the Liberal Democratic Party found it easy and even opportune to respond to the requests of the regions over the interests of the metropolitan governments.

Prime Minister Kakuei Tanaka's 1972 Plan for Remaking the Japanese Archipelago was to prove too ambitious and inflationary after the oil shock of 1973, but the gist of this plan for deconcentration continued to guide government policy.

Within Kyushu, Oita was the major beneficiary of these new trends. Oita was an extremely appropriate site. Bureaucrats concerned with closing the gaps between rich and poor prefectures could point to Oita as one of the poorest prefectures in the nation. As ships grew larger, many older ports did not have harbors deep enough to take the new ships, but Oita, though not yet a major port, was a planner's dream. The water along the edge of the shore at Oita City was very shallow and sandy from the silt deposited by the Oita and Ono rivers and could therefore be filled in to make a new industrial zone. Within a few hundred yards of the shore there was a sharp drop making the harbor ideally suited for the large vessels beginning to cross the Pacific.

The practice of filling in land along the Japanese seacoast was already well developed before World War II. Because foreign trade was so important, after the war land along the seacoast was earmarked for major industrial combines. Japan wanted the lowest transport costs as well as the cheapest energy. With factories built along the coast, raw materials could come straight from ship to factory and manufactured products could go straight back to the ships. In the 1960s Oita was earmarked as one of these areas. That led to what is arguably the world's largest landfill project.

It was by no means a foregone conclusion in 1961 that Oita would be selected as one of the new regional industrial cities. This required that the central government choose it over other applicants. Local politicians and businessmen had to demonstrate that they had the organizational know-how and the commitment to make it work, and large businesses had to decide to locate there. Companies would not decide to locate there until the landfill was well under way, and the landfill had to rely heavily on prefectural financing. Most leading prefectural officials in Oita as elsewhere had a Home Ministry background, and they tended to be fiscally conservative. Oita prefecture was in the red when the project was proposed, and these officials were reluctant to have a poor prefecture commit itself to such a huge and risky project. In many cities like Fukuoka the business community was willing and able to raise funds, but Oita's business community was weak and lacking in confidence.

The critical role in developing the project was played by a young director of planning in the prefectural government, Taiichi Sato. An able official who had grown up on a small farm in Oita, Sato had made his way to Manchuria after completing middle school. Because he had good rapport with local workers, shortly after he returned to Oita from the war he was placed in charge of labor problems. When labor unrest subsided he was put in charge of planning. His experience in dealing with labor problems had convinced him of the urgency of providing new jobs for Oita, which was then forty-fourth out of forty-six prefectures in per capita income. The idea of landfill for Oita had been discussed even before World War II, but no one had investigated carefully the appropriateness of the coastline. Sato contacted respected geologists and sponsored an ambitious survey. It concluded that Oita's coastline was appropriate.

Although Governor Kinoshita was cautious about whether Oita should invest in a project of such scale, he allowed Sato to make contacts with government and business leaders in Tokyo. Sato left no stone unturned, going to pork-barrel politicians who would benefit from such expenditures as well as to central government bureaucrats.

Within the central government bureaucracy, Sato found a powerful ally in Morihiko Hiramatsu. Hiramatsu not only came from Oita but his work in MITI had required that he be deeply involved in regional development. His wife's father had been mayor of the city of Oita, where the landfill was proposed, and through his former schoolmates in Oita he had maintained an interest in Oita developments. He gave Sato advice about how to develop proposals to the central government and whom to contact in the central government.

The bureaucrats who were later to form the nucleus of the National Land Agency were then in the Economic Planning Agency, the Construction Ministry, and MITI, and they liked what they heard from Sato. After suitable investigation, Oita became one of their candidates for expansion. When Oita developed appropriate plans, it was selected as one of the sites at the end of 1964.

With local petitions from Oita flooding Tokyo, the central government finally agreed that 80 percent of the initial funds were to be provided by central government loans, with about 20 percent to be raised by Oita prefecture. To obtain the necessary support in the government, Sato spent almost two years in Tokyo at the time when the New Industrial Cities Law was being written (1962) and cities were being selected for central government assistance. Landfill on the first pump-priming project, to be occupied by Kyushu Oil Company, through initiatives of former Oita businessmen, had begun in 1961, even before the new law was passed. It was crucial in getting the confidence of national officials and companies in the commitment and capacity of Oita to carry out the projects. In 1972 a second phase of landfill was approved and these two landfills were eventually to cover an area roughly twenty kilometers long and, at the widest point, some two to three kilometers wide.

Though enormously time-consuming, the actual work of the landfill was relatively straightforward. A large cement breakwater was built at the outer limits of the area to be filled in, and then water and sand were pumped in through a pipe from two nearby rivers. As sand built up in the area to be filled, the water gradually spilled over the cement barrier to the sea.

Once the landfill was under way, the task was to get companies to agree to build facilities. Besides the Kyushu Oil Company, the Kyushu Electric Power Company and Showa Yuka (a subsidiary of Showa Denko) were among the first to agree to come. Success, however, hinged on attracting a large steel company on lots #3 and #4, which together constituted about half of the first phase of the landfill. In 1964 Taiichi Sato and the governor were hopeful that Nippon Kokan would come. When finally the Nippon Kokan official negotiating arrangements with Oita failed to get his company's go-ahead, he encouraged his brother, Shigeo Nagano, then president of Fuji Steel, to undertake the project. Sato and Governor Kinoshita established good rapport with Nagano, one of the great business leaders of Japan, who found the conditions attractive and decided to move ahead boldly.

Unfortunately, prospects for the expansion of the steel industry began to fade soon after, and for seven years the future of the project was uncertain. The personal commitment of Nagano was crucial, for he had the influence in government and the business community to make things happen. Kinoshita's confidence in him sustained the project until it reached fruition in 1971. The two square miles of space were adequate to produce 12 million tons of steel per year without difficulty, but initially only a portion of the land was used to construct a plant with a capacity of 8 million tons. Before long, because of the excess of steel in the world market, the plant was producing only 6 million tons and employing fewer than 4,000 workers. Still, this played a major role in providing local employment.

By the late 1960s many Japanese were raising questions about the costs of rapid industrial development, and even in a poor prefecture like Oita, where the citizens desperately wanted more economic development, questions were raised about how much the project helped local business, how much pollution affected health and livelihood, and how much dislocation the projects caused. By the time landfill work began on lot #5, a local citizens' movement was organized to protest continued construction. Oita citizens, like citizens in the rest of Japan, had historically been passive before officialdom. Now local businessmen began to complain that all the help, including money raised locally, was going to large outside firms while nothing was being done for local business. In a sense, the industrial zone on the landfill was like a self-contained export processing zone, raw materials being brought in from elsewhere and products exported with only minimal contact with local businesses. Despite the efforts of local officials, it had been difficult to attract industries like autos that required a great deal of subcontracting. In response to local complaints, lot #5 was divided into some 120 sites for local companies to build on. This quieted most local businessmen but it did not quell other local opposition .

The five lots in phase 1 were filled in west of the Ono River, and in phase 2, plans called for lots #6, #7, and #8 east of the river, starting in 1971. Originally, local planners intended that shipbuilding or heavy machinery factories locate there, using the steel produced in lots #3 and #4. Mitsui and Mitsubishi had agreed to build such facilities on lots #6 and #7. The oil shock ended these plans, and Mitsubishi and Mitsui tried to find other, smaller projects to build on their lots.

Lot #8 became the focus of the opposition. A copper refinery not too far from the proposed site had caused serious pollution. When it was discovered that local areas had been polluted by the new steel and petroleum factories, local opposition jelled. When it became known that an aluminum company, almost certain to add to pollution, was being considered for lot #8, the opposition exploded. By then pollution was receiving front-page attention nationally as well as locally. Local planners had already tried to respond to the pollution issue by constructing a twenty-kilometer greenbelt separating the city from the factories on the landfill area along the shore. Next to the landfill was a band of shrubbery and trees fifty meters wide, then an artificial river thirty meters wide and a highway forty meters wide. In addition, the Nippon Steel Corporation planted almost a million shrubs and trees on its property.

Opposition to pollution gained support because it was an acceptable argument to represent deeper local interests, fishing and farming as well as business. A few people had been relocated in the earlier landfills, but some of them had invested their relocation payments in a transport cooperative servicing the new large plants, a business that turned out to be very successful. However, at the time of the second landfill, pollution problems in a nearby area, Iejima, required the relocation of about 100 fishing families whose land on shore had been passed on for generations. They opposed the development adamantly. Local farmers were, as one official put it, "half crying and half smiling." Some were happy to see that their children were finding new jobs in industry, but some were worried that too many industrial jobs were becoming available, that labor shortages would make it difficult for them to get one of their children to succeed to the family farm. Because copper refining had damaged mulberry leaves, some farmers and fishermen worried that their livelihoods might be affected. The combination of determined fishing opposition, some farming resistance, and city-dweller concern about pollution united in such opposition that in 1973 new construction plans for lot #8 were called to a halt. The opposition, supported by the National Environmental Agency, forced Governor Taki to agree to meet three conditions before resuming construction: obtaining local consensus, normalizing the fishing union, and meeting the standards of environmental assessment.

In 1975, Morihiko Hiramatsu, the MITI official who had assisted Oita's efforts in the central bureaucracy, retired prematurely because of internal MITI politics. He was immediately invited by Governor Taki to return to Oita as vice-governor. When the three conditions were met (some critics said they were met in letter but not in spirit), Governor Taki and Vice-Governor Hiramatsu resumed the project. When Taki retired, Hiramatsu was easily elected governor. His creative efforts in developing long-range visions to help the locality and his ability to keep broad support of different groups have made him a leader among governors.

The new factories generated by Oita's landfill constituted perhaps the most significant new industrial development in Kyushu since the establishment of Yawata in 1901. Within a decade afterwards, Oita rose from forty-fourth to thirty-eighth among prefectures in average per capita income, but it still was a poor rural prefecture with a large population on marginal farming land. Since the new factories were relatively self-contained, they did not provide much stimulus to other local businesses, but they did provide new employment and some secondary industrial and commercial fallout. The landfill project also provided new sites for the expansion of local industries. In short the combination of national policy, fortuitous local circumstances, and great local initiative brought tremendous vitality to Oita and indirectly to the Kyushu economy as a whole. By the early 1960s Kyushu's GNP dropped to 6 percent of the nation's GNP, but by the late 1970s it had risen to almost 8 percent even while the nation's GNP was rising.

8. ADVANCING FROM "SILICON ISLAND" TO TECHNOPOLIS ISLAND

With the Oita projects, Kyushu gained a solid base of heavy industry, but forward-looking leaders were aware that future growth would be in high technology and the service sector. They were searching for opportunities when transportation cost analysis unexpectedly put them in good position to expand high-tech manufacturing.

After the new rail trunkline, the *Shinkansen,* was completed in the critical metropolitan belt from Tokyo to Osaka in 1964, planners prepared to extend it the entire length of Japan. By 1975 the *Shinkansen* crossed through a short tunnel between Honshu and Kyushu, linking Fukuoka to Tokyo. Plans had been made to extend it to Kagoshima at the southern tip of Kyushu, greatly shrinking north-south travel time in Kyushu. In the late 1960s cost analysis had shown that it did not make economic sense to extend it to Kagoshima. Instead of complaining, Kyushu leaders had immediately begun clamoring for modern airports, which could be constructed at far less cost.

Until that time, only the very largest cities—Tokyo, Osaka, Fukuoka, and Sapporo—had large modern airports. The Transportation Ministry, responsible for air as well as rail travel and eager to take on new missions, cooperated with Kyushu in getting government support. Saga, a very small prefecture, could easily be served by the Fukuoka and Nagasaki airports. Fukuoka's airport was already satisfactory, but plans proceeded for all the remaining five prefectures. By the late 1970s all had modern airports capable of servicing large jets, although mountainous terrain caused them to be located as much as an hour from prefectural capitals. Kyushu could easily boast the best air transport in Japan.

When the airports were built, convenience for high-technology companies had not been an important consideration. But no sooner had they been built than electronics companies began looking for sites near modern airports to establish new factories. With small high-priced products for which speed of delivery was critical, these companies found the available air transport in Kyushu highly attractive. Planners who had helped place industries "next to the sea" (*rinkai*) to give Japan a comparative cost advantage were now siting these factories at airports, "next to the sky" (*rinkuu*).

When consumer electronics firms began to locate plants in Kyushu in the 1960s to take advantage of low labor costs, no thought had been given to integrated circuits. Matsushita, by this time the world's largest consumer electronics maker, decided to establish one plant in every prefecture to take advantage of local labor and to heighten the interest of all localities in their products. By 1970, Matsushita, Mitsubishi Denki, Toshiba, and NEC all had consumer electronics factories in Kyushu. As production of integrated circuits began to boom in the early 1970s, Kyushu was a natural location. Labor was plentiful, water supply adequate, the air relatively clean, and good airport transportation readily available. Before long, Toshiba had transformed its Oita plant into a semiconductor factory, NEC was producing semiconductors in Kumamoto, Oki in Miyazaki, and Texas Instruments in Oita. Kyushu, producing some 40 percent of the nation's integrated circuits, became known as "Silicon Island." While "Silicon Island" lacks the small innovative companies and research labs found in California's Silicon Valley, and advanced research is still done near Tokyo, it has highly modern production sites. Though workers require little more training than textile workers and receive scarcely any higher salary, the factories are far more immaculate than the best hospital surgical rooms.

For all the early excitement, semiconducters make only a modest contribution to the overall Kyushu employment picture. In the early 1980s these semiconductor factories together employed about 20,000 of Kyushu's 6 million workers. Yet just as the decision against modern rail transport led to modern airports, which in turn led to "Silicon Island," so the excitement of "Silicon Island" led to another new twist, a still grander vision.

Toshiyuki Chikami, mayor of Kurume, forty kilometers south of Fukuoka, had become interested in modern technology when he was an official in the Kyushu Productivity Center. As a mayor with a knack for publicity, he conceived a new vision for the middle-sized city in the information age and gave it a fetching new title, "technopolis." Incidentally, he thought Kurume could become a model "technopolis."

Chikami's vision fit the latest thinking of the community of Tokyo bureaucrats and intellectuals about the shape of an information society. Still concerned with excess crowding in metropolitan areas, they were advocating "regional renaissance" that would center on middle-sized cities (averaging 200,000 to 300,000 people). In an information age it followed that the regional city should become an information capital. Just as an essential element in social planning in the industrial era was equalizing access to wealth (among prefectures as well as among social strata), an essential element in social planning for the postindustrial society is equalizing access to information. Regional information capitals, "technopolises," would spearhead the extension of new information to all of society and prevent an "information gap" between the regions and the large metropolitan areas.

The term "technopolis" was picked up by the National Industrial Structure Council in its March 1980 report, even before it was carefully defined. In 1981, MITI decided to let each prefecture nominate one of its cities as a technopolis and to those selected as most appropriate, most ready to take advantage of the opportunity, the government would give special help. All seven of Kyushu's prefectures were among the nineteen prefectures proposing cities as technopolises. The Mitsubishi Research Center originally estimated that as much as 5 trillion yen of national funds might be available to help develop technopolises, but with financial shortfalls in the national government budget everyone recognized that this would be scaled down.

The nature of the new technopolises became a hot topic for private and public meetings of leaders, ordinary citizens, and experts. The idea was still evolving in the mid-1980s, as some cities began to try it out. Virtually all informed people felt it should embrace universal home information systems, community information resource centers, research centers, lifelong learning centers with ample offerings in high technology, and new high-tech manufacturing facilities. Planners aim to establish close links between local information centers and the best national and international research and information centers. To make possible more comfortable and interesting lives in an era of increased leisure, these communities will get new roads, parks, recreation centers and other facilities designed to strengthen community feeling. The expectation is that while certain regional cities will get special aid to be designated technopolises, other regional cities will follow their example with less national government help. Eventually every regional city will be a kind of technopolis.

Kyushu leaders continue to concentrate their energies on attracting industry, but they want new high-tech and information-related industries. Because Kyushu is likely to remain slightly more agricultural than the rest of the country, great emphasis is being placed on biotechnology. Since companies like Kyoto Ceramics have a solid base in Kyushu, ceramics and other new composite materials are being promoted. Quick in pursuing sectors that Tokyo planners designate as important for the future, Kyushu leaders are also seeking companies with laser and optical fiber technology.

Central government planners generally believe that Oita, with Governor Hiramatsu and his staff of progressive planners, has one of the best visions of a technopolis. Oita's technopolis will not be limited to the compact urban area but will include farmers, fishermen, and their families. Two large high-tech industrial parks have already been designated and they are attracting plants. The southern wing is located less than ten minutes by car from the airport, and the northern wing is next to a new superhighway that spans northern Kyushu from east to west, bringing it within an hour of the airport. Texas Instruments, Sony, and Canon were already located in the area when it was designated as the southern wing, and another American company, the Materials Research Corporation, the first foreign company to receive a loan from the Japan Development Bank, erected a factory there in 1983.

Matsushita and Dai Nippon Ink have located in the northern wing next to the superhighway. Although Oita is exerting itself to attract new industries, it wants industrial development to proceed at a modest pace so as to control a steady migration from the countryside, leaving enough children to look after farms and maintain a healthy rural society. It is looking for the *besuto mikusu* (best mix) between industry and farming, one that will permit industry to develop without destroying rural society.

For its villages, Oita started an *isson ippin* (one village, one product) campaign to get each village to make a product in which it can compete in international markets. Officials recognize that Japanese tangerines cannot always be protected from foreign oranges; therefore they will have to develop new products that can be internationally competitive. The village used as a model for the movement began flying fresh shiitake mushrooms to markets in Tokyo. In the first year, the average villager's income went up about 15 percent. Demand is far from being satiated, and many nearby villages are joining in producing shiitake. Prefectural and village leaders are exploring other such opportunities.

For the southeastern portion of Oita, which relies heavily on fishing, the prefecture is developing a "marinopolis," a technopolis adapted to a fishing community, including industry, recreation, and research. Local research on the transmission of musical sounds to attract different varieties of fish is already well developed, as are robots to feed the fish thus attracted. Robots at set spots in the ocean are designed not only to expand the fishing stock but to upgrade quality, using smaller fish to feed larger fish such as *hamachi,* which bring higher prices. Computer systems have been introduced to monitor water temperature and to study fish movements.

A 1982 personal computer show in Oita illustrates its effort to involve all groups of society in the information age. In planning the show, prefectural officials told computer companies that they were to have separate corners at the show with software programs of interest to key groups of local residents: students, farmers, housewives, small and middle-sized enterprises.

The process by which Kyushu revived was less than ideal, and many who participated can think of things they would do differently. Hundreds of people died in labor struggles and accidents. For years there was constant turmoil in government offices, in mining companies, and in people's private lives. The communities most centrally involved in mining—Tagawa, Iizuka, Omuta, and many smaller towns—remain scarred, physically and socially. There remain abandoned and run-down housing, the elderly, and younger people who are unable or unwilling to take part in the competitive struggle in other urban areas. Yet, considering the poverty of Kyushu at the time, the absorption of 3 million returnees and the loss of 200,000 jobs in mining alone, the revival of Kyushu is a remarkable achievement.

The success derived not from a single plan but from great efforts by many groups—national bureaucrats and politicians but above all local leaders in all circles—to reach consensus, find creative solutions, and pursue them vigorously. There is no magic way of getting consensus, and solutions reflect implicit power relationships. Nor do current Japanese solutions always reflect unchanging cultural characteristics. It is rather that many people now have a sense of responsi-

5

The Information Revolution: National Transformation

The Japanese approach to information industries began with the familiar efforts at sectoral catch-up, but in the course of a major policy review in the early 1970s the Japanese concluded that this sector had vast significance. Information industries would drive a new development comparable to the transition from agriculture to industry. In the course of the review, Japanese leaders consulted with the most knowledgeable people in the world, evaluated the strategies of major foreign powers and companies, estimated future needs of the Japanese people, considered new technologies likely to be developed within various time frames, estimated possible costs, evaluated the social, psychological, and political consequences, and considered possible new organizations for implementation.

The Japanese had reason to be proud of their transition to modern industry, in which they had succeeded beyond their hopes and at breathtaking speed. In the late 1940s half the nation had been employed in agriculture, but within two decades two-thirds of the farmers had moved out of agriculture. They accepted what they heard from the world's leading futurologists—that in the future capital would no longer be as important as knowledge and that the cutting edge would no longer be steel and automobiles but the computer, telecommunications, and the service sector. The question was how to devise strategies to speed the transition and enhance competitiveness. They concluded that they did not have to sacrifice industry any more than they had sacrificed agriculture and that they could use information to modernize industry just as they had used industry to modernize agriculture. Information could be useful everywhere to make Japan more competitive, and they would concentrate their resources and energy on the cutting edge: knowledge, information, computers, and telecommunications.

The rapidly rising educational levels of the population fit nicely with the new perspective. And just as leaders had moved to reduce the labor content in production as wages had risen, so the information industries would reduce energy requirements now that energy was becoming more expensive. They undertook the new transition with the same thoroughness and single-mindedness with which they had undertaken the transition to heavy industry.

The quest began in a new international economic climate that required some adjustments. In the 1950s and 1960s, Japan could use tariffs and other formal mechanisms to protect growing industries, but in the 1970s, with the new pressures of internationalization, Japan had no choice but to reduce or remove formal tariff barriers. The term *kokusanka* (substitute domestic production for foreign) did not lose any of its positive connotations, and the basic assumptions of economic policy remained unchanged: Borrow as much foreign technology as possible, buy foreign manufactured goods when necessary in the interim, and build up competitiveness. The challenge with formal reduction of trade barriers was to find new ways to protect the home market and reduce purchases of goods and services in high technology, in which Japan hoped to catch up until the country became competitive, when natural market forces would increase exports and restrain imports.

The transition to knowledge industries became infused with an added meaning. For many Japanese, it was the final assault in the 100-year effort to overtake the Western powers. As the race became more intense, people from all circles rallied to the cause. Scientists and technicians who had been dubbed "copiers" by foreign rivals were out to prove that they could be as creative as anyone. Businessmen accused of "receiving government assistance" sought to prove that they had succeeded by their own efforts. Bureaucrats accused of unfair protectionism were out to prove that they were abiding by international rules and that they could manage innovation as well as borrow it.

The process of modernizing shipbuilding and steel had been extraordinarily complex, but these sectors were nothing compared to becoming the world's leader in information. It required a vastly more complex research program. Information was not a single industry but a vast array of industries and technologies. Leadership would require not only the development of new industries but the remaking of old industries. It would require not only the expansion of the service sector but its reorganization. It would affect not only work life but also home life. Japanese planners, impressed with the scope of change, believed it was indeed a "revolution," which required yet another national transformation.

1. REORGANIZING FOR GROWTH: SPLITTING BUREAUCRACIES AND REVIVING COMPANIES

At the end of World War II, Japanese leaders had concluded that America was the most advanced nation, and they therefore endeavored to have some Japanese group follow developments in each major sector of American life—whether government, business, academic, even recreational. Computers, which would become the entering wedge of the information revolution, were of minor importance at the time, but they were no exception. By 1955, MITI had already organized a Research Committee on the Computer to ensure that it kept informed about American computer developments.

Even before then, by 1953, scientists at Tokyo University had begun attempting to develop computers with vacuum tubes. Tokyo University Professor Eiichi Goto, who was to become a major leader of Japanese computer research, developed the parametron, a circuit element earlier invented by Von Neumann, and this was further developed jointly by the University of Tokyo and Nippon Telegraph and Telephone (NTT). At the time, the parametron seemed promising to Japanese leaders, and Hitachi and Fujitsu used it as the basis of their first generation of computers. In 1954 scientists at AIST's Electrotechnical Laboratory (ETL) began a new project to explore the transistor, then at the cutting edge of new developments in the United States. By 1957, a team of scientists at ETL under the direction of Shigeru Takahashi had assembled a transistor-operated computer, the Mark IV. At this point the initiative was passed to private industry for commercial application of ETL advances with only a minuscule subsidy because at the time computers had low priority.

Consumer electronics companies, except for a brief foray by Matsushita, showed little interest in computers until the late 1970s. MITI believed consumer electronics companies could develop with little government help, as indeed they did, and they found expanding markets and higher profits in the consumer market. Besides, once the government became heavily involved in the computer industry, neither these fiercely independent companies nor the government believed it would be easy to work together.

Rather, NTT, AIST and the communications companies took the lead in computers. Communication switching gear had a great deal of technology in common with computers, and the large communications companies were prepared to make the necessary investment. These firms had long experience in collaborating with the government during and after World War II in the tight-knit communications community under the technical and administrative leadership of the Communications Ministry. The Ministry had led the introduction of telephone and communications equipment ever since the founding of its research lab in 1891 with the cooperation of Western Electric. During the 1930s, as Japan moved toward independence from foreign technology in wireless, telephones, electricity, and power transmission, the communications firms had accepted the leadership of the Ministry and during the war even produced primarily for the Ministry.

Soon after the war, as communications grew and proliferated, bureacracies were divided and reorganized, structures became more complex, and organizational rivalries replaced the earlier tight-knit community. One major split came in 1949 when the Communications Ministry was divided into the Ministry of Telecommunications and the Ministry of Posts. In 1952, at the end of the Occupation, Japanese made the first of these into a public corporation, NTT, and placed it under the second, which was renamed the Ministry of Posts and Telecommunications (MPT). Because NTT's officials had until then been bureaucrats themselves and because it became a large, rich organization, NTT in fact enjoyed considerable independence from its ministerial supervisors. In 1953, NTT's international wing, Kokusai Denshin Denwa (KDD), further branched off to become an independent company.

A second split occurred between electronics and communications. The electronics industry, which through the war had also been under the Ministry of Communications, was given to MITI, because it was regarded as industrial promotion. MPT retained communications, to assist telephone development of NTT. This second split required a parallel split in the research community working on electronics and communications. Those in the Communications Ministry laboratory working on electronics went to form a new lab, the Electrotechnical Laboratory (ETL), under AIST. Most former researchers remained to work on communications in the old lab, renamed Electrical Communications Laboratory (ECL) and led by NTT under the bureaucratic supervision of MPT. Though the cleavage between electronics (MITI and ETL) and communications (MPT and ECL) seemed reasonable at the time, it turned out that technological developments knew no such boundaries. When the technological distinctions between computers and telecommunications became blurred, so did that between MITI and MPT and between ETL and ECL, providing more than ample opportunity for struggles over turf, funds, and new technology.

Just as Japanese studied foreign products carefully and then tried to make them a little better, so they studied foreign organizational models and then tried to improve on them. NTT modeled itself after AT&T, and its lab, ECL, modeled itself on the Bell labs, but the Japanese felt that AT&T's overwhelming reliance on a single supplier, Western Electric, removed the stimulus of competition and left the telephone company too dependent on one company. They believed that distributing contracts among several companies that also had to compete in commercial markets would force companies to give better performance and enable NTT to get better service and quality at lower prices.

Four communications companies, all to play a central role in computer development, became the main suppliers to NTT. To jealous outsiders, they were known as the "NTT family," although the extended NTT family included nearly 300 suppliers. During its heyday until the mid 1980s, when family relations were attenuated as NTT became more open to competitive bids, family relations were strong but complex, a blend of parental benevolence and strictness toward children and of competition and cooperation among siblings.

NTT's history of technical leadership, its size, and, in the early decades after the war, its contacts with Bell Labs gave it unquestioned technical preeminence even while critics complained of arrogance, excessive bureaucratism, inefficiency and excessive costs. Companies wanted to be part of the family in order to share its technology and to produce for its massive orders, and NTT was accustomed to expect ready compliance and high standards of performance. Yet companies do bargain with NTT and try to define contracts to accord with their commercial needs. NTT cooperates with individual companies in developing products, but, recognizing that valuable commercial secrets are involved, it takes great care to see that secrets of one company do not go to another. By retaining some of its highest technology and not passing it out too freely, NTT endeavors to keep the respect and cooperation of the companies. Of course, more than one company may work on specific projects, requiring a sharing of technology, and members of one company talking with personal friends in another get a sense of what others are doing even while they are competing for contracts.

Within the family, NEC (formerly known as Nippon Electric Corporation) is known as the "favorite child." Founded in 1899 as a joint venture between Western Electric and a Japanese trading company, NEC has been Japan's preeminent communications company. NEC began importing telephone equipment early in the century and then manufactured equipment that Western Electric designed. It gradually began developing its own communications equipment and in the 1930s broke foreign connections and produced overwhelmingly for the Communications Ministry. NTT's first president (1952–60) was Takeshi Kajii, former NEC president, and after retiring in their fifties more former NTT officials have gone to work for NEC than for any other company.

Hitachi is a much more diversified company than any of the other major communications firms. It has a solid base in industrial machinery, heavy electrical products and consumer electrical products, as well as shipbuilding and communications. It profits from affiliation with other Hitachi firms in shipbuilding, metals, and chemicals. Because it is the wealthiest of the four and least dependent on NTT, it is closer than the others to being a stepchild.

Fuji Electric Company, which was started in 1923 by Furukawa Mining as a joint venture with Siemens, was a highly diversified electrical equipment company until 1935, when Fujitsu, specializing in electronics and communications, broke off. Fujitsu is therefore smaller and less diversified than NEC and Hitachi. With a narrower resource base, it had to assume more risks to remain in the computer race, but because its key technologies were close to those of computers and because of the persuasiveness of a dedicated and talented computer specialist in the company, Toshio Ikeda, it chose to bet on computer development. As the only major Japanese company with more than half of its business in computers, it has pursued computer marketing and technical development with a special fervor.

Oki, the fourth communications company, founded in 1881 as Japan's first manufacturer of telephones, was commited to computers and computer-related products, but was not as strong as the big three. As a smaller company, almost entirely in the communications field, Oki is very dependent on contracts with NTT. It tends to be very cooperative with NTT and, while not the strongest child, it is certainly the most obedient and NTT therefore regards it as the most lovable.

Until the 1980s, when consumer electronics companies entered computers in a major way, three other companies with varying degrees of commitment to computers joined Oki in the second tier of computer companies. Toshiba, a strong, diversified company established in 1875, ranks second to Hitachi in electrical appliances. It worked closely with General Electric, which now has more than 10 percent ownership. It is loosely affiliated with the Mitsui group as NEC is affiliated with the Sumitomo group. It had not concentrated on computers as much as had companies in the first tier. Matsushita, the largest electronic appliance company, retained some interest until the early 1960s, when the level of investment and risks grew very large. It then concentrated in the rapidly growing consumer electronics market until the late 1970s, when it returned to computers. Mitsubishi Denki, while a strong company, had been busy producing heavy machinery, industrial products, and other electronic products often related to the Mitsubishi group, and these commitments were much stronger than to computers. It lost interest in the early 1960s but in the late 1970s returned and quickly advanced to a leading position in office computers.

As in the opening of robotics and other new industrial sectors, when computers began developing, MITI worked closely with private industry and other specialists to define the field, determine the optimal organizational structure, and bring the appropriate companies into an association to work on common problems of research, information gathering, and product and market development. Emerging large fields may require their own laws, but in 1957 computers were far too small to receive such attention. However, in 1957, as applications using transistors led to a boom in electronics, the Electronics Industry Act helped pave the way for transistor development. Paralleling the new Electronics Industry Association of Japan (EIAJ), an Electronics Industry Section was established within MITI's Heavy Industry Bureau to provide direction for this new industry. The new act incidentally provided for computers and assigned responsibility for computer development to MITI's new Electronics Industry Section. NTT, the common carrier, did not have formal authority to develop the computer industry, but nothing prevented it from working with its suppliers to develop computers for its own use.

2. OPENING THE DOOR PARTLY, 1960

In computers MITI confronted a basic problem like the one previously confronted in the machine-tool industry. Major Japanese industrial companies, to compete with the West, needed modern data-processing services, but Japanese computer makers were not yet able to compete with Sperry-Rand (Univac) or IBM and were not likely to achieve that level soon. At the time, Japan did not allow foreign companies to have dominant positions in joint ventures, let alone wholly owned subsidiaries in Japan. But IBM was in an unusual position because some large Japanese companies were already using IBM products and others increasingly needed them, and IBM insisted on establishing a wholly owned subsidiary.

In 1960, despite strong opposition within MITI and many business circles, MITI permitted IBM to establish a wholly owned subsidiary. In return IBM agreed that its patents available for licensing to companies in the United States (by a 1956 American court decree) and later in Europe would be available for licensing on the same basis to interested Japanese manufacturers. Although IBM-Japan became a Japanese company and was soon to have 100 percent Japanese employees, unlike Japanese subsidiaries in the United States, it was regarded as a foreign company, excluded from—indeed the target of—collaborative Japanese computer efforts.

Although Hitachi and Toshiba were as large as IBM, within the computer field IBM was so dominant that Japanese computer company leaders and MITI bureaucrats, lacking the usual methods for keeping out competitive foreign products, had to work harder to find ways to restrain the necessary but frightening giant. Over the years MITI and IBM reached an uneasy modus vivendi. IBM operated by MITI rules that restrained its activity, kept MITI informed of its plans, and hired former bureaucrats whose loyalty may have been more to MITI than to IBM. MITI observed formal correctness while trying to protect and strengthen IBM's Japanese competitors.

Like the United States, Japan is concerned with the dangers of monopoly, but on the whole MITI uses more flexible means to assure competition than resorting to antitrust law. It often does things to strengthen the number two and number three firms in a sector when one company is dominant. One logical way to deal with IBM was to encourage alliances between Japanese companies and IBM's foreign rivals. Within several years, virtually all Japanese computer firms had found foreign allies with whom to share technical assistance and licensing arrangements. Hitachi teamed up with RCA in 1961, Mitsubishi with TRW and NEC with Honeywell in 1962, Oki with Sperry-Rand in 1963, and Toshiba with GE in 1964. Only Fujitsu, for the moment, remained independent of foreign technology, and in the meantime was accorded a special status as a purely Japanese company. As in other industrial sectors, foreign partners were not allowed to have substantial equity participation or any control over domestic computer production.

A customer wishing to buy a foreign computer had to explain why the computer was needed and get MITI's approval to import. If MITI judged a domestic system adequate to perform the task, it advised the customer to purchase a domestic machine. When IBM sought MITI's permission to produce a new model, if the IBM model was considered too similar to a model a Japanese company could produce, permission was delayed or withheld. In the 1960s, because domestic machines could not meet the sophisticated requirements for services like banking and airline reservations, such customers were allowed to buy foreign machines. MITI was aware that it could not investigate each request thoroughly, and it wanted to provide incentives for companies to purchase domestic machines. A Special Tax Treatment Law for the benefit of strategic industries was applied to the computer industry from 1961 to 1966, giving special depreciation allowances to companies purchasing domestic machines. Another law allowed the domestic producer adjustments for losses in purchasing old domestic machines when replacing them with new ones.

IBM offered customers leasing arrangements. In 1961, Japanese computer makers, with assistance from MITI, established the Japan Electronic Computer Corporation (JECC) to buy computers from Japanese manufacturers and lease them to users at subsidized rates. JECC borrowed funds from commercial banks, trust companies, and life insurance companies, but half of its assets were provided by the Japan Development Bank, which provided some 364 billion yen between 1961 and 1978. Loans were renewed in 1978. The system has remained unchanged since 1961: Only domestic manufacturers may sell machines to JECC, foreign content of machines is strictly limited, and IBM-Japan is counted as a foreign manufacturer.

In 1962, to narrow the technological gap between Japanese computers and the IBM 7000 series, MITI organized FONTAC, a computer-development program with the technical leadership of ETL and the participation of Fujitsu, Oki, and NEC. At the time, however, MITI vastly underestimated the research effort that would be required to keep pace with foreign computer advances.

3. LAUNCHING LARGE-SCALE COMPUTER RESEARCH, 1965–68

In November 1964 a large-scale computer developed under the FONTAC program was ready for testing, but this was hardly cause for satisfaction, for just seven months earlier IBM had announced its 360 series with compatible machines of varying sizes. The new series showed that the technological gap between IBM and Japanese companies had grown. Concern was heightened by GE's purchase in the same year of France's Machines Bull, leaving Britain as the only country besides the United States with a viable computer industry. Greater efforts were required if Japan was to keep its computer industry.

Companies are not always eager to accept MITI's leadership, but Japanese computer companies were then worried about survival and eager to cooperate. For the first time, MITI bureaucrats defined the computer situation as a crisis, precipitating a whole new system for large research projects. Such a major decision required consultation and study by an advisory committee of senior government officials, business leaders, and academics. MITI lost no time. By September 1964, some five months after IBM's announcement, an advisory committee to AIST, the Industrial Technology Council, had held a series of meetings, carried out background studies, and recommended a major integrated research program to develop important new technology, including computers.

The recommendation served as the basis for establishing within AIST a new National Research and Development Program, administered through a new office, the Large-Scale Project Office. Technical leadership for a project remained with the appropriate AIST lab, but these labs were not equipped to provide the broad coordination among companies, government offices, universities, and research centers. This was provided on the staff side by AIST's new Large-Scale Project Office and on the broad public advisory level by special subcommittees of the Industrial Technology Council. Since that time, on the average, one or two new large-scale projects have been begun each year. The super-high-performance computer project was one of the first three projects inaugurated in 1966 and far more important for international competitiveness than the other two, desulfurization technology and MHD (magnetohydrodynamic) power generation.

Meanwhile another advisory council, the Electronics Industry Council, had been meeting to provide further inputs of advice for the forthcoming computer research project. In its final report of April 1966, the Electronics Industry Council concluded that Japanese computer companies would have difficulty competing with IBM without government assistance. The report recommended strengthening JECC, rationalizing the production of peripheral equipment, and developing programs for training systems analysts. It also recommended a concerted research program, with the close cooperation of bureaucrats, academics, and the private sector, to develop a super high-performance computer. The super-high-performance computer project, eventually costing some 100 billion yen over six years, was not huge by international standards but in Japan was then unprecedented. Some fifty researchers from ETL and the participating firms worked at project headquarters at ETL, but much more work was assigned to private companies to do internally.

New patterns of project organization were required. Although patterns of government and private business cooperation may sound all the same to outsiders, among participants the differences are crucial. Most large projects of this kind in Japan since then have passed on public money to the company either by a form of "matching grant" (*hoshokin*) or "research contracts" (*itakuhi*, sometimes translated as consignments).

Matching grants go to firms that put up some of their own research funds. The grants assist in developing projects that are risky or expensive and might otherwise not be undertaken, but the company is allowed to keep the patents and market the product. Such grants are used when commercial payoff is likely, and the firm can thus be counted on to work enthusiastically. Theoretically the grants are loans to be repaid to the government if the results are profitable, but in practice they have rarely been repaid.

Research contracts are used to produce generic processes or products more remote from immediate commercial application. The funds come entirely from the government, and the firm works on the government's behalf. The government specifies precisely what the firm is to do. Patents belong to the government, which may license them to any firm or to selected firms. Because the work is done for the government and has less clear commercial advantage for the firm, it is understood that companies do not exert themselves as much.

The super-high-performance computer project was not new basic research. It had an urgency but it also had modest goals, for Japan was then far behind. The aim was to master foreign technology and to use the foreign model to assemble a large-scale computer with attached software and peripherals so Japan could remain in the computer competition. The project was sufficiently remote from commercial application that the government financed it entirely, made specific assignments to companies for certain specified research, and took rights to patents.

The art of the AIST official in charge of a project is to mobilize others to define and implement a project that will keep competing companies cooperating while pushing ahead the state of science and technology. Defining a project requires many rounds of delicate and complex negotiations to find in what areas competing companies can be expected to cooperate with enthusiasm. Companies generally want to take part in the projects because they receive funds and keep up with technology. Even if they don't get specific secrets, by working with government researchers and with people from other companies they can follow developing technology and have some idea what competitors are doing. Furthermore, they know that MITI officials will use their power to award licenses, grant approval for plant sites, and mediate with lending institutions to reward companies that are cooperative. Thus even companies ahead of rivals and reluctant to share technology in joint projects feel it wise to take part.

The trick is to define projects in which the competitors will work well together. Negotiations to achieve this may seem endless, but once agreement is reached the paperwork is almost nonexistent. The assumption is that people can, within considerable bounds, be trusted and that they will perform better if given considerable latitude to do what is needed to get results. A project that in the United States might require several hundred pages of precise legalistic wording is handled in MITI with a one- or two-page document.

Patterns of administration to be used in later projects were developed within the super-high-performance project. Research contracts for group projects involving several companies require ongoing negotiations among companies beyond the span of control of a government office. Therefore, AIST has the companies involved in the project establish a research cooperative *(kenkyuu kumiai)*, and the cooperative members work out among themselves the complex details of scheduling and division of labor and funds. The appropriate lab under AIST first works with the companies in defining the project and continues to provide technical leadership and generally does final testing. The research contract is negotiated with the cooperative, which in turn disburses funds to the individual firms.

AIST considered having each firm send personnel to the cooperative administrative staff, but company rivalries, variations in office procedures, and coordination proved so difficult that AIST allowed one company to serve as project secretariat *(kanji gaisha)*, with the idea that there would be some rotation of the secretariat among companies in subsequent projects. Naturally, AIST chooses for the secretariat a company it believes it can work well with. The company that serves as the secretariat has the advantage of knowing what all other companies are doing and of receiving extra funds to cover administrative costs, but it also has its reputation on the line with the success or failure of the project. Therefore, as a project goes on, the company serving as the secretariat tends to assume more responsibility and other companies less. As secretariat for the super-high-performance project, AIST chose Hitachi, a company with strong computer capability that had worked closely with MITI in heavy electrical equipment. During the first year only a small number of researchers were involved, and ETL worked closely with the companies in defining the project. In the middle years of the project, as it reached the height of activity, sub-projects were assigned to various companies, universities, and government labs.

During these middle years, it became clear that more efforts were required in software than originally anticipated, and this eventually took some 47 percent of the project budget. In order to let software developments proceed while their people concentrated on hardware, NEC, Fujitsu, and Hitachi joined to form a new company, the Japan Software Company. By virtue of developing an operating system and programming software packages for the project, overnight it became Japan's largest software house. Funding levels were low, relations with sponsoring companies did not turn out well, and labor relations were soon unpleasant. Unknown to the project leaders at the time, not only MITI officials but a number of young Communists judged computers to be a key future industry; they found jobs in this software company and proceeded to use the company as a place to pioneer labor activity in high-tech areas of the future. Before long, Japan Software was dissolved and companies pursued their own software development.

The super-high-performance project had originally been intended to last five years, but in 1970, as the consortium of companies and government agencies was about to start the final year, the next shock, the unveiling of the IBM 370 series, hit. IBM could offer a broad range of services at cost advantages and RCA and GE decided to give up their flagging computer businesses. Although Japanese companies had collectively made great strides as a result of the super-high-performance project, they had not yet committed themselves to the final product when the 370 was announced. After considerable debate, they extended the project for one year to build more memory capacity.

Still, IBM's new capacities were so impressive that project leaders realized few large users of computers in any country would want to risk buying a computer that forced them to give up IBM software, as well as their own in-house software already developed on IBM machines, and risk being left behind the new IBM developments. If Japanese computers were "plug compatible," they might have a chance to woo customers who would not have to take the risks of leaving the IBM system. Project leaders therefore made the landmark decision that the final machine assembled as a result of the project would be compatible with IBM machines. It may have constrained their system designs but it gave their hardware a wedge to enter the market.

In the final stages of the super-high-performance project, there was disagreement as to whether one company or two would put the system together. ETL officials believed that Hitachi, the project secretariat, had a technological edge over Fujitsu and decided that only Hitachi should put the system together. Until that point, Fujitsu had been proud that it was the only company without foreign technological ties, but it had begun to wonder. At that point it was clear that the project should pursue an IBM-compatible strategy, and an opportunity presented itself. In 1971 one of IBM's brilliant computer designers, Gene Amdahl, left IBM and set up his own company. He and the Fujitsu computer specialist, Toshio Ikeda, had known each other for some years and in 1971 their relationship blossomed. In 1972, when Amdahl's new venture was floundering financially, Fujitsu rescued Amdahl and invited him to Tokyo for a series of ten lectures to Fujitsu leaders and the two companies thereafter played a key role in developing IBM-compatible technology. After Ikeda's death, Amdahl gradually came to believe that Fujitsu had taken advantage of him to get technology, but the company he founded marketed Fujitsu computers in the United States.

In Japan in 1972, as the super-high-performance project drew to a close, the term "computer" still meant large mainframe computers. Here Japan was still substantially behind IBM, but the frantic collective activity had enabled Japan to remain in the computer race. It also had allowed AIST to move down the learning curve in how to organize large collective research projects.

4. MODERNIZING TELECOMMUNICATIONS, LATE 1960s

In the 1960s and 1970s, in Japan as elsewhere computers and telecommunications developed largely on separate paths until new technology in the late 1970s blurred boundaries, creating a single field that Harvard Professor Anthony Oettinger called "compunications" and NEC's Koji Kobayashi called "C&C" (computers and communications). From 1954, when NTT's great leader Yonezawa accepted the assignment of the computer industry to MITI, until the late 1960s, NTT concentrated on communications and played a minor role in computer development. Yet NTT was not unaware of developments because politicians and bureaucrats expected that all important relevant agencies be represented in national projects, and NTT representatives took part in all AIST computer projects even if bad relations sometimes made the representation pro forma. Furthermore, the companies supplying NTT were the same ones working on AIST projects, and technological advance anywhere—at NTT, the companies, or AIST—were soon reflected elsewhere in the chain.

Within communications, the powerful technical leadership of the Ministry of Communications over commercial companies was if anything strengthened in the postwar period as it was transformed from the Communications Ministry (1945–49) into the Telecommunications Ministry (1949–52) and into NTT (1952). As commercial companies did not revive until the mid-1950s, the most talented graduates in communications from the end of the war until the mid-1950s therefore overwhelmingly tried to enter what became NTT. This generation of talented people led the technical modernization of Japanese communications, especially after Yonezawa's visit to AT&T in 1950, and dominated NTT leadership until the mid-1980s.

From 1945 until the late 1960s, NTT was busy repairing Japan's war-damaged telephone facilities and extending them to meet the explosive increase in demand that accompanied economic growth. When NTT began its first five-year plan for telephone services in 1952, there were approximately 1.5 million subscriber lines. In 1978, with the completion of the fifth five-year plan, NTT had basically achieved universal service with 35 million lines.

By the mid-1960s, as the rate of growth in telephone service began to slow and the company accumulated funds, NTT began to devote more attention to new technology. Beginning in 1966, and for a period of ten years, for example, NTT sent more than forty researchers to AT&T and Bell Labs for periods of six months or longer to learn about its new technology.

NTT wanted to install computers for its own use, and in May 1968 it set up an architecture committee composed of its own research people and some of the ablest engineers in Hitachi, Fujitsu, and NEC. As beloved as Oki was by NTT, Oki, with less bargaining power, agreed to all its computer activities in a joint venture, Oki-Univac. While Univac did not have majority ownership, from NTT's point of view the joint venture was a foreign company. NTT had a strong national identification dating from wartime days under the Communications Ministry, and while Oki remained a favorite supplier, Oki-Univac lost out with NTT.

By July 1968, NTT's architecture committee had defined the system specifications. Thereafter the committee worked closely with NEC, Fujitsu, and Hitachi engineers as the companies began producing the test computers and bringing them into a systems configuration known as DIPS-1 (Denden Kosha Information Processing System). Not totally unlike the process at ETL, NTT made the specifications and then the companies developed the prototypes and returned them to ECL for final debugging. But NTT wanted its own design and, jealous of MITI and ETL, wanted to develop its own computer capabilities.

Although the DIPS-1 series was not very useful, it enabled NTT to begin some on-line systems. DEMOS (Dendenkoosha Multi-access On-line System), begun in 1971, provides information and calculations for science, technology, and engineering, primarily for businesses. DRESS (Dendenkoosha Realtime Sales Manage System), begun in 1970, provides businesses with calculations to control sales, inventory, and production. Because personal checks were not highly developed in Japan, transactions among branch banks, their main office, and other banks required an on-line system. NTT and Fujitsu developed an appropriate system, ZENGIN, in 1973, and ZENGIN was eventually linked to the international SWIFT system for interbank transfers. When ZENGIN went into operation, it was the most advanced computerized banking system in the world. In 1964, Japan National Railway (JNR) launched its own on-line system linking nearly 2,000 terminals and providing more than 2 million seat reservations per day; NTT later took over its administration as well. Companies producing the equipment for NTT thus had an opportunity to get paid for their costs in this expensive period early in the learning curve, taking advantage of new technology both from AIST projects and NTT labs. And NTT could plan for later DIPS series that were to be far more useful.

5. COOPERATING FOR INTERNATIONAL COMPETITION, 1971

At the beginning of the 1970s the Japanese government realized that to keep world markets open for its exports it would have to liberalize partially even "infant industries" like computers that were not yet internationally competitive. Computer companies naturally resisted. Japanese political leaders were able to delay liberalization until April 1976, allaying foreign complaints and overcoming domestic resistance by offering the computer companies some 60 billion yen between 1972 and 1976 to prepare for liberalization. The companies realized it might be in their interest to heed MITI's urgings to cooperate not only for research but for production, but they were very wary of one another. As soon as political leaders decided to buy off company opposition, MITI bureaucrats moved quickly to tie the subsidy to cooperative production projects, a move that politicians accepted. The new law developed by MITI in 1971, the Specified Industries Law for the Electronics and Machinery Industries (Kidenhoo), was for "developing technology and reorganization," a bland statement of MITI's strenuous efforts to push companies into cooperative projects.

The "project" aimed to commercialize the super high-performance computer, just completed. In naming the new project, MITI, tired of always chasing behind some IBM machine already in existence, wanted a more forward-looking image. It was not yet as bold as it was to become a decade later when it responded to fourth-generation machines by announcing a fifth-generation project. IBM called its new series announced in 1970 the "3.5 generation," halfway between integrated circuits and very-large-scale integrated circuits. MITI called its new project to promote company cooperation and commercialization the "3.75 generation" project.

MITI's program for company cooperation, arrived at through laborious negotiation, linked the six major computer companies into three groups. Fujitsu and

Hitachi had already decided on IBM-compatible computers, and it was therefore logical to link them together. Hitachi was to develop two large machines, an M-170 aimed at meeting IBM 370-158's performance, and an M-180, approximately twice as powerful as IBM's 370-168. Fujitsu was to develop two machines, one smaller, an M-160, and one larger, an M-190.

MITI's efforts at pushing cooperation tend to work best when companies are short of funds and need help, when the companies concerned have a history of cordial relations, and when the research and information to be shared is basic and is only remotely related to commercial success. None of these factors applied to Hitachi and Fujitsu. For a brief period in early 1974 they had a joint-venture marketing company, Facom-Hitac, Ltd. But the spirit of competition was greater than that of cooperation. The Hitachi M-180 and the Fujitsu M-190 were announced together in 1974, but in September 1975 Fujitsu announced an M-180II to compete with Hitachi's M-180, and Hitachi announced an M-1060II to compete with Fujitsu's M-160. From then on, it was market warfare. When Fujitsu announced an M-200 in 1978, Hitachi responded with an M-200H, and when Hitachi announced an M-280H in 1980, Fujitsu countered with an M-380 in 1982.

From a technological perspective, the link between NEC and Toshiba was also logical. NEC had formed a relationship with Honeywell in 1962 because Honeywell's H-200 computer was considered an excellent machine for the time. NEC therefore concentrated its energies on developing communications, relying on Honeywell for computer development. When General Electric left the computer business in 1970, Honeywell bought GE's computer technology. As Toshiba had worked with GE in computers since 1964, it was natural that MITI should link NEC and Toshiba.

The relationship between NEC and Toshiba worked more successfully than that between Hitachi and Fujitsu. NEC developed models 200, 300, 400, and 500 in the ACOS series. Toshiba developed models 600 and 700, and the two cooperated in the largest models, 800 and 900, announced in 1976. In 1974 they formed a joint venture NTIS (NEC-Toshiba Information Systems), in which NEC owns 60 percent and Toshiba 40 percent, for the marketing and servicing of the ACOS series.

The two other major computer companies, Mitsubishi Denki and Oki, were weaker computer producers. Oki, troubled by financial difficulties, was by then out of the large mainframe business and concentrated on small computers, peripherals, terminals, and office equipment. Mitsubishi Denki, having potential access to the many Mitsubishi-related firms, many of which then used IBM machines, went for an IBM-compatible strategy and concentrated on office machinery. It was therefore appropriate for them to cooperate in the COSMO series, designed for offices, Mitsubishi developing the central processing units and Oki the peripherals.

Until the 1970s, Japanese companies had avoided direct competition with IBM, which was allowed the large mainframe market. Japanese companies had confined themselves to making smaller machines except for some special models for NTT and Japanese government offices, which did not purchase foreign machines. The new technology from the super high-performance project, government aid from 1972 to 1976, and the limited cooperation in the 3.75 project helped Japanese companies to move upscale to compete directly with IBM and better protect their home market as domestic demand expanded and liberalization proceeded.

6. MASS PRODUCING PERIPHERALS

In the auto industry, MITI had encouraged specialization among parts manufacturers in order to develop economies of scale to prepare for foreign competition. In the computer field, it encouraged similar cartelization and specialization among those making peripheral equipment.

Ordinarily when a new sector opens up, before technology has stabilized and before it is clear which Japanese firms have the greatest potential, MITI is happy to see all-out competition. When technology begins to stabilize, MIT considers cost competition the critical factor, and tries to do what it can to speed up the process by which a few strong companies get economies of scale: weeding out the weak, standardizing products, and encouraging specialization among firms. This was especially true in the late 1960s and early 1970s in preparation for allowing foreign firms more market access and more opportunities to set up wholly owned subsidiaries in Japan. Standardization in peripherals became easier after 1964, when IBM's 360 series became a single product line. The decision in 1970 to go plug-compatible helped give further stability to the peripheral market. This new stabilization provided the opportunity for strong Japanese companies to excel at what they do so well: move quickly to get a high-quality product, devise excellent cost-saving production techniques, mass produce, accept small profit margins, engage in forward pricing for market development, and overwhelm the competition.

In 1969, MITI formally organized a cartel to standardize the design of peripheral equipment where technology had stabilized, thus assuring the stronger companies of markets for mass production. MITI decided that by 1969 the technology for various types of punch-card and paper-tape equipment had already stabilized. The next year, it determined that line printers and magnetic drums qualified.

During the 1960s imports of central processing units generally paid 15 percent tariffs, but in 1970 as Japan began expanding its peripheral production, duties on peripherals were raised from 15 to 25 percent. In 1972, with standards stabilized, to encourage economies of scale it began a five-year project of modest scope— 4.6 billion yen—to subsidize the development of key peripherals.

The largest computer companies were concentrating on the central processing unit, and many of the former second tier of computer companies or related strong electronic companies concentrated on mass production of peripherals, producing printers, disk drives, floppy disks, cathode-ray tubes (television screens), terminals, and other equipment, just as they had previously succeeded in other consumer electronic products.

7. INVESTIGATING JAPANESE LANGUAGE PECULIARITIES, 1971

Even before the technology from the super-high-performance computer project passed to private companies for commercial development, research leaders in AIST and ETL were considering what new technology to explore that might be commercialized three to five years hence. One problem that required much more work was the input and display of the 90 kana (syllable designations) and 2,176 Chinese characters in common usage.

They realized it was a highly complex task that would require many years of research. Computer companies were motivated to pursue their own hardware development but basic research to allow computers to use Chinese characters required government aid if it were to advance quickly. Even then the initiative came more from ETL technicians than from companies or bureaucrats. Not only company officials but MITI bureaucrats in the Industrial Electronics Division who reflected industry views dragged their feet.

The key technical problem, long studied at Bell Labs and elsewhere, was getting the computer to recognize and process patterns whether inputted through voice or written word, and the project was therefore named PIPs (Pattern Information Processing System). Funds were provided by the government, and research contracts were issued. Toshiba, a strong company with good relations with MITI, supplied the secretariat.

The stubbornness of the research problem caused the project to be extended for a second five years, until March 1981, and it eventually cost some 22 billion yen in government aid.

The project achieved considerable technical success. By the end, researchers could distinguish some 2,176 printed characters at the rate of 100 characters per second with 99.9 percent accuracy. They could distinguish the 96 handwritten alphabet, numerical, and *kana* characters with a 99 percent accuracy at the rate of 400 characters per second. They could distinguish some 100 words spoken separately by a variety of male and female speakers with 99 percent accuracy with one second recognition time per word. They made comparable advances in picture recognition and three-dimensional object recognition. The researchers judged that they had closed the gap with the United States in image processing, and that their speech-recognition work was at or above levels of other countries.

Yet the extension of PIPS for a second five years and the final results had so little immediate commercial payoff as to make companies and their defenders within MITI critical of the project organizers and of ETL in general. Of course, PIPS can be justified for promoting contact between companies that speeded up information exchange or for giving advanced research training to young people who would later contribute to their own companies. Even skeptics acknowledged that the government should help explore promising but risky avenues of research for it saves the companies from having gone down the same blind alleys entirely at their own expense. But in research projects as in production, Japanese have high expectations and PIPS was judged unsuccessful. By the mid-1980s when the results of PIPS were being commercially developed, the project was regarded, in retrospect, more favorably.

8. SUCCEEDING IN SEMICONDUCTORS, 1976–79

The dedicated effort of Japanese working together to develop computers by protecting their own market, borrowing technology, focusing research efforts, and guiding product development to get economies of scale finally paid off in a big way in the late 1970s, almost fifteen years after they had identified it as a major concern. The timing was fortuitous but perfect. Japanese semiconductors had established a beachhead in the U.S. market in 1977 and 1978. In 1979, when the United States suffered a severe shortage of memory chips, Japanese producers, with products incorporating the results of the new VLSI (very large-scale integrated circuit) project (1976–79) were ready to fill the gap.

The project goal had been clear from the beginning. Japanese leaders expected IBM to launch a new generation of computers by about 1980. They expected the new IBM computers to be fourth-generation machines using VLSIs rather than LSIs. The threat of being left behind by new IBM advances and the strategic importance of computers for the information society led Diet leaders not only to support a vigorous national effort but personally to urge NTT, MITI, and company leaders to work together. Planners at AIST conceived a fourth-generation project that would begin with semiconductors and move on to a later phase of research on the remaining requirements of fourth-generation machines: operating systems, software, and peripherals. Although in 1976 planning had already begun on what became the second phase (1979–83), its shape was still sufficiently unsettled that bureaucrats initially announced only the first phase, the semiconductor project.

Japan was already highly competitive in semiconductors used in the electronics industry, where it then dominated the world. However, in semiconductors for computers, despite progress in the super-high-performance computer project and a small, focused 3.5 billion-yen-per-year semiconductor project (1972–74), it was still behind. The VLSI project focused on memory chips, which are used in great quantity in computers and which can be produced much less expensively in massive quantities. They were therefore strategically important in reducing computer costs and in permitting volume sales. As VLSIs were at the heart of commercial needs, companies were prepared to contribute to the project, and by then planners had more experience as to where to draw the line between cooperative and independent work. Some work was carried on in a central lab and two applied labs, but in large part the government relied on individual firms to carry out the work. MITI made matching grants, allowing companies to keep most patents. In addition to government overhead and personnel expenses, the government contributed some 29 billion yen for the project and private firms some 43 billion.

The choice of firms to participate in the project reflected MITI's long-range strategy. Oki, a major producer of semiconductors and a participant in previous computer projects, was excluded. The project was not just to build semiconductors but to contribute a crucial link in building strong vertically integrated companies that, like IBM, were capable of producing everything from semiconductors through hardware and software. For this it required companies with great financial and personal resources, and Oki lacked the requisite strength. Oki was by no means discarded, because it continued to concentrate in peripherals, facsimiles, and other office equipment, and NTT later sent management and shared technology with its beloved but weakened child to enable it to produce viable semiconductors. But the big game favored strong, vertically integrated firms able to adapt instantly to new technology anywhere along the line.

Furthermore, with vertical integration, even without nontariff barriers, it would be difficult for foreigners to sell semiconductors or other computer parts in the Japanese market. Although Japanese companies in the project did specialize in producing certain kinds of chips and sold specialized chips to one another after the project was over, by the end of the project they bought very few chips from foreign companies. Japanese companies continued buying such items as testing equipment from foreign companies, which had unquestionable technical superiority, when only small quantities were required, but Japanese companies were determined to produce even these remaining items before long.

Because ETL facilities were too small for a project of this scope, for the first time such a project needed an outside lab with appropriate facilities. Such facilities were in companies, but worry among them about advantages to rivals led to six months of discussions before the companies, organized as a VLSI Technology Research Association, agreed to locate in a wing of the NEC central lab in Kawasaki. About 100 researchers, a few from ETL but most from the participating companies, spent the full four years working there on the basic VLSI component and manufacturing technology. For applied work, the companies were grouped into two independent companies, each with its own lab. Some 320 (from Fujitsu, Hitachi, and Mitsubishi Denki) worked at a new Computer Development Lab and some 350 worked in a lab already established for the 3.75 project.

The work included examination of all aspects of semiconductor production: microfabrication, materials science, semiconductor design, process technology, test and characterization techniques, and device design. A considerable amount of the early expenses were for purchasing the most advanced semiconductor manufacturing and test equipment from the United States. As in many cases of Japanese advance, the project concentrated on a strategically critical but limited product segment with clear standard specifications: 64K RAM (random access memory chips that could hold more than 64,000 bits of information) to replace 16K RAM, then the state of the art. They would also develop technology to lay the basis for 1 megabit D-RAMs.

For project management the key problem was handling the narrow line between cooperation and competition. At the central lab, which worked on problems farthest from application, project leaders insisted that each subteam include members of several companies, but each subteam was dominated by the company from which its head had come. Employees from Hitachi, Fujitsu, and Toshiba led microfabrication teams, a Mitsubishi employee led the processing technology team, and an NEC employee led the testing devices technology team. (An ETL employee led the crystal technology team in addition to being responsible for overall technical leadership.) As things moved closer to application, the two applied labs had responsibility, but much of the work was taken back to the five individual companies, for cooperation became more difficult. Of course, work led directly by ETL and some generic work was jointly patented, but some 84 percent of the 1,000-odd patents deriving from the project went to individual companies or employees of those companies.

In 1979, just as the firms began commercializing the results of their research, IBM was going into production with its 4300, and because its own 64K-RAM chips developed problems it suddenly had to buy massive amounts of 16K-RAM chips. American semiconductor makers had meanwhile not expanded production owing to the economic slowdown, so they were not prepared for this unexpected demand. Japanese companies had just expanded, and by the end of 1979 had captured 40 percent of the American 16K-RAM market. It is impossible for outsiders to know what percent of total VLSI production is done within IBM, AT&T, and other computer companies and not marketed, but by 1982 Japan had captured some 70 percent of the world's 64K-RAM market.

Because few Westerners had been following Japanese developments, Japanese success came as a surprise. The scope and strategic importance of the Japanese achievement of 1979 along with NTT's display of a 256K RAM in the same year sent shock waves through Silicon Valley, surprising specialists and shaking confidence in American technological leadership. Even after the shock waves subsided, American semiconductor companies were left with great difficulty in matching prices, and they feared that Japanese success would be repeated in more advanced memory chips and in microprocessors. In the meantime, American computer companies bought Japanese chips because they were of high quality and low price, and available in times of shortage. But some feared and experienced cases when Japanese suppliers gave preferential delivery of newly developed semiconductors to their own in-house computer divisions, giving them a competitive advantage over foreign rivals.

9. REDUCING THE SOFTWARE GAP, 1979–83

By 1979 Japanese industry leaders were confident that they were ahead of Europe. In their view, America had dissipated much of its lead by being too free with its technology, a mistake they were determined not to repeat. They were confident that they had narrowed the hardware gap with IBM, and the new hue and cry was "the software gap." As the VLSI project was drawing to an end, it was officially called phase 1 of the "next (fourth) generation of computers," and phase 2, for the "promotion and development of technology," focused on systems software. Both in the narrower meaning of software (systems software and applications software) and in the broader meaning, the information processing industry (including data processing, programming, and servicing), MITI had been concerned about software since 1969 and began its first software five-year plan in 1970. There were still software gaps, but when MITI put software on center stage in 1979, the Japanese were already farther along than most foreigners realized because they mistakenly equated lack of independent software companies with lack of software.

To Japanese software specialists, greater attention to their area seemed overdue. Japanese companies like NEC, trying to sell computers abroad in the late 1970s and early 1980s, lacked the software to gain significant market share while foreign companies, even without state-of-the-art hardware, were selling well because of software. Furthermore, Japanese leaders, always looking for the biggest areas of growth, noticed that software revenues were growing some 20 percent per year, faster than hardware revenues. Makoto Hattori, then president of the Japan Software Industry Association, estimated that nonhardware costs in Japan were only 50 percent of total information-related costs compared to 80 percent in the U.S. and therefore had great room for growth.

Japanese practices made it difficult for independent software houses to grow rapidly. The software industry had burst on the U.S. scene in 1969 when IBM began "unbundling," charging separately for its software and hardware products, enabling independent software houses to provide software packages and services while computer companies provided hardware. In Japan, however, large computer companies wanted to maintain very close relations with users, including customizing some software for them. Users regarded certain services as the responsibility of their supplier and it seemed like crass commercialism to charge for it.

Furthermore, just as large Japanese firms rarely use outside lawyers, accountants, and consultants, who might leak secrets of company operations to competitors, so they avoid giving independent software specialists access to sensitive data. When necessary, Japanese users prefer to train a substantial staff of in-house software specialists who can not only preserve secrets but who understand all the inner workings and therefore better adapt to the firm's needs.

Despite the small number of independent software houses, the software specialists in Japanese computer firms and in user firms are often very sophisticated. In some areas of manufacturing like continuous steel casting that require large amounts of software engineering for manufacturing, Japan is without peer. As many as several hundred highly skilled software engineers were required to work several years to develop one of Japan's dozen large continuous casting steel plants. The ZENGIN system for banks, the Japan National Railway system for on-line rail reservations, and Nihon Keizai Shinbun's program and Asahi's NELSON program for newspaper editing are among the most advanced systems in the world.

MITI's concern is not with software programmers in large user companies or with developing small software firms that dispatch personnel, for these services will grow with commercial need and do not require national programs. MITI's aim is rather to raise the general technical level of software specialists, to develop systems software, and to strengthen software firms capable of developing creative software applications of general applicability.

In 1969, as IBM began unbundling, the Information Industry Subcommittee of the Industrial Structure Council of prominent citizens and MITI staffers prepared a report on future directions for the Japanese information-processing industry. The report, submitted in May 1969, became the basis of MITI's first software five-year plan, including creation of the appropriate infrastructure. Within MITI itself, a Data Processing Promotion Division was established, one of three divisions in the Machinery and Information Industries Bureau, to supervise the expanded activity in data processing. In May 1970, as consultations between MITI and private firms gradually defined the new field, the Japan Software Industry Association (JSIA) was formed with thirty-two software companies as charter members. In the same year, the Information Technology Promotion Law was passed, and a new governmental agency, Information Technology Promotion Agency (IPA), was established.

IPA was a creative effort to promote Japanese-style firms that could fulfill the same function that vigorous independent software houses fulfilled in the United States. Although some Japanese companies were pioneering in venture capital, most Japanese leaders, government and private, found venture capital unattractive. Not only did it encourage split-offs that troubled the large firms that were the nation's strongest competitors, but the cost of venture capital was excessively high. Better to find another way with less risks, lower costs of capital, and less wild profiteering. With the cooperation of the three long-term-credit banks, IPA worked out a system whereby specialist committees under it reviewed applications from software companies wishing to create software programs. IPA guaranteed bank loans to these small independent software houses at low rates of interest. A loan guarantee fund of 2.08 billion yen was created with some 1.05 billion yen from the government and a matching fund from the three long-term-credit banks. The amount lent out was not to exceed ten times the guarantee fund, that is, 20.8 billion yen. The small software companies often had cores of talented older people, often retirees from strong companies, and with this kind of financial backing they could also recruit talented young people otherwise unwilling to join small, insecure firms.

In addition, IPA accepted applications from these software houses to develop software programs of high technical quality and broad applicability. Specialists working with IPA selected the most worthy applications, and then the government issued research contracts and controlled the resulting patents to ensure their wide applicability. The government tried to push rapid diffusion of results by publicizing them to interested groups and offering the packages at modest prices. The income from the sales was used to support further development of new work. By the end of 1981 some 127 projects had been funded. Many of them were for adaptations of basic computer language and for development of general systems of data handling with wide applicability.

Because the small firms had not generated the breakthroughs that MITI had hoped would advance the field, in 1975, for its second software five-year plan, MITI moved to establish under IPA a private company, the Joint System Development Corporation (JSDC), which opened the following year. IPA continued to fund projects lasting one or two years while JSDC provided a framework for firms jointly to undertake larger projects of three to five years' duration.

Seventeen core companies, generally the strongest independent software houses, formed JSDC to develop common production technology. By 1983 two more core companies were added and 105 other companies cooperated with JSDC in its efforts. By then JSDC had a fund of 2.66 billion yen from private and government sources to provide interest for overhead, with additional project funds coming from the government and member firms. Funds are also available for multiyear projects from bicycle racing funds, channeled through a conduit, the Software Industry Promotion Association, that in turn offers contracts for multiyear projects that include intelligent editor, computer languages, machine translation, and data base development.

IPA's major project for 1976–81, a 6.5-billion-yen Software Production Technology Development Program, aimed to develop program modules for editing and assembly needed for automating software production. The hope was to leapfrog foreign software developments, improving both productivity and reliability. The project did develop some new languages, but although extended a year beyond the original five years planned, it did not achieve the desired breakthroughs and therefore work continued within companies and in the fifth-generation project.

For its third software five-year plan that began in 1979, Japan planned to expand work on software packages, drawing on the new Software Promotion Law enacted the previous year to help prepare for new developments.

Software packages then constituted about 50 percent of America's software development effort but less than 5 percent of Japan's. MITI aimed to raise this to 20 percent by the end of the plan in 1984. Special incentives and a network of software companies were to help achieve this goal.

Beginning in 1979 special tax incentives were provided for companies developing systems software and certain applications software. In the same year, IPA inaugurated a special Program Reserve System whereby software companies selling a program could place 40 percent of the income into a taxfree reserve fund for four years to be used in the meantime for the development of software programs. To receive such credits, companies were required to register their software programs, and this had the additional merit of making possible an up-to-date listing of available software programs, thus encouraging the rapid dissemination of new ones.

In 1982 a Software Development Insurance Fund was created to help small companies that could not afford to employ their own software specialists. Worried that these small companies might not be able to pay for software development they requested, software companies had sometimes hesitated to fill such requests, and the new fund eliminated this bottleneck.

One of the major efforts in the third software five-year plan was to raise general technical levels to speed dissemination of new information systems. In 1981, IPA established a Software Maintenance Engineering Facility, with an initial five-year grant of 5 billion yen, to help users in such tasks as data-base management, control systems, network controls, and basic support facilities. The facility has on-line capability to service the requests for help from smaller software houses. At the same time, IPA also established a Software Technology Center, a permanent research and development facility for software engineers dispatched from mainframe producers, software houses, research institutes, universities, and computer users wanting to upgrade their software technology skills. It was hoped that the facility would speed the spread of new technology from the laboratory to commercial firms.

The major effort of the third software five-year plan was phase 2 of the fourth-generation computer project (1979–83), primarily for systems software development by the five large integrated computer companies of phase 1. During the second half of phase 2 they were joined by Oki, Matsushita, and Sharp working on peripherals. These eight companies formed the Electronic Computer Basic Technology Research Association (ECSTRA). Funding organization was similar to the VLSI project. The phase 2 budget was 47 billion yen but, in view of national budget deficits, the government lowered its portion from 50 to 45 percent. Since operating systems provide the interface with the machine, linking the machine with memory management, data-base management, and high-level languages, the work is done by engineers close to hardware development. This area attracts some of the most talented engineers, and they made considerable progress, although not with the spectacular commercial results of the VLSI portion of the project. In fact, as revealed in Hitachi's and Mitsubishi's acknowledgement of stealing secrets from IBM, Japanese firms were troubled by the difficulty in producing timely systems software for new generations of IBM-compatible machines.

Meanwhile, leaders of the large integrated companies and MITI officials, drawing on a successful pattern of Japanese organization, developed a new vision of how to match foreign independent software houses. Zaibatsu "groups" had found that specialized firms, linked in a network, combined the advantages of specialization with access to timely information and mutual assistance.

Like Zaibatsu groups, Fujitsu, NEC, and Hitachi would each spin off software subsidiaries specializing either in a functional specialty or a regional locality. The functional specializations would include such areas as medicine, biology, agriculture, industry, education, family affairs, publishing, recreational games, communications, and small business. Until the early 1980s about 70 percent of Japanese software business was in the Tokyo and Osaka areas, but these regional subsidiaries would be poised to take advantage of the growth in regional computer business anticipated to begin in the late 1980s. The parent computer company would have far more power than any postwar zaibatsu firm, but the software subsidiaries would be small enough to have a good span of control, independent enough to be innovative, and close enough to a network to share information. Since each of the three networks would have a parallel set of software subsidiaries, each subsidiary would have competitors in rival networks, and this competition would drive them to high performance. It reflected a familiar Japanese approach: cooperation for more effective competition.

Fujitsu is spinning off six to ten subsidiaries a year and has announced that it expects to have 100 functionally and regionally specialized subsidiaries by 1990. NEC and Hitachi expect to form subsidiaries at a comparable rate. Influenced in part by the thinking of American specialists, the companies believe that an optimal size for a software company is about 200 people. They typically begin subsidiaries with nuclei of thirty to fifty people, mostly recent retirees and temporary assignees from the parent companies, which by the 1980s were large mature companies that could spare the personnel. They then expand primarily by taking new school graduates. Although the most talented young engineering graduates still prefer to work at the parent companies on hardware problems, the prestige of software is rising, and those challenged by rapid growth opportunities come to these new subsidiaries. Meanwhile, parent companies like Fujitsu, which in 1982 built a new software building for 1,700 employees at the base of Mount Fuji, are rapidly increasing their software capabilities.

The late chairman of the Japan Software Industry Association, Makoto Hattori, had a vision of strong independent software companies producing generic software, with a range of more specialized companies producing applied programs. In these new software company networks, the parent computer company, in addition to doing systems software for its machines, aims to develop some generic software and to facilitate transfer of new ideas and technology within the network.

Company and MITI officials are convinced that competition among firms in given fields will lead to waves of software application as competitors move with great speed to follow when one company introduces popular innovations. When some hotels, for example, began to use automated billing, automated recording of outside phone calls, and automated calculation of drinks taken from hotel-room refrigerators, others moved quickly to do the same. Similar waves of automation have spread through various types of banks and insurance companies. Japanese computer companies are convinced that coming waves of automation in government offices as well as private companies offer a fertile ground for rapid expansion of their software subsidiary network.

These efforts reflect the great skill of Japanese leaders in devising innovative new frameworks that make for high company performance. In the mid-1980s the Japanese still had problems in systems software, and Japanese firms acquired technology in ways that most Japanese, if fully informed, would acknowledge as improper in order to do well in certain "decisive battles." MITI was reluctant to move quickly to give high levels of protection to foreign software companies entering the Japanese market and the effect was almost the same as protecting an infant industry from foreign inputs. Yet the main trend was conscientious and careful work that greatly advanced software capacities on a broad front. By 1983, as phase 2 of the fourth-generation project and the third software five-year plan drew to a close and major computer makers rapidly expanded their new software subsidiary networks, talk of the "software gap" began to recede.

10. ENTERING THE "MICON" MARKET, 1980s

In Japan until the late 1970s, "computer" meant large mainframe computer, and all of MITI's research projects were for large computers. Aside from Mitsubishi Denki, even the minicomputer market was not well developed.

Globally, IBM still had more mainframe business than all Japanese companies combined, and Digital Equipment Corporation (DEC) and Control Data Corporation (CDC) each had more computer business than any Japanese firm. Yet within the Japanese domestic market, second in size to the U.S. market, Fujitsu, Hitachi, and NEC continued to grow rapidly. There are no official statistics, but in 1979, according to *Nihon Keizai Shinbun*, Japan's *Wall Street Journal*, Fujitsu edged out IBM-Japan to gain the largest share of computer sales within Japan. To be sure, many Japanese government and public corporations bought only domestic machines and regarded IBM-Japan as foreign. NEC, whose computers had fallen behind in the early 1970s because Honeywell, on which it relied for computer development, did not keep pace; revived quickly in the late 1970s as it developed its own computer skills. Although it is difficult to compare the sales of Hitachi, which leases far more of its own machines than do other companies, NEC edged out Hitachi in computer sales in 1982. Hitachi, although taken aback by the discovery that its employees had stolen secrets from IBM, remained a strong company, with rapid advances in technology, a large consumer sales network, and impressive capital resources.

As steady as was the growth of large mainframe computers, at the end of the 1970s and in the early 1980s growth of this business could not compare with the explosive growth of the microcomputer, soon abbreviated affectionately as "micon." In 1975, only four years after Intel developed the microprocessor chip, Japan had formed, after the usual discussions to define the parameters of the new field, a Microcomputer Systems Industry Association, which by 1981 had forty-nine member companies. Although in the early 1980s Japan still had to rely on foreign suppliers like Intel for advanced microprocessor designs, the domestic market for micon had grown from 4 billion yen in 1978 to 25 billion in 1980, when Japanese companies sold 300,000 micons. During the early 1980s sales roughly doubled each year.

The explosive improvement of microprocessors had paved the way for a revolution in Japanese offices. The typewriter, which had long dominated Western offices, was not widely used in Japanese offices because mechanical and electric typewriters could not easily incorporate 2,000 characters. Japanese typewriters on the eve of the micon revolution had been large, clumsy, expensive, and difficult to use (requiring a six-month training program), and were therefore used only by a small number of specialists. Because Japanese offices then still relied overwhelmingly on handwriting, copy machines had spread like wildfire, and the diffusion of facsimile machines far outpaced that in the United States.

Advances in microprocessors made possible in the early 1980s, for the first time in history, a popular Japanese typewriter. Technologies continued to evolve, but an ordinary office worker could now learn quickly how to type in *kana* (syllables) on a typewriter-sized keyboard to get a word to appear on a screen in *kanji* (Chinese characters). If several characters had the same sound, several *kanji* would appear on the screen and the typist could with one more push of a button select instantly from the several. Certain software programs even analyzed context up to several words before given words to eliminate or reduce alternatives to the correct *kanji*.

Until recently, Japanese offices have been very inefficient. Because of this backwardness and the size of the new technical leap, Japanese leaders are convinced that the micon revolution will have a profound impact in the offices of Japanese manufacturing and service companies. In government offices, think tanks, and company headquarters, leaders and rank and file are considering the implications of the revolution with the same enthusiasm and thoroughness that characterized such other major changes as the early introduction of state-of-the-art manufacturing systems.

New forms of equipment and organization are being tried, although most companies expect to retain marked flexibility through the 1980s to allow for new technology. At the very least, however, the new office will make widespread use of micons, display screens, printers, copiers, and facsimile machines. Already many corporations are hiring fewer young women straight from high schools and liberal arts backgrounds and more from two-year technical colleges with strong training in mathematics, computers, and other office technology. This new revolution, which will reduce office costs and create new capacities to handle information, is being given great weight by Japanese leaders, bureaucrats, and businessmen thinking about world trade. Because international protectionism for manufactured products diminishes the opportunity for export increases despite Japanese competitiveness, they see a great future in export of services as Japan gradually undertakes the same kind of reorganizations that have taken place in manufacturing.

MITI has not played an important role in developing micons. As with consumer electronics, the area does not require great assistance by the government to develop, for many companies like Sony, Matsushita, Sanyo, Ricoh, Sharp, Canon, Casio, Epson, Fuji-Xerox, Oki, and Sord, as well as the large computer companies like Fujitsu, NEC, Hitachi, Toshiba, and Mitsubishi Denki, have the resources to do it on their own. MITI officials, thinking of national policy, are more concerned about issues like standardization of equipment, rapid diffusion of information, experiments with new office equipment and reorganization, public training, and public acceptance of new equipment.

In 1967 to help speed public diffusion of information and appropriate training and reorganization as new technology comes on stream, MITI established the Japan Information Processing Development Center (JIPDEC), a nonprofit, public-private institution. Among its tasks are surveying public demand for computers, sponsoring conferences, providing a clearinghouse for computer information, handling public relations for issues like privacy and secrecy, and maintaining contacts with relevant foreign groups. Since microcomputers and home computers involve this broader public, JIPDEC endeavors to anticipate and forestall possible public resistance to rapid expansion of information age technology.

Surveys of public attitudes suggest that at first the "pasocon" (personal computer for home use) will not expand as rapidly as the office computer. Small businesses and professionals are at least as eager as large companies to utilize the micon, and among large companies those with many branches, like retail chains, are expected to be among the first to diffuse them widely.

At some point, beginning in the late 1980s and early 1990s, home micon use will take off, after NTT opens its lines to private branch exchanges (PBXs) and new services are developed. Exactly how it will be combined into a home information system is at this point still unsettled, but no one doubts that as a consensus is reached, at some point after micons are widely diffused in offices that the pasocon market will expand very rapidly.

Given the price-cutting and rapid changes in American home computers in the early 1980s, Japanese companies postponed serious efforts to enter the American market. The great success of vigorous English and American micon producers in their own home markets made Japanese entry more difficult, even in the mid-1980s, than entry into the television and audio equipment markets had been in an earlier period, but Japanese producers did not give up the hope that as technology stabilizes their capacity for low-cost, quality mass production will gain them significant entry at an opportune time. In the meantime, their success in standardized products gave them a dominant position in micon peripherals and components, both at home and abroad.

Technological change is now so rapid that national and company plans undergo constant reevaluation and change. When it first developed the Walkman, Sony was delighted. Several years later many leaders of the audio industry wondered whether the success of Walkman and its imitators compounded their difficulties with the saturated audio market, for many customers satisfied with Walkman felt it unnecessary to buy large, expensive audio systems. Even successful computer companies worry that they are far more vulnerable to technological change than is heavy industry. The cost of processing one bit of information has decreased by millions of times since Univac was first produced in 1951. Will technological advance and intense competition reduce costs and eliminate the need for many kinds of machines and perhaps even some occupational specialties? Regardless of or perhaps because of these uncertainties, Japanese companies and bureaucrats feel they have no choice but to rush on to the newest technologies.

11. EXPANDING THE RESEARCH BASE, 1980

By the 1980s increased income enabled Japanese computer companies to afford more research. Some companies estimated that the private sector was spending twenty times as much on computer-related research as the government. Yet the need for research continued to expand, and government officials, surveying their role, felt that even modest government grants would mobilize collaborative efforts to keep abreast of foreign competition. Researchers at ETL, ETC, and elsewhere were attacking new theoretical problems like inference, logic, and linguistics. Aside from work under NTT, the biggest national efforts begun in the early 1980s were four AIST-led projects, three of which are:

1. *A project to develop new materials to be used by industry in the 1990s, the Next Generation Fundamental Industrial Technologies Program.* One portion of this, the New Function Elements, was allotted 25 billion yen to develop new electron devices for semiconductors. The project was to attack three problems: superlattice elements, three-dimensional elements, and environment-resistant elements. Fujitsu, Hitachi, and Sumitomo Electric worked on the first project, developing techniques to form multilayered superlattice elements in which each layer was only a single atom thick. NEC, Oki, Toshiba, Mitsubishi, Sanyo, Sharp, and Matsushita worked on three-dimensional elements to increase the density of elements per chip forty to fifty times over existing levels. Toshiba, Hitachi, and Mitsubishi Denki worked on the final project to develop circuits with integrated 30,000 transistors per chip, capable of withstanding radiation levels of 10 million rads, and others capable of withstanding temperatures up to 300 degrees centigrade to be used in specialized areas like atomic energy and space.

2. *A project to develop an Optoelectronics Applied Measurement and Control System.* Under ETL leadership, Fujitsu, Hitachi, NEC, Toshiba, Mitsubishi Electric, Matsushita, Furukawa and Sumitomo Electric are organized into an Engineering Research Association of Optoelectronics Applied Systems to develop optical and electronic elements that can be incorporated into integrated circuits. With an initial grant of 18 billion yen, they established a joint research laboratory in October 1981 in the Fujitsu Laboratories in Kawasaki.

3. *A project to develop the supercomputer, the High-Speed Computer System for Scientific and Technological Uses,* with an initial allocation of 23 billion yen. Participating companies (Fujitsu, Hitachi, NEC, Toshiba, Mitsubishi Denki, Matsushita, Furukawa, Oki, Sumitomo, and five others) are organized into the Association for the Development of High-Speed Scientific Computers. The association does not have even a centralized lab but issues contracts to companies and sponsors meetings to exchange information. Since silicon dioxide-based devices are encountering fundamental limits of gate switching speeds, the companies began exploring alternatives for high-speed logic elements, particularly Josephson junctions, HEMT (high electron mobility transistors), and gallium arsenide. Present computers process information sequentially, but the new challenge is to develop a machine capable of performing different kinds of analysis simultaneously.

At the time the project began, the world's fastest computer was made by the American company Cray, but given the modest efforts on supercomputers at Cray and Control Data, Japanese companies believed that with their large systematic project they could soon get the world lead. By 1983 various Japanese companies, Fujitsu, NEC, and Hitachi, were claiming the world's fastest computer, even before their products were debugged. Rather than buy the Cray, Japanese users, partly on government advice, awaited Japanese products. Meanwhile Japanese claims helped the U.S. Department of Defense attract project funds to maintain technical superiority. Many doubt the commercial feasibility of supercomputers since potential users within Japan are estimated to be fewer than fifty, but Japanese leaders believe that spin-offs for mainframes and the prestige of having the world's fastest computers justify the project. These three projects may turn out to have far more impact on the shape of the computer field than a fourth project, which has received far more attention, the fifth-generation computer project.

12. LEAPING AHEAD TO THE FIFTH GENERATION, 1990s

As early as 1977 and 1978, as the phase 2 software project got well underway, bureaucrats and advisers were actively debating where to go next in computer research. The headquarters for the debate was MITI's Electronics Policy Division, which had much greater political ambitions than the two other divisions of MITI responsible for computer development—the Data Processing Promotion Division responsible for software and the Industrial Division responsible for coordination with industry. The debate involved researchers, academics, bureaucrats, and, through the media, the public.

Proud leaders within the Electronics Policy Division, humiliated by projects that were always in IBM's shadow, wanted a grander vision with Japan leading the way or, as more diplomatic spokesmen put it, "making its contribution to world science and technology." Concerned with foreign, and particularly American, reaction to continued Japanese subsidization of computer research, these bureaucrats thought that a grand vision, with some foreign participation, might reduce foreign objections and ensure domestic funding.

Electronics Policy Division bureaucrats were not technical specialists, and many skeptics questioned whether efforts to achieve "artificial intelligence" by duplicating human reasoning and perceptual processes would pay off. For twenty-five years the field had attracted a dedicated group of American researchers but it remained controversial. The idea of making user-friendly machines that would respond and answer in natural human speech or writing seemed too risky to win the enthusiasm of industry leaders and their allies among MITI's Industrial Electronics Division bureaucrats. But Electronics Policy Division bureaucrats were determined, and they found an advisory committee headed by Professor Motooka of Tokyo University that could define feasible research goals and persuade enough people about the potential importance to justify the risks.

Kazuhiro Fuchi, then a forty-six-year-old section head at ETS, had become friendly with Motooka when they were advanced researchers at the University of Illinois some twenty years earlier. As chairman of the basic theory group planning the fifth-generation project, Fuchi had written one of the background papers for the advisory committee, giving his views of problems that deserved future study. He had a reputation for being a creative and able administrator; the committee liked what he said and selected him to be director of the research center.

The question of how to make Japan more creative had been a favorite topic since the late 1960s. An argument often used by frustrated young people held back by arbitrary and stodgy elders was that, to make Japan more creative, talented youth needed more leeway. The United States succeeded, they argued, because of the opportunities it gave to ambitious young people. The average age of the first forty researchers assembled to begin exploratory research in April 1982 was thirty-one. Many section leaders were over thirty-five, but many researchers were under thirty. To be sure, they had solid training in science and engineering (of the first forty, thirty were trained in electrical engineering, six in physics, four in math), and they would work on hardware issues. But they would also work on "user-friendly" issues, the psychological, linguistic, and cognitive issues linked with hardware. Project leaders felt that older researchers lacked appropriate training and flexibility to start completely afresh. They established in Mita (downtown Tokyo), completely separate from any company's or government's laboratory, a new research lab known as the Institute for New Generation Computer Technology (ICOT). Although they have a high-level advisory committee and another working level academic advisory committee, ICOT has more independence than previous projects.

For young Japanese working on the project, the freshness of the issues, the international attention, the potential of achieving breakthroughs and putting Japan ahead of the West in computers, lends an aura of excitement and grandeur to the mission.

Yet the remoteness of the project from foreseeable commercial applications, the gap between research goals and known technology, the youth of the researchers, the project's independence from established research centers provoked more controversy than any other research project provoked. Senior researchers thrust aside for youth charged that the project was a political show. Companies contributing funds lamented that the project was too risky. Software specialists claimed that, despite its professed concerns, it was just another hardware project. Those excluded from the project charged that while MITI required companies to send top people they could only judge this by paper credentials (i.e., whether the person attended Tokyo University) and that companies often sent not their best people, whom they reserved for internal research, but the worst of those with the best paper credentials. Fujitsu, which felt that it was in the lead in many of the announced research areas, was about as enthusiastic about participating as IBM would be in a similar joint research project in the United States.

Unlike any other government-sponsored research project, the fifth-generation project was launched with an international conference, held in Tokyo in October 1981. No Japanese project had attracted more foreign interest, and responses of foreigners were as varied as those of Japanese. Some engaged in research on artificial intelligence proclaimed that ICOT was boldly investigating precisely what the United States ought to study. Some sounded the alarm that the Japanese were now overtaking the rest of the world in high technology. Others believed that artificial intelligence was not a promising line of inquiry and that the project was hopelessly vague and ill-defined. Foreign companies and governments were ambivalent about whether to take part, not sure that this would be an important project, cautious that foreign participation might be a one-way street, and yet wanting to be part of a project that had the potential for being in the forefront of world technology. Indeed, the basis of foreign participation was difficult to resolve, and in the first phase of the project all the researchers were Japanese. In the end the forces of narrow nationalism in Japan proved too strong, and in 1983,

MITI decided that there would be no foreign participants, although rather than announce this MITI announced new plans to have meetings between researchers from ICOT and those from other countries to discuss results.

As in most major projects, the first year or two was devoted to defining the problem. Though some 10 billion yen were allocated for the initial phase of the project from 1981 through 1984, even the level of eventual funding was then unclear. Despite the uncertainties, the goals had a certain coherence. "User-friendly" software would enable a wide range of users to have ready access. A machine capable of making inferences would be linked with a machine capable of handling vast data bases. The goals for the first phase of constructing prototype machines were met right on target.

Initially researchers had been divided into task forces exploring: (1) machines capable of making logical inferences and solving complex problems of a symbolic nature while using parallel processing; (2) knowledge-base systems that would permit analysis of more complex problems; (3) intelligent interface systems between the central system and natural language (voice, written, and picture image processing); (4) appropriate software systems and architecture; and (5) basic applications systems, such as translation between English and Japanese of specialized texts with 85 to 95 percent accuracy and other data systems that would permit answers to more complex questions. The second and greatly expanded phase of research was launched in November 1984 with the second international conference.

Meanwhile, away from the public eye, NTT's ECL researchers were working on many of the same kinds of problems. Since by the mid-80s NTT had access to $3 billion annual income and a $.3 billion annual research budget, it was able to fund a tremendous amount of research, and by the 1980s in fields related to computers and telecommunications it had even larger research staffs than AIST and it was able to recruit larger numbers of talented young people. Although foreigners were focused almost entirely on the fifth-generation project, NTT was in addition developing another vision for the information era.

13. DEVELOPING THE INFORMATION *SHINKANSEN:* INS, 1990s

NTT's vision for shaping the 1990s, although subject to modifications as plans mature, appeared as predictable as the fifth-generation project was unpredictable and illustrates another kind of national coordination for the information age. It draws on a technological and financial base already secured. Its potential for shaping Japanese society in the twenty-first century is at least as profound.

As in many areas, Japan's success stems not from being faster to identify the problem but from a more thorough, broad-based examination of all issues and a bolder more unified long-range strategic plan. In fact, partly because of jurisdictional disputes between MPT and MITI and between NTT and private companies as well as questions of deregulation and liberalization, many Japanese user services like value added networks still lagged behind those in the United States in the mid-1980s. But the Japanese are confident that they will have a superior, more uniform system in the 1990s that will offer more universal services accessible to everyone in the society. In the new, more open era beginning in the mid-1980s, NTT also could not dominate private companies and remain closed to foreign bidders the way it once did. By the 1980s the private market was much larger and some companies like NEC, Hitachi and Fujitsu had great capital resources and research facilities. With the gradual opening of NTT lines to private exchange branches in response to pressures from the Japanese business community and from foreigners, NTT was often competing with these private companies for user services. This and the gradual opening of NTT to non-family bidders weakened relations within the NTT family. Despite these confusions, which retarded developments in some areas, Japan maintained great telecommunication potential. Unlike the situation in the United States, which suddenly opened AT&T without even seriously considering the impact on international competition, the plans for opening NTT in 1980 and for making NTT a private company in 1985 were developed so as to keep a strong unified system and to restrain entry of competitive foreign products to allow Japan to catch up.

The dominant vision for the new telecommunications age, timed to draw on France's Simon Nora-Alain Minc report in 1978 and England's Carter report in 1979, was embodied in a report prepared for the Ministry of Posts and Telecommunications by NTT's senior bureaucrat, Executive Vice President Yasusada Kitahara, presented internally within NTT in 1980, and to the public in 1981.

By 1981 the decision was made to rely basically on fiber optics and digitalized equipment for Japan's future communication system, with satellites playing a supplementary role. Because optical fiber is very expensive, sparsely populated countries will use a higher proportion of satellite communication, but Japanese planners believe that the density of service in Japan will make good use of the tiny optical fiber cables no larger than a human hair that can each carry some 10,000 ordinary conversations. Compared with satellites, fiber optic cables are unaffected by atmospheric changes, far more durable, and more suitable for maintaining confidentiality.

Japanese planners introducing new national programs commonly talk about establishing experimental points that expand into lines, then lines that expand to cover the entire surface. NTT began by laying optical fiber in Tokyo and by 1984, as with the *shinkansen*, the first trunk line linked Tokyo and Osaka. By the late 1980s all small cities in the nation will be linked by trunk lines, and by 1995 the network of branch lines will cover the entire surface of Japan's four main islands. A fiber-optics cable to span the Pacific is planned for the late 1980s. Satellites will be used primarily for linking remote islands, for foreign communications, for backup in case of earthquakes and other emergencies, and for events like Olympics requiring vast increases of temporary service.

Opinion in Japan was sharply divided about whether to buy foreign satellites and to rely on foreign launching vehicles or to develop Japan's own rocket capacity and risk delaying the launching of communications satellites by as much as five years. By the summer of 1983 an advisory committee recommended the development of Japan's own rocket-launching capacity. After Japan's Number Two Communications Satellite was sent up in early 1983, plans called for a larger, half-ton satellite by the late 1980s. Planners estimated that it would take until the mid-1990s before Japan would have the rocket capacity to launch a satellite as large as two to four tons (and capable of handling 100,000 to 200,000 circuits, the estimated minimal size needed to make them commercially viable). NTT and KDD are trying to restrain foreign companies' satellite communications services entry into Japan until they are better able to compete. Broadcasting satellites involve no such difficult strategic issues. Number Two Broadcasting Satellite, a direct-broadcast TV satellite, was launched in 1984 and Number Three is scheduled for about 1989.

The transformation to digital switching equipment is scheduled to coincide roughly with the laying of optical fiber telephone lines. NTT officials vastly underestimated how fast digital equipment would become cost-competitive, but Japan is standardizing equipment in an effort to catch up and forge a unified national system. As fiber-optic cable lines are expanding, gradually the separate lines for different services—telex, computers, facsimile—will be linked together. The aim is to link all these services by 1995. It is estimated that the system will eventually cost about 20 trillion yen, and that NTT can easily invest the 1.4 trillion yen needed to achieve this.

CAPTAIN (Character Pattern Telephone Access Information Network System), a fixed-image teletext system similar to the British PRESTEL system, with fixed-image information on a TV screen in response to pushing *kana*, letter, or number keys, was developed in the late 1970s to provide content to the Information Service Network, INS. The television screen can present some 3,000 Chinese characters, graphs, *kana*, English letters, and numbers. Newspapers, broadcasting companies, publishers, advertising agencies, finance and insurance companies, travel agencies, and department stores cooperated with CAPTAIN to provide news and weather information, stock information, banking services, travel information, mail-order requests, games, and educational materials.

Trials began in the Tokyo area from late 1979 to early 1981, with expanded service trials from 1981 to 1984. Plans for expansion to national levels are scheduled to parallel the expansion of fiber-optic telephone lines and the digitalization of communication equipment. Continuous surveys are being made of public attitudes and demands to avoid England's mistake with PRESTEL in overestimating the proportion of home users. The proportion of Japanese home users, like England's, is expected to be less than in the experimental trials of the BILDSCHIRM system in Germany, where the popularity of catalog sales lifted home demand. The expansion of home banking in Japan is expected to speed up home demand eventually until the services are virtually universally available.

Japanese expect that two-way communication linking homes with one another and other facilities through on-line systems and electronic mail, providing access to data bases, will also be virtually universal when the system is complete about 1995. By then homes are to be equipped with telephones, facsimile machines, data terminals, video terminals, and printers, all connected with INS. Backing these up will be specialized centers for business telecommunications, home telecommunication, and information processing.

Just as the expansion of railroads in the nineteenth century and of highways in the twentieth stimulated the American economy, so Japanese expect that their information *shinkansen* will have an enormous stimulating effect on their economy. Although aware that Europe and North America will be linked by similar systems, they believe their system will be universal more quickly. They confidently expect that, just as the *shinkansen* was the most up-to-date rail transportation when it was completed in the mid-1960s, their information network system will be as modern as any in the world on the eve of the twenty-first century.

Japanese bureaucrats and manufacturers of telecommunications equipment are confident that the difficulties and uncertainties of foreign companies getting contracts with NTT will keep purchases from foreign companies at a modest level. Indeed, in 1984, four years after the agreement was signed, NTT purchased some $140 million worth of foreign equipment, over 3 percent of its procurement. Soon after AT&T was opened in 1983 Japanese companies were able to sell several times as much telecommunications equipment in the United States each year as American companies were able to sell in Japan.

Japanese companies happily spend a considerable amount of R&D funds in response to peculiar NTT demands because they have every reason to expect that they will make substantial profits when NTT procures great quantities of supplies from them. Since 1980, NTT has done a great deal to make the procurement process formally open, but foreign companies with advanced technology, observing past cases in which foreign companies were required to submit ever more detailed specifications of products without ever selling and then seeing NTT family members develop similar products, were slow to respond. Furthermore, they are doubtful that spending a great deal of time to develop products suitable for the Japanese market will pay off in sizable sales. Companies with digital equipment and fiber optics for sale reported no signs that NTT would buy from them regardless of the quality and price of their product.

Many NTT leaders want to demonstrate that NTT is ready to procure quality goods by fair open standards so foreign markets will be open to Japanese telecommunication products, but many NTT officials, some of whom expect to work in NTT family companies after retirement, feel comfortable dealing with Japanese companies with whom they have excellent long-standing relationships. NTT complains that foreign goods are below quality and that foreign companies don't design products for their needs. Foreign firms complain that NTT uses peculiar specifications in unpredictable ways to exclude them and that even when NTT makes a purchase it is to acquire know-how or display tokenism rather than to acquire substantial amounts of products over the long haul. Japanese leaders believe that the privatization of NTT in 1985 creates a more open market. Japanese firms hope that NTT's capacity to set national standards and procure great quantities of equipment and their own dynamism will enable them to gain a dominant position in the world telecommunications equipment market.

14. COMPETING FOR LEADERSHIP: MPT AND MITI

The linking of computers and communications everywhere requires readjustment. A computer company like IBM, despite considerable communications experience, must develop new capacities as it expands its communications equipment and services. AT&T, with quality technology but without experience producing and selling computers for the competitive marketplace, confronts even greater adjustment pains. The Japanese are confident that Fujitsu, NEC, and Hitachi, with long experience in communications and computers, are in strong positions for the new era. Japan's biggest problems center on MITI and MPT (Ministry of Posts and Telecommunications). The original division of labor, with MITI responsible for the computer industry and MPT responsible for supervising NTT as the common carrier but not authorized to develop industries, is simply no longer tenable. Just as Japanese companies live by market share, so ministries live by jurisdictional turf, and ministerial loyalty can be just as steadfast as company loyalty. The struggle between the aggressive, internationally experienced MITI and the more reserved MPT, accustomed to administering postal and telephone monopolies, pervades all aspects of telecommunication and computer policy.

The labs, ECL and ETL, have competed from the time they were split in the late 1940s but the competition intensified when NTT began linking computers with communications in the late 1960s. Both labs conduct research on all aspects of ICs, computers, and software. Theoretically, on large government research projects ETL and ECL coordinate their activities and assign people to work on each other's major projects. In practice cooperation is at best superficial for they not only duplicate research topics and equipment but withhold information from each other, plot and fight over budgets, academic advisers, new recruits, company researchers, and access to politicians.

ETL tends to have a more open, academic atmosphere and therefore attracts people more interested in basic research, whereas ECL focuses on telecommunications products. In the early years, when ETL had the strong leadership of Makoto Kikuchi, who led transistor development, and Hiroshi Wada, who guided the development of electronic calculators, ETL attracted outstanding people. Some of them now lead the fifth-generation project. In recent years, the growth of NTT's revenue base has enabled ECL to expand much more rapidly. For example, in 1981 NTT had about 5 trillion yen revenue and a research budget of about 70 billion yen. In 1983, whereas ETL had about 700 people, ECL had over 2,000, located at four sites: Musashino (their oldest site, with a general lab and digital switching), Ibaragi (near the atomic energy facility of Tokaimura, fiber optics), Yokosuka (software and computers), and Atsugi (their newest site, semiconductors). ECL's superior depth, budget, and equipment, and its ability, as a public corporation, to offer higher salaries than a government lab like ETL give it an edge in attracting talented graduates. NTT's huge procurements and the desire of firms to keep NTT happy also give ECL an edge over ETL in getting the firms to send their best researchers for joint projects. The public prominence of ETL's fifth-generation and supercomputer projects help counter these advantages, but ECL's successes have affected ETL's morale.

Although the same companies work in both ECL and ETL projects, ECL still tends to work most closely with companies in its traditional family while ETL project leaders tend to be firms not in NTT's inner family. Hence it was Hitachi (the least central NTT family member) that served as the secretariat for the super-high-performance project and Toshiba for the PIPS project.

Perhaps the most serious policy dispute between the two ministries over the years has centered on the question of opening up NTT lines to outside users. As early as the 1960s, MITI and the business community, represented by Keidanren, pushed hard to develop programs of time sharing that would require NTT's opening its lines to allow private firms to compete for services provided by NTT. Their pressure strengthened as NTT's refusal led to Japan's falling behind foreign competition. The disputes between MPT and MITI are generally resolved at the highest political levels in favor of MPT, for NTT has had powerful political support. Local communities that want help in modernizing communication facilities or in getting frequency band assignments contribute to Diet members' campaign funds, and politicians getting these donations want to keep good relations with NTT and MPT to get favorable action. Some politicians fear that if NTT were private or entirely open, their roles as middlemen and these political contributions would disappear. MITI's political support is weaker and less single-minded.

In the 1970s, the opening of NTT procurement beyond its family became an international trade issue. The United States, urging the opening of NTT to outside bids, found itself on the side of MITI, and MITI was not unhappy to use foreign pressure to help open NTT. Although MITI was able to get support for a formal agreement between Japan and the United States to open the telephone companies in both countries for competitive bids in 1980, many NTT officials dragged their feet.

In the early 1980s, when the government began privatizing some public corporations to reduce budget deficits, the business community supported by MITI pressured to make NTT a private company. It was commonly believed that Hisashi Shinto, the great shipbuilding modernizer, was made head of NTT because he would not oppose such a move. NTT could argue that, unlike the Japan National Railway, it was not in debt, and that telephone service and telecommunications research were strong, while atomic energy research was behind because of the splitting of the electric power companies. Those who favored privatizing argued that NTT's rates were too high, that strong unions had made NTT inefficient and excessively rigid, and that bad management had created a cash-flow problem, forcing NTT to go into debt to pay dividends to the national treasury.

Another battleground between MPT and MITI is cable television. MITI took the first initiative toward cable TV in the late 1960s with a consortium engaging in exploratory research. Once MITI's planning attracted attention, MPT argued that such a project was within its jurisdiction. The Ministry of Finance, wanting to avoid duplication, used budgetary leverage to get MITI to cooperate with MPT and NTT, but they achieved little success. Political leaders at the highest level then ruled that the project was within MPT's jurisdiction and NTT and MPT set up an experimental cable TV program in several hundred households in a huge new housing project, Tama New Town, on the outskirts of Tokyo. They chose a new developing community with the idea of using local two-way television service as a way of building community spirit, an important goal for the new media. They provided local programming, a library of programs for rebroadcast, many informational services, electronic newspapers, and photoduplication service.

MITI continued to want its own project. When optical fibers were discovered, permitting far more lines in a small space and hence a richer range of services and feedback, MITI had a strong case for starting its own project. MITI was allowed to begin its project in another new town, Higashi Ikoma, in the Osaka area, on the outskirts of Nara. MPT's and MITI's competing projects were quite similar and provided a wide range of services of high technical quality that were both very well received. The problem was that they were extremely expensive to operate, and there seemed to be no way by which most of their services, except for some of the still-image data base incorporated into the CAPTAIN system, could be commercially viable on a national scale.

Most foreigners, and the Japanese Ministry of Finance as well, consider duplication between MPT and MITI wasteful. To the participants, however, the situation is more like a relationship between two competing companies. Companies do not ordinarily consider it wasteful if they duplicate facilities or research of another company as long as they achieve reasonable economies of scale. The Japanese did not plan to have the two ministries compete and duplication is often unnecessary, but many Japanese who know both ministries well believe that the rivalries, like those between private companies, are a desirable stimulus to high performance.

Since the late nineteenth century, Japanese society has measured the success of bureaucrats concerned with various sectors of the economy by the achievements of their sector. This accountability provided the personal drive for bureaucrats that sustained a tradition of governmental assistance to industry. Beginning at the same time, American society measured the success of comparable bureaucrats not by the achievements of the sector under them but by how well they enforced the rules, and this sustained a tradition of adversarial relations and control over industry. The Japanese bureaucrat responsible for the success of his sector has a powerful incentive to help his team do well against rivals, foreign or domestic, and it is the same incentive that drives the competition between MPT and MITI.

15. TOKYO, THE WORLD INFORMATION CAPITAL?

Leading Japanese bureaucrats surveying the international scene see information not as an end in itself but as a vehicle for increasing productivity, national influence, and national welfare. They expect to use information to keep their manufacturing capacities at world levels and to drive the revolution that will make their service sector as competitive in the 1990s as their manufacturing sector became by the 1980s. The 1982 report of the Information Subcommittee of the Industrial Structure Council suggested that Japanese leadership in information would give them very important bargaining leverage with other countries. They want to use information to assist the aged and infirm in achieving ready access to help. They want medical records and useful diagnostic information readily available throughout the nation. They want information systems that will permit an ambulance to take a person to the nearest appropriate hospital with the most relevant equipment. They want warning systems for storms and natural disasters.

Japanese leaders realize that computers and the new information *shinkansen* are merely the pathways for making Tokyo the information capital of the world. They aim to provide content by expanding their lead in collecting useful information around the world and to improve its analysis, classification, and distribution to those who can best make use of it.

Japanese leaders are making every effort to anticipate and guide the impact of information on society. Relevant Japanese government agencies are constantly undertaking social surveys and commissioning appropriate studies. Of course, they are tracking problems of systems security, invasion of privacy, information thefts, and unreasonable concentrations of information power, and devising programs to cope with them.

They also want to maintain universally high educational standards so that everyone in the society can have ready access to information. One of the biggest issues being discussed is how to ensure universal distribution of information throughout the society. Japanese planners believe that Japan is a successful well-integrated society partly because, without welfare programs that discourage some from working, they have provided opportunities to ensure a relatively equal distribution of wealth. By providing high levels of education to virtually everyone, they have also kept educational disparities to a minimum. They are convinced that, as information replaces wealth as the key source of advantage in a new age, information equality will be a key issue. They are determined to ensure that everyone in the society is able to use computers and other tools that give ready access to information.

With the world's best-educated work force, with the world's largest trading companies collecting the information, with the world's best-informed bureaucrats leading the government, and with the rapid application of the world's most up-to-date technology, they are increasingly optimistic about their ability to make Tokyo the information capital of the world.

6

Japan's Learning Curve for Managing Global Competition

Japan's success in global competitiveness derives not from particular plans or targets but from skills acquired step by step. The skills could not be acquired suddenly by Japan or any other country for they rest on experience, analyses, and relationships developed over many years. Just as individual firms move along a learning curve as they acquire skill in making a new product more efficiently, so Japanese leaders since World War II have gradually learned to be more effective in guiding adaptation to global markets.

1. DEFINING THE NATIONAL INTEREST

The basic skill from which all else stems is thinking through the implications of global competition for all aspects of national policy. The Japanese persevered to acquire this skill because of the shock of being cut off from imports near the end of World War II. Starving, shorn of colonies, sorely in need of technology and continuous imports of raw materials, they realized they had to export to survive. But they did not suddenly understand the implications. Tens of thousands of Japanese leaders—politicians, businessmen, media representatives, academics—some by government design, but often by their own initiative, forged this understanding by years of foreign travel, study, analysis, and discussion. They learned how to frame the basic question, "How should Japan respond to the difficult problem of ———?" and enlist the best minds, within Japan and from around the world, to gather relevant information and consider what Japan should do.

To import needed raw materials and technology, they had to make products that could compete on world markets. Being ambitious for their country, they wanted to minimize foreign control of capital and production and wherever possible to add value to products in Japan. They were not willing to accept Japan's position of comparative advantage of 1945: low quality goods produced at low labor costs. They wanted to raise the wages and standard of living of their population, and this meant gradually raising their sights to achieve new comparative advantages.

They learned where their capacities stood in world markets. They learned to find where they had the best prospects for export, and how to distinguish those areas like steel, transistors, semiconductors, computers, and telecommunications that were strategic for other developments. They learned how to encourage businessmen to concentrate their efforts in areas of future growth where they had a chance of making it within a short span of time. They learned how to upgrade their skills as they concentrated on successively more complex areas. They gradually learned the logic of selecting new fields, the pacing of their development, and the inputs of technology, capital, personnel, and managerial know-how required to catch up in each new field. They learned which sectors, like consumer electronics, could develop with minimal government aid and which, like shipbuilding and steel, required more government help.

They explored ways to keep their costs as low as possible. To keep down transport costs, they learned to select the best coastal areas for heavy industry, areas where foreign materials could be brought in and goods exported with minimal breaks in transport routes. They concentrated on shipbuilding and shipping so as to cut the cost of ocean transport and avoid being at the mercy of other countries.

They explored energy costs and went for the lowest in the world. They encouraged the development of several key suppliers of each key raw material, not only for security of supply but as bargaining leverage to keep costs down. They encouraged the development of friendships—national, company, and personal—to assure the stability of these ties. They devised ways to get raw materials, not processed goods, and they learned how to group orders from Japan to get the maximum leverage in obtaining these raw materials on the most favorable possible terms.

They learned how to encourage a high savings rate and to help low-cost capital flow to areas of high priority. They were willing to wait and generate their own capital rather than permit foreign capital to play a major role. As a whole they found that, compared with stock equity, bank loans permitted better control and lower cost of capital while allowing companies to take a longer time horizon, and they made bank loans easier than stock equity. They learned to provide government backing so when capital was short, companies could borrow far beyond their assets from banks motivated and able to make wise investment decisions. They learned to direct the flow of capital to priority areas through a combination of public and private banks, but they also learned to allow enough leeway to the financial market and stock market to permit others to take initiatives in areas they considered promising.

They learned that they needed to train some scientists and engineers to world levels to absorb new technology, but they found it was usually far cheaper to purchase the technology through patents or licensing or to engage in reverse engineering than to perform basic research themselves. On the frontier of technology, they found that it was in the national interest if some Japanese company or consortium pursued each important promising approach, either by its own work or by contacts with leading foreign researchers, and was poised to move once the technology became commercially feasible. They have generally found it less important to be first to market with a new product than to move quickly as soon as technology begins to stabilize, improving the product by new engineering design and lowering costs through advances in process technology.

They have learned that in most sectors Japan does best when there is a small group of highly competitive companies with great resources able to achieve economies of scale. In consultation with companies, the government can play a helpful role in providing a predictable environment and facilitating the solution of problems, but they learned that competition between healthy companies is the greatest driving force for success in international markets. These companies can cooperate when it is in their interest, but they hone their competitive skills within Japan while preparing for other battles abroad. The sector remains strongest when they specialize to develop high levels of expertise but are linked with outside information networks that open new opportunities and push them to compete against the world's most advanced producers. Sectors are stronger when companies do not diversify to areas unrelated to their main work, do not have to worry about takeovers, and are less distracted by opportunities for manipulating rules, taxes, or accounting procedures. Rather, they concentrate on cultivating the best possible employees to prepare for global competition by producing the most strategic goods of highest quality at the lowest price.

They initially protected infant industries from inundation by foreign competition but learned to phase liberalization so as to prevent continuing inefficiencies, secondary effects of higher prices on other Japanese industries, and foreign trade retaliation. Although not necessarily national policy, sectoral associations and sometimes officials responsible for those sectors learned to find formal and informal ways to discourage foreign businessmen from establishing successful large-scale operations to manufacture or sell foreign products.

National leaders have learned how to identify the highest feasible level of training for all citizens so they can share a high level of common knowledge while selecting the ablest for the jobs most important to the country. They have learned how to fashion a national school system and lifelong education and training programs to achieve national goals. They have learned to follow changing national manpower needs and to devise forward-looking programs to prepare the population for these changing needs.

They have learned how to acquire information from around the world—studying patiently, translating, traveling, inviting world experts—and how to provide networks to facilitate the flow. But they have also learned how certain groups can scan it, digest it, and disseminate it to all those in Japan who might make use of it.

Leaders have gradually developed criteria to select issues important for long-range national development and bring them to the top of the national agenda. They have learned that all serious issues can receive ongoing attention but that it takes several years of sustained attention to reach a national consensus on a top issue (like closing the coal mines, responding to the oil shocks, or launching the information era). They therefore concentrate on two or three top issues at any point. Scheduling of issues may be determined by external events, such as shortages of key materials and foreign protectionism, but people in each sphere are constantly evaluating major issues in their sphere and selecting those that deserve the attention of others. Leaders have learned how to move an issue on the national agenda toward resolution, assigning it staff work, gathering information, and consulting with key groups to obtain useful inputs, minimize resistance, and broaden the national commitment to the solution eventually agreed to.

In large organizations, government and private, they have learned to recruit and cultivate small groups of unusually talented people whose job it is to think of the organization as a whole. These people acquire experience in all important parts of the organization and, as they mature and develop skills, are sent to be leaders of all parts of the organization. They can thus be flexible in reorganizing and rethinking for the good of the organization as a whole rather than being rooted in particular sections or particular specialties.

Japanese leaders have learned that all these processes can be guided but not controlled at the highest levels. Leaders can nudge and coordinate when their actions rest on national consensus, but much of the initiative must remain with individual companies and local groups. National leaders have found that they keep a wide base of support when they heighten awareness of common problems, accommodate to various interest groups, and find ground rules for resolving disagreements. Individual companies pursue their own interests, sometimes in conflict with national interests, but they have a high level of awareness of how their role fits in with national goals and know that they will get better cooperation from other groups in Japan when they adjust their behavior to the flow of forces associated with the national interest.

2. GROUPS IDENTIFYING COMMON INTERESTS

Just as leaders in all circles have thought through and continue to think through the logic of what is good for the nation, so representatives of endless combinations of different groups meet with each other to explore interests in common. Not that groups in other countries do not, but with few worries about antitrust laws and with great value placed on keeping open positive networks, Japanese groups do it more.

Even in Japan, companies in the same sector bristle with competitive spirit and are wary of rivals. But companies have gradually learned how to keep certain secrets and protect their interests while at the same time building a basis of trust and defining satisfactory rules of the game to define how and where they can cooperate when it is in their interest to do so. Through experience they have learned how far they can cooperate in information gathering, research and development, marketing, specialization to get economies of scale, on size of political donations, on relative wage increase, on proportion of graduates admitted from key universities. They can agree on common parts producers who can then acquire economies of scale, reducing costs for all, and when to buy one another's specialized products even while they compete fiercely in other areas, both at home and abroad.

The government has learned to help manage this competition, encouraging sectors to work together for common goals by rewarding those who cooperate—through distribution of permits, approval of licenses and patents, concessionary loans, interpretation of tax issues, and procurement and research contracts—and by punishing those who do not. At the same time the government encourages the flow of inside information, making it difficult for companies to engage in oligopolistic practices not in keeping with consumer and national interests.

Just as companies in a sector learn to cooperate, so most major companies in a sector tend to have strong links with suppliers and purchasers, while companies in a "group" (like Mitsubishi and Mitsui) are linked around a main bank. They have found that relationships of trust among themselves and other companies speed the flow of new information and expand the range of opportunities available to them while reducing their "transaction costs," the worry and costs of inspecting one another's products, mutual checking, complicated accounting, legal fees, and risks of law suits. Mutual trust expands the range of possible solutions that might be achieved through cooperation in case of unexpected developments not enumerated in previous agreements. These considerations are sufficiently important that companies will not easily turn to a third party offering goods at lower prices unless it promises a long-term relationship that will lead to similarly low transaction costs.

Banks have developed a system for making short-term loans to particular companies to give them options and leverage, but the ordinary expectation is that they will keep a long-term relationship with a given company. They therefore tend to be much closer to the company than are American banks and to give greater scrutiny to the quality of the leaders, the personnel system, the technology, and the long-range prospects. This not only makes for wise long-term decisions on bank loans but helps reinforce company considerations of long-term strength.

Although companies tend to have closer relationships within a "group" or with contractors and subcontractors than do overseas competitors, within the rules of the game companies can also form relationships with counterparts in other groups or with firms with no group affiliation for large-scale projects. And they have gradually developed skill in discerning which firms can be linked quickly in large-scale projects. The government is ready to assist in large projects where the national interest is clearly involved, convening meetings, facilitating low-cost finance, troubleshooting, rewarding companies that cooperate, and creating obstacles for those that do not, but the initiatives are overwhelmingly from the individual companies, which have learned how to make the best use of the many frameworks for cooperation.

3. MANAGING SECTOR DEVELOPMENT

The sector (like shipbuilding or machine tools) is the basic building block of Japan's approach to global competition. The firms in the sector and the bureaucrats concerned, along with a community of media representatives, politicians, and other interested people with special knowledge, have gradually acquired the skills of sector management at all stages of development.

1. Forming a new sector. When a new field (such as television, computers, robots, fiber optics) opens up, leaders work to decide which firms are central to its development. They have learned how to form different associations for the sector, usually one for the handful of leading companies and one for all firms in the sector.

They have gradually learned how to establish ground rules to select the head of the association. If a sector has one dominant company, the head of that company is commonly selected as head of the association, assuming that that company takes a gentlemanly role, exercising restraint in its own ability to dominate the sector. If there are two or three companies of approximately equal size, the headship of the association might be rotated among them or it might be given to the head of a smaller company who enjoys the respect of the other company heads. The leading groups of these associations, the bureaucrats in charge of the sector, and the community of others then have the responsiblity of thinking through the logic of everything that will help the sector. As the sectoral associations are established, government offices are reorganized so that some unit is assigned clear responsibility for the success of the sector and interfaces with the private sector.

2. *Setting the sector agenda.* As these leaders think through the logic of their position, they consider what information, research, technology, personnel, and funding is needed for the healthy development of the field. They meanwhile explore foreign markets, work out cooperative arrangements to get market information, and work with trading companies, JETRO, and other organizations to help build up foreign markets. They gradually set up their agenda of appropriate timing and divide tasks among the companies, bureaucrats, related groups, and even outsiders with special contributions to make. Although new sectors develop their own agendas and change them to respond to new developments, new sectors can now learn more rapidly by drawing on the experience of other sectors.

3. *Getting technology and capital.* Various task forces, often highly informal, learn how to gain information on technological developments around the world that might affect their sector. They explore the kinds of patent and licensing arrangements and research projects that will open up the technology desired. Similarly, they examine the financial needs of the field to consider possible bottlenecks and joint projects that might cut developmental costs for all while not curtailing individual competitive efforts.

4. *Moving to scale.* Ordinarily as a field opens up, many companies explore the field, a "hundred flowers bloom," and everyone is encouraged to try anything. As technologies begin to stabilize in preparation for mass production and international competition, it is possible that the strongest and most successful companies in the early stage will be given special assistance in moving to acquire economies of scale. Special concessionary funds may be given to a small number of firms for new facilities. Government regulations about minimal facilities licenses may be imposed so that small companies are encouraged to merge in order to meet the standards and move more rapidly to mass production. The government may also support cartelization and specialization of production to hasten the move

to mass production as well as providing special incentives for purchasers or leasing arrangements to ensure sustained demand to speed up the mass-production process.

5. *Public acceptance.* Leaders have also learned how to prepare for public acceptance of important new products, performing a function that supplements advertising. Leaders sponsor public-opinion polls, provide background information to key opinion makers, and deal with issues like safety, pollution and displacement of workers.

6. *Managing decline.* In sectors leveling off or declining, companies and the government have gradually learned to find ways to reduce production while keeping the most competitive, slimmed-down parts of the sector. In these areas of structural decline, government and business leaders have learned to share responsibility for developing multiyear plans for reducing numbers of personnel and finding appropriate training programs that lead to new employment opportunities.

4. RESPONDING TO FOREIGN PROTECTIONISM

As exports of Japanese products have grown, the Japanese have become more skilled in handling the political as well as the economic side of foreign market penetration. In international markets they have learned to bargain most for keeping foreign markets open for goods that were strategically important for Japanese exports. In the United States, they have learned to keep in touch with congressional staffers to anticipate congressional voting as well as dealing with the administration in the White House. They have learned to deal with a number of law and public relations firms, which employ important former officials of both political parties, to provide access and influence in representing their views. They have developed comparable contacts in other foreign countries. They have learned how to wait until the last minute when congressional votes about to be taken would be unfavorable to their interests and then propose voluntary restraints giving them much greater flexibility in managing changes than would be the case if they were bound by rigid legislation.

They have learned to send to foreign countries emissaries who get positive foreign reaction and to make arguments that are meaningful to the particular audience. In countries in which the behavior of certain Japanese arouses criticism, they have learned to exert social pressure on the "ugly Japanese" to reduce foreign resentment. They have also learned how to cultivate key foreign groups to reduce opposition and a climate of international sympathy for their point of view.

5. DIFFICULTIES

Foreigners want very much to believe that there are weaknesses in the system, and of course the Japanese do make mistakes in placing their bets and in failing to anticipate certain changes. If there are systematic errors, commonly repeated, I would suggest that they are primarily one of two types:

1. *Overexpansion.* The eagerness of the leaders involved to take advantage of all possible opportunities has led in many cases to overexpansion of new facilities, leaving a sector with excess plant and equipment. Though sectors have had ways of scrapping facilities, a number of them have had problems of serious excess capacity.

2. *Excessive de facto protection of certain sectors.* Particular sectors resisting the penetration of foreign products have had success in developing certain tests and practices that make foreign penetration difficult or impossible. Now that leaders are committed to free trade, it is difficult to overcome habits and institutions that had come to be taken for granted. And it is awkward and sometimes impossible to overcome interest groups resisting the market penetration of foreign goods and displaying virulent nationalism. It is sometimes even awkward fully to inform the Japanese public of the concrete problems suffered by foreigners. It is somewhat easier, under foreign pressure, to restrain Japanese exports. Because Japanese are so competitive internationally and because resistance to foreign goods can have such a large impact on the hardening of foreign protectionism to Japanese goods, it is unfortunate for Japan that it cannot further overcome its own resistance to liberalization of markets for capital, manufactured goods, and agricultural products.

On the whole, however, the commitment to global markets, the clear assignment of responsibility for managing change, and the broad involvement of relevant groups permit great flexibility. It makes possible a broad range of responses to problems not possible in countries that rely more exclusively on unguided market forces and social and political pressures. Japan's extensive experience in successful response now enables it to learn even more quickly as it confronts new problems.

Part Three

SUCCESS, AMERICAN STYLE

7

NASA: All-Out Mobilization

by Ezra F. Vogel and Jonathan Kaufman

Many observers do not believe Americans are capable of the dedication and government-business cooperation that the Japanese, with their sense of urgency about national survival, were able to impart to shipbuilding, machine tools, and "compunications." American businessmen do not believe their government can provide effective leadership, and consumers doubt that U.S. companies are still capable of making high-quality goods that can compete in international markets. The mood of pessimism is the same, whether expressed in a frantic search for the quick fix or an almost desperate search for familiar ways in hopes that something might work, or a lashing out at Japanese, who are accused of not playing fair. Pessimism about U.S. competitiveness is only one aspect of Americans' doubts, doubts about our institutions' ability to function effectively and our ability to wage a war on crime or poverty or poor schools or a national budget and trade balance out of control. Is there any reason to hope that Americans, finally aware of the seriousness of their competitive problems, might mobilize to respond effectively? Is there any hope that the Japanese economic challenge might mobilize America in the same way that the Soviet space challenge did? It is worth reviewing how we found our way to unite to respond to that challenge.

In retrospect, getting a man to the moon may seem to have been inevitable, but such hindsight obscures the enormous effort involved, an effort larger and more complex than anything the Japanese have attempted, including shipbuilding and compunications. When plans for the moon shot began, no one could be certain that the flight would be successful or that Americans could surpass the Russians in space efforts, to say nothing of ensuring the safe return of the astronauts. Public support for getting a man to the moon did not alone guarantee success. Not only scientific and technical, but political, managerial, and organizational obstacles had to be overcome. Although reasonable men may disagree about the decision to spend billions of dollars on the Apollo project, no one can deny the capacity demonstrated by Americans to find effective ways of working together when persuaded of the need to do so.

Americans' commitment to the effort began almost immediately after the Soviets launched Uri Gagarin, the first man in space, on April 12, 1961. Within a few days President John F. Kennedy told his advisers, including National Aeronautics and Space Agency head James Webb, "If someone can just tell me how to catch up. . . . There is nothing more important." On May 25, 1961, he announced that America would "commit itself to achieving the goal, before the decade is out, of landing a man on the moon and returning him safely to earth." On July 20, 1969, Neil Armstrong radioed, "The *Eagle* has landed." Americans had won the race to the moon, and four days later they returned safely to earth.

1. CREATING A POLITICAL BASE

Until October 1957 space had not aroused a great deal of interest in the American public, or in American political leaders. To be sure, science-fiction writers and others had galvanized a small following, but that was hardly a basis for a political program. Military rocket and missile specialists and other groups of scientists were dedicated to their work, but their work was not assigned high priority by others.

Among specialists, one of the big issues had been whether satellites should be placed under military or civilian control. Under military control, efforts could be centralized and unnecessary duplication avoided. Space clearly had military purposes, and in the context of the Cold War and Russian advances, Army, Navy, and Air Force leaders could all make the case to have a large role in space developments. To gain the cooperation of American scientists who had second thoughts about taking part in atomic bomb and other military research and to gain the cooperation of other countries, the Apollo project, many believed, should be a civilian effort. The issue came to a head in 1955 during planning for the International Geophysical Year (IGY) that was to begin on July 1, 1957. In April 1955 the United States announced plans to launch a Vanguard satellite during IGY. Although the Army rocketry team under Wernher von Braun was farthest along in related work and very much wanted to build satellites, satellite development was separated from missile development and located under the Naval Research Laboratory. Missile development was for military purposes and was given high priority. Satellite development was to have no military mission.

It could therefore get the cooperation of civilian scientists and gain the respect of the international scientific community for IGY, but it was also given lower priority because space development was not then considered a race.

Among specialists, neither the Soviet technical achievements in space nor their political implications were unanticipated. As early as 1946 a prescient Rand Corporation report anticipated the world political reaction to Soviet success in launching a satellite before the United States. It was long known that outstanding Soviet rocketry experts whose work predated World War II had been joined by a sizable group of German experts captured at Peenemunde in 1945, and that they had been making substantial technical progress. In 1955, after the United States announced its satellite plans for 1957, the Soviet Union announced that within two years it would launch a satellite larger than the one planned by the United States. As the International Geophysical Year grew near, the Soviets made a number of announcements of their plans that were picked up by American specialists and even by the American press, but they attracted only minor attention.

Despite forewarnings in the press, on October 4, 1957, when the Soviet Union launched the eighty-kilogram Sputnik I into orbit, the American public suffered an enormous shock. On November 3, the Soviets launched Sputnik II, carrying a dog in a payload totaling 508 kilograms. Thrown on the defensive, the United States then hastened to get its 1.5 kilogram satellite launched, and on December 6, amid full coverage by TV cameras and the world press, Vanguard failed on the launching pad. On January 26, 1958, another Vanguard launch was attempted and postponed. Wernher von Braun and his Army team meanwhile were given permission to launch a satellite of their own, and on January 31 they successfully launched Explorer I, with an 8.5 kilogram payload. When Vanguard III was finally launched on March 17, it was an anticlimax.

President Eisenhower's initial reaction to Sputnik was to play down the impact of the Soviet achievement. He had not considered satellite development a matter of military or political urgency, and he was dubious about the military or scientific value of turning space development into a race. He had long believed in the importance of reducing government spending and was reluctant to have the government commit itself to a costly new program. In addition to these convictions, which predated Sputnik, he felt it important to respond calmly and not add to doubts about U.S. capacity to meet Soviet challenges around the world.

But the Soviet achievements in space were too spectacular and too daunting to enable even a President with impeccable military credentials to reassure the American people. Coming just at the time when Americans were beginning to have doubts about their military superiority over the Soviet Union, Sputnik became a symbol of Soviet power. As recently as 1953 Secretary of State John

Foster Dulles had advocated the doctrine of massive retaliation in the event of a Soviet attack. But by 1957 the Soviet Union had acquired nuclear weapons, and experts advocating more defense expenditures then warned of a missile gap. Sputnik's success proved that nuclear weapons could reach the United States. In its report submitted just a few months before Sputnik, the Gaither Committee, appointed by Eisenhower to evaluate civil defense shelters, warned that if the United States did not change its policies it was in danger of becoming a second-class power.

The problems Sputnik created were not just psychological. A few weeks after the launching of Sputnik I, Mao Tse-tung in Moscow, ready to take advantage of the Soviet's newly demonstrated power, proclaimed the superiority of the East Wind over the West Wind and prepared to invade Taiwan. In the wake of the British and French failure in the 1956 Suez campaign, the USSR itself appeared poised for a Middle East adventure.

Despite his surface calm and his determination not to be drawn into a space race, Eisenhower in fact moved quickly, albeit in low key, to respond to the Sputnik challenge. He ordered the acceleration of the ballistic missile program and a hardening and dispersing of missile sites. In February 1958 he created within the Department of Defense the Advanced Research Project Agency, bringing together under unified management missile, satellite, and space R&D. He began giving unprecedented attention to scientists. The President's Science Advisory Committee, which had been a stepchild of the Office of Defense Mobilization, was transferred to the White House. James Killian, president of MIT, was named to the new post of Science Adviser, and he doubled as chairman of the Science Advisory Committee. Prominent scientists were invited to the White House to advise on strengthening national scientific efforts. To increase funding for scientific research, the National Defense Education Act was passed to assist in the training of needed manpower, and new efforts were made to upgrade the science curriculum in secondary schools.

Eisenhower also launched broader staff studies, and in March 1958 he made his proposal for strengthening space efforts. He recommended that space leadership be concentrated in civilian hands, in the National Advisory Committee for Aeronautics (NACA). NACA, founded in 1915, had played a major role in the development of airplanes and air travel and then had about 8,000 employees. Its functions were to be greatly expanded and its space programs accelerated.

Eisenhower's five-month delay in making recommendations and his low-key approach had given Democratic opponents and some Republicans an opportunity to raise questions about the vigor of the administration's space effort. Many politicians responded to the opportunity, and the one who did so most vigorously and successfully was Senator Lyndon Johnson. Johnson, aware that one did not directly challenge a military hero President about security matters, undertook a low-key effort of his own.

Johnson believed in the desirability of a space program for national defense and he also sensed an opportunity to project himself onto the national scene. Reflecting broad sentiment in the Senate, he advocated a much stronger program than the administration originally wanted, and this was reflected in the National Aeronautics and Space Act, passed in July 1958. The mandate of NACA was greatly expanded, and in October its name was changed to NASA (National Aeronautics and Space Agency). The principle of civilian control of space efforts remained unaltered.

With strong Senate support, Johnson also advocated a council to push space development, interposed between the President on the one hand and NASA and the Department of Defense on the other. The National Aeronautics and Space Council was soon established. Including the President, secretaries of State and Defense, heads of NASA and the Atomic Energy Commission, and four other persons, it played a role in coordinating congressional and bureaucratic efforts. It came as no great surprise to many that Lyndon Johnson was made a member of the council or that when, under President Kennedy, he became its head it played a major role in pushing for space efforts.

As part of the new upgraded program, in the summer of 1958 manned space flight was assigned to NASA, and in October the Wernher von Braun team was transferred from the Army to NASA and assigned the task of developing a strong booster capable of launching manned satellites. Other institutions were formed to interface between NASA and the scientific community, Congress, and other groups. The National Academy of Sciences had a committee responsible for planning the International Geophysical Year Satellite Program, and in June 1958 this committee became the nucleus of a new Space Science Board to channel advice from the scientific community to the government for space developments. Not all scientists were very enthusiastic about such an expanded space role, both because they feared that a single-minded concentration on a space race would be detrimental to the well-balanced development of science and because they were reluctant to be drawn into such politicized activity. Nonetheless, key scientific leaders who believed in such research and prestigious scientific institutions were centrally involved from the beginning.

In July 1960, NASA announced plans for manned exploration of outer space, but two months later Eisenhower still refused to budget funds for the program. Yet he and his administration had pushed forward the careful examination of what would be required for such an undertaking and begun programs that were later to prove crucial for its timely success. A NASA committee formed in 1959 and named after its chairman, Harry Goett, was assigned the responsibility for reviewing such issues and making recommendations for the future. The Goett Committee accepted the mission of a lunar landing as the long-term goal of manned space flight and considered the research and technical developments necessary to achieve it by 1970. One decision NASA made in 1959, to develop a new fuel using liquid oxygen and hydrogen to achieve greater thrusts, was later to prove especially crucial. Despite Eisenhower's low-key approach, sufficient technical progress was made under his administration that at the beginning of the Kennedy administration on February 7, 1961, a special committee chaired by George Low to review the issues could announce that "No invention or break-through is believed to be required to insure the overall feasibility of safe lunar flight." The group found that the mission could be accomplished during the decade.

During the presidential campaign of 1960, Kennedy criticized Republicans for their lack of vigor in pursuing space development. U.S Information Agency analyses in October 1960 confirmed that throughout the world the United States was judged to lag behind the USSR in space and had suffered a loss of prestige. Yet in the early months of his administration Kennedy was preoccupied with other matters such as Laos, and he took no new initiatives on space. Indeed, Kennedy's first meeting with James Webb, held on March 22, was called by the NASA administrator to protest that the budget allocated to NASA by the administration was not sufficient to meet minimal needs of the agency. Meanwhile, Kennedy had assigned staff members to look into issues related to NASA. A report by Jerome Wiesner, Kennedy's science adviser, had been critical of NASA for its poor organization and large number of technical failures. In the session with Webb, therefore, Kennedy gave Webb no positive answers, wanting to consider the issues further.

Kennedy received accurate intelligence information warning of Soviet plans for launching a man in space. He was given more than a week's advance notice of the approximate date of the launching, and the night before the launching Jerome Wiesner informed him that the launching was expected that night Washington time. Kennedy and his staff made no decisions to step up NASA activities or to diffuse the potential impact of the Soviet launching before it took place.

As with the launching of Sputnik I and Sputnik II, the impact on April 12, 1961, of the Soviet's launching of Vostok I carrying Yuri Gagarin into space was instantaneous and overwhelming. Papers around the world heralded the Soviet success and the American failure.

Participants in White House discussions during the days following the flight later described the atmosphere as one of crisis. Although the decision to launch a lunar landing was never explicitly linked by the President to the Bay of Pigs fiasco, participants testified to the impact of the following week's failure of the

Cuban invasion on the crisis atmosphere at the White House. In view of Soviet success and his own failure, Kennedy clearly needed a dramatic step to rally American morale and demonstrate America's determination to remain a world power.

Six weeks later, Kennedy committed the United States to manned space flight within the decade. He could draw on work of the Eisenhower administration, but he saw the decision in much broader terms. Kennedy felt keenly the threat of Soviet power and wanted to demonstrate American strength and determination in a way that did not risk military confrontation. Nothing better symbolized Soviet success and American failure than space achievements, and no words could take the place of American success in space. An activist by instinct, Kennedy sought the moral equivalent of war and found it.

After the Gagarin flight and the Bay of Pigs, Kennedy called together his science advisers to determine whether the country could possibly leapfrog the Soviets with an even greater space spectacular. White House studies indicated a moon shot would cost up to $40 billion, one half of the 1960 federal budget. Many scientists within NASA opposed a manned lunar landing, believing robots and computers could do a better job for scientific purposes and for less money and with no risk to life.

During the course of these deliberations, on May 5, Alan Shepard, flying in a Mercury capsule, became the first American in space. He returned safely and his success gave heart to those who advocated manned lunar flight. Although Shepard's flight had been suborbital and had lasted only fifteen minutes, compared to Gagarin's eighty-nine minutes, Shepard's success was a tremendous boost for the space program.

The Space Council, which had begun meeting on April 20 under Vice President Johnson to consider an appropriate plan, concluded that a landing on the moon was the first dramatic space development in which the United States had a better than fifty-fifty chance of beating the Soviet Union. On May 8 the Space Council's report went to the President and on May 25, in an address billed as the second State of the Union address, Kennedy said, "This nation should commit itself to achieving the goal, before the decade is out, of landing a man on the moon and returning him safely to earth. No single project in this period will be more exciting or more impressive to mankind . . . and none will be so difficult or expensive to accomplish. . . . In a very real sense it will not be one man going to the moon . . . it will be an entire nation. For all of us must work to put it there."

2. BUILDING A FLEXIBLE ORGANIZATION

Keith Glennan, the first NASA administrator (from August 1958 to January 1961), had been trained originally in electrical engineering and had served for almost twenty years as president of Case Institute of Technology. He had worked in Navy laboratories in World War II and thus had experience in dealing with the military. As a member of the Atomic Energy Commission, he had adequate knowledge of the Washington scientific community. He was considered a sound administrator who insisted on taking the time necessary to build a solid basis for scientific research and engineering development. He had made it easy for Webb to replace him by virtue of his efforts to leave the organization in good shape and by writing a number of thoughtful memoranda posing options.

Webb was anxious to make good use of the staff he inherited, and he was pleased to retain the services of Hugh Dryden. Dryden had been director of NACA from 1949 to 1958 and had stayed on as deputy administrator under Glennan. A scientist who had spent most of his career in government, he was an invaluable repository of institutional information and an able administrator.

Kennedy moved cautiously in choosing Glennan's replacement because of disagreements among his staff about the right qualifications for a NASA administrator. Some wanted a skilled scientist with administrative experience, others wanted it the other way around, but Kennedy eventually sided with those who believed political savvy was most important. A number of persons turned down the job before Kennedy enlisted the services of Webb.

An administrator with acknowledged political sensitivity, Webb had had broad experience in running large organizations, in business as well as in government. He had served three years as director of the Bureau of Budget under Truman. He had, moreover, strong political support. He was recommended for the job by Robert Kerr, then head of the Senate Committee on Aeronautical and Space Sciences, and strongly backed by Lyndon Johnson. While serving as head of Educational Services Inc., which had promoted a new high school physics course designed by MIT faculty, he had come to know many scientists and was therefore judged acceptable by the President's Science Adviser. Webb's appointment was rushed through Congress and he was sworn in as NASA administrator on February 14, 1961, some two months before Gagarin's flight and some three months before Kennedy's speech making the moon landing the national goal.

In office, Webb quickly demonstrated not only a clear understanding of the big picture—what was needed to get a man on the moon—but also an appreciation of the second-order impact of decisions. He was concerned about scientists' complaints that NASA was taking too much talent from the reserve of scientific manpower and therefore he set up a program to expand the pool. He was interested not only in getting a man on the moon but in contributing to basic science in the process. He was bent not only on assisting universities but on developing new patterns of government-university cooperation. He was alert to the economic impact on the firms with which NASA had contracts and to keeping firms healthy. He anticipated the commercial applications of new technology deriving from space exploration. He gave attention to developing appropriate organizational forms to coordinate these complex efforts and to having them analyzed by social scientists and recorded by historians.

Webb's genuine interest in these second-order issues was reinforced by his awareness that he needed the support and cooperation of these various groups and of the public, which wanted to feel it shared in the achievement. At the same time, Webb wanted a measure of independence from these organizations and this required a staff sufficiently competent to evaluate advice coming from the outside. The public interest in space and NASA's large budget made it easy to attract a staff with the requisite competence in the appropriate specialties.

Perhaps the greatest organizational challenge confronting Webb was managing NASA's extraordinary range of activity amid utter uncertainty as to developments. Issues like location of facilities, specifications for all stages of the rocket, the nature of the subprojects to be contracted out, and the negotiations with prospective contractors required hundreds of talented administrators working as one. Unlike the traditional bureaucracies, which could rely on tables of organization and give assignments to units and positions with some consistency, NASA required more flexibility. Rather than a bureaucratic structure, teams had to be assembled to work on programs and projects and then reorganized and reassembled for new programs and projects with different requirements. As new issues developed, the staff had to reorganize and solve the problems regardless of the specialty in which they had originally been trained. Unlike mature manufacturing organizations, in which production of a given item achieves some scale, NASA was generally building one of a kind or at best doing short runs. To be sure, these problems of organization were not unique, for they are found in greater or lesser degree in most research and development firms. But in NASA they existed on a grand scale, with more public visibility, and with an unusually high degree of pressure for long-term results. Nevertheless, the combination of a fresh new bureaucracy with little established red tape, able administrators, and a clear, measurable goal allowed them to accomplish what other organizations of comparable size could not.

Participants in NASA recall that it was anything but a well-oiled machine. New issues were constantly arising and disagreements abounded between headquarters and local centers, between contractors and NASA, between scientists inside and outside, and among strong personalities who identified with their specialties or units and doubted that their value was truly appreciated. People who did not get along had to work together. Engineers who wanted to move more rapidly toward production disagreed with scientists who wanted to generate more data and take the time necessary for contributing to basic knowledge. Webb considered that one of the greatest contributions of NASA was learning how to manage an organization of this type, and he was eager to seek and use the advice of organizational specialists.

No sooner had Webb taken office than he set up a task force to consider administrative reorganization. The task force found, for example, so many layers between headquarters and regional centers that regional centers had difficulty seeing the agency point of view. Within regional centers, field officers reported to special program officers in their own specialties, but specialties were not always well coordinated. In the first major administrative reorganization, implemented in November 1961, the field offices were made accountable not to an intermediate program officer but directly to Robert Seamans, the associate administrator in Washington, thus strengthening agency coordination. Because the one associate administrator could not supervise field officers in as much detail as a number of program officers could, field officers were in fact given more room for maneuver. So as not to strain the span of control within NASA as activity expanded, a larger proportion of work was contracted out to universities and private firms. Other reorganizations followed from time to time.

The years after 1961 were especially busy ones, and an enormous group of very talented people with a clear and compelling sense of mission accomplished a tremendous amount of work in a very brief time.

3. GETTING COOPERATION FROM SCIENTISTS

NASA had more trouble with university scientists than with businessmen. University scientists were accustomed to working independently, carrying out their own research and publishing at their own pace. NASA required them to accept topics, timetables, and large teams of co-workers not necessarily of their own choosing. Scientists had been encouraged to take part because NASA required expanding scientific frontiers, but in practice many scientists felt that basic research was pushed aside for expediency. However, the most basic question was whether NASA helped or hurt other scientific research. Webb and others could reasonably argue that the space effort, by increasing interest in science, benefited the whole field, but many scientists in other areas feared that it cut into their areas, distorting the nation's science efforts by draining talent as well as funds into a one-sided effort. The opposition became stronger in the late 1960s when the Vietnam War led to financial stringencies and NASA's budget overruns threatened to affect other areas. If only a certain percentage of funds wasted in

NASA could be used to develop their own academic disciplines, how much more science and mankind would benefit. So argued many outstanding scientists, such as Philip Abelson, vocal editor of *Science* magazine.

As much as the aura of NASA may have given a general boost to science, if one were devising a project to develop science, NASA would not have been it. NASA was designed for national and international political objectives and at key points these objectives made a difference. Scientists were of course correct that NASA created imbalances. Between 1960 and 1970, for example, the number of astronomers in the United States tripled to 2,500. Many were lured to the field by NASA funding, which by 1967 was underwriting 40 percent of American astronomy Ph.D.'s. As NASA's largest programs drew to a close and opportunities in astronomy shrank, many of those drawn to the heady world of space exploration in the 1960s found themselves without employment.

Yet for all the differences in perspective and needs, NASA succeeded in devising many different ways to gain the cooperation of scientists of widely different interests, positions, and working styles. NASA was so big, required so much scientific work, and financed so many projects that scientists and NASA came to rely on each other and developed what NASA's associate administrator for space science and applications, Homer Newell, called a "love-hate relationship." NASA's scope required a new class of scientist entrepreneurs and politicians who could not always retain the respect of those who received less funds and those who stayed in the labs. NASA needed scientists in many roles: administrators, advisers, consultants, employees, contractors, visiting researchers. The agency made use of advisers at the very top level, at the smallest regional project level, and at all levels in between. Panels from the prestigious National Academy of Sciences were assembled to identify priorities in lunar exploration and to assess the cost effectiveness of using satellites for such varied activities as predicting the size of the world grain crop, detecting agricultural diseases caused by water pollution, and improving navigation. An Astronomical Missions Board made up of outstanding astronomers set guidelines for science-oriented programs connected with spacecraft flight. A Space Science Steering Committee composed of distinguished outside scientists advised NASA's own scientists and acted as a review board for proposals on space-related experiments.

NASA encouraged members of advisory boards to take more active roles than did advisers in many organizations. They were encouraged to visit the factories doing work for NASA and supervise and inspect the design and quality of goods produced. Although the policy was not universally liked by its own administrators, NASA encouraged outside scientists to become intimately familiar with agency affairs, both organizational and technical. It hired some outside consultants to come to NASA once a month to review a broad range of programs and others to come as often as three days a week.

For its own staff, NASA wanted high-level scientists and engineers as well as entry-level staff. It had difficulty recruiting top-flight scientists from the best universities to work full-time and therefore worked out a variety of flexible arrangements. It was, however, very competitive in recruiting young people. Before the end of 1961, NASA embarked on a country-wide effort to recruit some 2,000 scientists and engineers. Webb had persuaded Civil Service authorities to give the agency considerable flexibility in appointing new employees and increasing the salaries NASA could offer. As a result, some 88 percent of the people recruited by NASA earned as much as or more than before they joined. Because NASA grew so rapidly in the early years, chances for promotion were very good.

Just as outsiders were sometimes frustrated that their advice was not more frequently followed, so scientists within NASA occasionally resented self-serving pronouncements by arrogant outsiders lacking due appreciation for overall priorities and for the difficult choices among mutually exclusive options. Despite continuing frustrations, however, there was constant communication, and participants on both sides testify that they made serious efforts to accommodate to the advice and positions of others and profited from the experience.

In addition to the standard programs of contracting out research projects to universities and bringing in outside advisers for internal research, NASA endeavored to develop innovative programs that would not only benefit NASA but have other useful secondary impact. Among the programs sponsored by NASA were the following:

1. *Doctoral fellowships.* So as not to diminish the general national pool of scientists, NASA offered some 1,000 fellowships each year to train engineers, mathematicians, and physicists. These figures were derived from the Gilliland report on the need for scientific and technical personnel, prepared in 1962 when NASA was setting up its program. The report estimated that to meet national needs for 1970 about 4,000 scientists with doctorates would have to be added each year. NASA accepted about one-fourth of this as its fair share, based largely on its relative share of budgets compared to other federal research programs, each of which was to help in the training of scientific personnel. The agreement illustrates the capacity of the U.S. government to find ways to divide responsibility for training to meet national manpower needs. Although many scientists and others continued to complain that federal programs with attractive fellowships pulled students away from other valuable pursuits, NASA on balance undoubtedly helped increase the reservoir of manpower in science fields.

2. *Postdoctoral fellowships.* Beginning in March 1959, NASA offered opportunities for leading scientists from universities and businesses to work alongside NASA scientists on projects of their choosing. The fellowship program was administered by the National Research Council of the Academy of Sciences and

over the years gave opportunities for several hundred academics to work in NASA settings.

3. *Grants to universities.* In 1962, when universities began requesting larger grants to erect new facilities, Webb began to develop a new conception of how such facilities might also be used to benefit local communities. Grants would be made not simply on the basis of contribution to NASA but on the basis of how much the university would help its geographical area "in utilizing for its own progress the knowledge, processes, or specific applications deriving from the Space Program." By 1966, Webb began planning to wind down the university facilities program because he was disappointed that universities had not been more creative in finding ways to help their regions and also because it was becoming clear that the Gilliland Committee had overestimated the needs for new scientific personnel. Although Webb's grander visions for local development applications were not fully realized, the program did play an important role in developing university research capacities.

One example of the creative effort to link scientists within and outside NASA was the development of a Theoretical Division at the Goddard Space Flight Center by Robert Jastrow, an enterprising and articulate physicist. Not satisfied with his ability to attract first-rate scientists to the Center, he rented offices and computing facilities near Washington's National Airport to make them more accessible for outside scientists. Here he was able to attract leading scientific specialists to conduct seminars, to engage in research for a period of time, or to respond to research or plans for research by NASA staff. His thought was that constant contact with the ablest scientific minds would be an important stimulus to NASA in generating new ideas. Aware of the limited number of first-rate academic scientists in the Washington area, he set up another office in New York, where he could take advantage of close relations with the best universities in the greater New York area.

By thus keeping the agency open to constant stimuli from the outside, NASA was able to reduce problems of parochialism and smugness, and to take advantage of some of the best work and best scientific minds in the country.

4. GETTING COOPERATION FROM BUSINESS

Traditionally the government had tackled such large public projects as Apollo by employing the "arsenal" method. It built factories, hired workers (usually away from private industry), and supervised production. In the late 1950s and early 1960s, however, the Department of Defense had come to believe that the arsenal method disrupted the economy and denied the government the lower costs obtainable by having private companies bid against one another. The government therefore in general moved away from the arsenal method to the opposite extreme: contracting out entire projects to private companies, giving corporations most of the responsibility for quality control and product supervision. Most of the country's ships, airplanes, and arms were then built this way.

NASA's method differed from both of these. Webb decided, in effect, to make the whole country his arsenal—paying private companies to build the millions of semiconductors, electronic components, and other products that NASA needed, but getting NASA people closely involved with company work and keeping a close eye on quality and costs while the work was going on. This approach required a group of hands-on managers within NASA to go out and work with private companies. Recruitment of high-level industry executives was essential if they were to have the skill and the respect of industry to make this work, and it was backed up by the 20,000 NASA scientists and engineers. A July 1969 *Fortune* article acknowledged that "NASA's governmental team for Apollo is unusual in being, if anything, more knowledgeable than industry about space engineering, so the two sides can meet in an atmosphere of mutual respect."

In the early stages of negotiating with a company for a contract, technicians were organized into Source Evaluation Boards, which went out to review the competency of firms competing for contracts. The Evaluation Board, made up of a small team of technical people, reported its recommendations to the top three executives of NASA, who then made a final decision taking into account NASA's broader needs as well as political factors.

Procurement for the Apollo project began in July 1961 after a meeting in which NASA officials made preliminary explanations to a meeting of some 1,200 representatives from 300 companies. The next month a smaller group of companies was briefed on more detailed requirements. NASA in effect told these potential contractors that the agency itself would have no capacity to design, develop, and manufacture rockets and space capsules. Moreover, it would have only a limited capacity to build the instruments to go inside the vehicles. Thus private industry would build the rocket that went to the moon.

In September bids were requested from several large contractors. NASA's eventual decision was to choose three contractors—Boeing, Douglas Aircraft, and North American Aviation—each to build one stage of the Saturn V rocket. Any one of these contractors might have been able to build the entire rocket, but incorporating three large contractors into the space program made long-range sense politically and economically. Dispersing contracts around the country broadened the number of congressmen with an interest in NASA, and incorporating large contractors into the NASA program from the beginning widened the talent pool that could be drawn into future projects.

At times, the problem facing NASA was not which contractor to pick but how to find any contractors at all to perform certain complex tasks. In such cases it tried to select potential contractors and help them acquire the needed expertise before issuing the contract. Some of the technology NASA demanded was so advanced or so costly that only one large company—for example, IBM or General Electric—was capable of making the product. NASA could still induce competition in some of the stages, a technique known as "parallel development." The agency could separate, for example, concept, design, and preliminary construction stages, ask several contractors to work on one of the early stages, and evaluate their progress before going on. This gave NASA the benefits of industrial competition while protecting the companies from sinking millions of dollars into a project NASA might reject. On one occasion several computer companies were competing to develop an advanced electronic system. After several months it appeared that IBM's design was far superior and that it would win the eventual contract. Rather than encourage companies to continue to pour money into the project, Webb showed all the competing companies IBM's design. It was clear that IBM would develop a superior product and therefore the other companies pulled out.

Determined to ensure the largest possible pool of resources, NASA officials often found appropriate smaller contracts to give to companies that had lost out in competition for bigger contracts, thus retaining their expertise and their interest in NASA for possible future projects. Two-thirds of NASA's contracts went to smaller companies, although the dollar value of these contracts represented only about 10 percent of NASA's budget. Webb was convinced that keeping up contacts with so many companies magnified the ripple effect of NASA, inspiring broader technological innovation.

NASA officials soon learned that they could adapt to new developments more easily if, instead of giving very precise specifications that allowed little flexibility, they discussed their goals with contractors and then combined considerable flexibility with close supervision. NASA personnel often visited contractors in order to try jointly to find ways to develop better products. They became involved in day-to-day administration of contract, cost analysis, review of subcontracts, plant inspection. When North American Aviation won part of the Apollo booster project, for example, NASA moved 100 of its employees to the company's Downey, California, manufacturing facility. A similar office was set up near GE facilities in Daytona Beach, Florida, and a third in Boston to facilitate cooperation with universities and high-tech companies in the area.

NASA chose, however, not to try to administer all aspects of all the thousands of contracts by itself. The agency turned over many of its administrative responsibilities, such as property administration, consent to subcontracts, and audit procedures, to the Defense Supply Agency and the Defense Contract Audit Agency, leaving NASA free to concentrate on technical and research questions.

Concerned with the safety of astronauts, NASA had no choice but to set the highest standards for reliability and performance. Manned missions for NASA had to have a 90 percent chance for complete success and a 99.9 percent chance for survival of the crew. This meant that certain key components of electronics and computers could have less than one chance in 100,000 of failing. Few companies at the beginning of the 1960s could meet these standards, and NASA established a panoply of inspection teams to improve products and production facilities. The Microelectronics Reliability Program, for example, established standards for semiconductor devices, and NASA inspected the production facilities of all semiconductor suppliers, including companies like Motorola, Fairchild, and Texas Instruments that were to play such key roles in developing semiconductors.

The usual problems of contract research—cost overrun, design change, poor quality, misunderstanding—were all present. An enormous range of types of contracts—fixed-price, cost-plus, cost-reimbursement, cost-sharing—was used. However, beginning in 1963, incentives for performance and cost reduction became the cornerstone of contracting policy, providing a relatively effective method for stimulating quality, low cost, and timeliness. Even more than before 1963 every effort was made to develop contracts that lent themselves to incentives and to use provisions for incentives as widely as possible. In 1962, NASA was administering some six incentive contracts, but by 1967 it was administering some 200. In short, NASA's approach was a combination of technical help, advice, and supervision with flexibility in achieving the mission and with, as NASA officials gained contracting experience, incentives for speed, performance, and quality.

5. MAINTAINING PUBLIC SUPPORT

Given the size and complexity of the effort and the pluralism of the American political process, NASA needed to keep the active cooperation of very diverse groups, and in this it was basically successful. Webb recognized that the most essential support was that of the President, and Kennedy's and Johnson's early public commitments were central to that support. In the early 1960s, when key Air Force and Department of Defense officials questioned the wisdom of letting so much space activity develop outside their control, Webb's personal good working relationships with Secretary of Defense McNamara, Deputy Secretary of the Air Force Roswell Gilpatric, and Air Force Secretary Eugene Zukert stood him in good stead. His experience as head of the Bureau of the Budget undoubtedly gave him an advantage in managing the process of getting his desired appropriations. NASA also made political compromises with key congressmen to keep the firm support of Congress. NASA contended with constant scrutiny from advisory committees, industry, universities, scientific organizations, management consultants, military and other government offices, and the media. This required development of a very substantial public relations program to satisfy the needs of all these disparate groups.

The popularity of space research and NASA's skill in cultivating congressmen made Congress so supportive that in the early years it gave NASA virtually everything it wanted. But as the Vietnam War began to strain the government budget, Congress began to review NASA's budgets with increasing care. Then in January 1967 what NASA officials had most feared, the death of astronauts, occurred in a disastrous fire on a launching pad, threatening public support for manned space flight itself. Although workers engaged in NASA projects had been killed in accidents before then, their deaths had been treated as ordinary industrial accidents. A heated debate ensued in which critics argued strenuously that unmanned flight could yield at least as much scientific information with less risk and at far less cost. Congress cut subsidiary projects, those not essential to landing on the moon, but remained committed to manned flight.

After mid-1967 it was clear that new budgetary constraints would deny NASA a sizable research and development mission once the lunar landing took place. In 1968, four months before the end of the Johnson administration, Webb, bitterly disappointed that NASA could not take on new missions and had to face continuing budgetary constraints, resigned. Public support was sufficient to permit NASA to get a manned Apollo craft to the moon, but no public relations effort that NASA might mount thereafter would be enough to continue its mission.

6. DIFFUSING TECHNICAL AND ECONOMIC BENEFITS

It is impossible to make any precise assessment of the commercial usefulness of technology developed by NASA. NASA carried on a very sizable public relations effort to show this usefulness, but the issue remains a subject of widespread disagreement. There is no way to measure, for example, the economic value of technologies developed through NASA that would not have been developed otherwise. It is impossible to estimate opportunity costs, work that might have been accomplished had these companies and these individuals not worked on NASA projects. It is almost impossible to measure the effects of their training of people who took part in NASA programs compared to the effects of the training they might have had elsewhere. Likewise estimating the effect that technology and management techniques acquired by the participants had on later work would have to be mostly guesswork. It is even difficult to estimate how much the assured demand from NASA orders had on the willingness of a company to invest in new R&D facilities. Yet it is not impossible to hazard certain general conclusions about the impact:

1. *Many new products were specifically developed by companies for NASA projects*, although most of them had modest commercial impact.

2. *In certain broad areas, substantial new advances were made.* Perhaps the most comprehensive study of these areas is that of Eli Ginzberg and his associates, who analyzed contributions to weather forecasting, astronomy, and the development of the computer industry.

Weather forecasting has been transformed by weather satellites and by mathematical models developed in good part through NASA. Some economists have estimated that weather-related losses in the United States amount to billions of dollars a year and that perhaps one-sixth of this could be prevented by better forecasts and perhaps 40 percent more from a combination of forecasts with increased protection measures. Ginzberg and associates conclude that substantial economic gains are likely as a result of these advances made by NASA.

In academic fields the greatest advances were made in astronomy. Because the number of American astronomers tripled between 1960 and 1970 in good part because of NASA, the field has been vastly transformed.

The Apollo guidance computer required extensive miniaturization, and NASA's progress in this area was among the most striking of its successes. NASA's willingness to pay for developmental costs of semiconductors played a major role in the development of the semiconductor industry, and the high level of demand helped companies move down the experience curve and product economies of scale. Costs fell dramatically from $50 for an integrated circuit in 1962 to $2 in 1968. Space and defense demands together accounted for 35–45 percent of semiconductor sales for each year between 1955 and 1961 and over 70 percent of annual sales during the first four years of integrated circuit production. One survey of private scientists and engineers conducted in the mid-1970s put the commercial value of NASA's contributions up to that time in four fields— integrated circuits, gas turbines, multilayer insulation, and computer simulation —at between $2.3 billion and $7.6 billion in 1974 dollars. Yet at the time of the lunar landing in 1969 these successes were not yet apparent.

3. *In communities with NASA facilities, NASA had a marked economic impact,* especially in smaller communities with weaker economies. Ginzberg and his associates note that the sums NASA spent in Houston and New Orleans were comparable, but that in New Orleans, with a weaker economy, the agency had a very great secondary impact. In one small community, Huntsville, Alabama, NASA had an enormous impact. In addition to immediate employment effects, it served as a community catalyst, spurring development of a new industrial park and a major rejuvenation of the local community.

4. *The impact of synergy, of bringing people together, was, though incalculable, undoubtedly considerable.* One can argue, as NASA supporters did, that bringing people together with clear and demanding performance targets provided great cross-fertilization that could not have been achieved otherwise, especially in smaller independent firms.

5. *Finally, NASA had little success in assisting in the transfer of technology to firms that did not have NASA contracts.* In his review of NASA's reporting service and its ten Regional Dissemination Centers, Samuel Doktors concludes that the success in diffusing information to smaller firms and to localities far from NASA facilities had only limited success. The universities more remote from NASA facilities had little experience in working with industry, which therefore made little use of the centers. Clearly greater efforts would have been required to make such programs a success.

7. LESSONS FROM SPACE

In fulfilling its mandate to get a man to the moon within the decade, NASA was undeniably successful. NASA leaders were able to identify a project that was technically feasible, to maintain strong political support, to create an innovative and effective organization, and to coordinate a vast array of activities necessary for getting a man on the moon. One important reason for this success was the capacity of government officials to provide creative leadership in joint work with business and academe. Private industry was able to offer the efficiency of the market system, the drive of the profit motive, and expertise in research, development, and manufacturing. Government was able to provide the more general knowledge of how each segment of the private sector fit into the national whole, to adjust incentives, and to create a system that made the partnership effective. It was not simply a spectacle but an extremely complex effort in which Americans cooperated and excelled.

Judging by NASA's experience, it is difficult to predict which technologies will succeed and which will have substantial commercial application. The frontiers of knowledge are filled with uncertainties. Yet if one were to devise a program primarily designed to stimulate the American economy, one could undoubtedly, with far less money than was spent on NASA, devise research that would have enormous impact.

But NASA has potentially great significance in illustrating what the United States can do in bringing together government and business to work for a goal when the political will is there. As John Logsdon says in his very careful analysis in *The Decision to Go to the Moon*, "The lunar landing decision was not a unique event, one with no relevance to understanding how the resources of American society can be mobilized by its political leadership toward other national goals. . . . In my judgment the experience of the lunar landing decision can be generalized to tell us how to proceed toward other great new American enterprises." The question is how to dramatize the problems of American competitiveness, potentially far more serious in its consequences than space, to mobilize a similar wide-ranging and cooperative effort.

8

Agriculture: Export Promotion

by Ezra F. Vogel and Kevin Murphy

If NASA suggests what Americans can do when they unite to achieve a specific target, American agriculture illustrates how government can help a large private sector when it has strong political support, an able corps of specialists with a long-range perspective, and a framework for public-private cooperation.

Public-private cooperation in agriculture extends to many areas, but the one most relevant to international competitiveness is that of global marketing. MITI has been aptly described as "an elite corps that works well with the private sector to help it prepare for international competition," but the description fits the Foreign Agricultural Service of the U.S. Department of Agriculture (USDA) just as well, and it has been just as successful in helping American agriculture adapt to growing world demand as MITI has been in helping Japanese industry do the same.

Since World War II, the world has witnessed a dramatic transformation of its food system. Breakthroughs and new applications of technology in seed varieties, fertilizer production, refrigeration, transportation, processing, distribution, and management have permitted world agricultural production to keep pace with rapid increases in world population. And despite strong political pressures by farmers in many countries to erect barriers to agricultural imports, agriculture has been internationalized at every level: inputs, production, procurement, processing, storage, transportation, marketing, and distribution. American agriculture has been just as successful in remaining competitive in world markets as our industry has been unsuccessful, and the U.S. government has been just as active on behalf of agriculture as it has been inactive on behalf of industry.

The globalization of the world food system brings benefits to both producer and consumer countries, leading to specialization, economies of scale, the availability of wider varieties of food at lower prices, and international assistance at times of local shortage. But it also makes both producer and consumer more dependent on international markets and therefore vulnerable to unpredictable changes in world economics and politics. Given the vital importance of a reliable food supply, countries dependent on food imports have often become anxious and determined to maintain a measure of self-reliance. Farmers in producing countries that have trouble meeting the competition apply political pressure to keep out competitive goods by erecting artificial barriers in the form of tariffs, levies, subsidies, import monopolies, cartels, troublesome inspection procedures, and boycotts. In times of world food shortage, as in 1972–74, consumers suffer and some suppliers prosper, but in times of excess supply when prices drop, as in 1979–82, consumers benefit and suppliers may suffer.

As an agricultural exporter that has expanded production to meet new international demand, the United States faces new problems: Overexpansion of productive acreage has in places exhausted and eroded soil and dangerously lowered groundwater levels. The increase in borrowing to invest in supplies and equipment to meet increased demand has made the individual American farmer more vulnerable to sudden drops in world prices. Opportunities for export sometimes raise domestic food prices and may even create food shortages.

As a whole, American agriculture responded quickly and successfully in adapting to these changes. Efficient and productive American agriculture is a success story envied and emulated throughout the world. Recent success has led many to believe that America has always been a large agricultural exporter, but this is not the case. As late as 1959 the United States was actually importing a larger value of agricultural goods than it was exporting. The United States was then exporting only $4 billion worth of agricultural goods, but during the next two decades the value of exports multiplied ten times, to over $40 billion in 1980. By then, the United States had a trade surplus in agricultural goods of some $23 billion but a trade deficit in other goods of about $50 billion. The country's farmers, less than 4 percent of its population, were producing enough trade surplus to offset about half of its trade deficit in all other goods.

These advances were made possible by annual increases in agricultural productivity, increases that in recent decades have been far more rapid than during the 1930s and World War II. At the end of World War II, America had more than 6 million farm families, and the average farm was less than 200 acres. In 1980, there were fewer than 2.5 million farm families, and the average farm was more than 400 acres. While the farm population was dropping to less than half, farmers were increasing production rapidly enough to provide food for an expanded American population and at the same time to increase the proportion of goods exported from 10 percent to 30 percent. In the decade 1949–59, production per farm worker per hour increased 85 percent; in the decade 1959–69, 77 percent; and in the decade 1969–79, 92 percent.

The growth of exports was made possible by the growth of world demand for agricultural goods, but America outpaced other strong agricultural producers like Australia, Canada, and Argentina in adapting to these opportunities. By the late 1970s more than 50 percent of the grain, 50 percent of the soybeans, and 30 percent of the cotton entering international markets was produced by American farmers. From the mid-1960s through the 1970s, more than two-thirds of the food aid throughout the world came from the United States. Although the United States produces only about 2 percent of the world's total volume of rice, in recent years America has been responsible for 20–25 percent of the rice traded in international markets.

While important American industries, such as steel and automobiles, failed to anticipate the changing dynamics of the world market, American agriculture was able to anticipate the changes and adjust appropriately. USDA did not dictate to farmers what they should produce, but it played a crucial leadership role that included coordination, information gathering, strategic analysis, education at home and abroad, market development, formulation of trade policy, and arranging of export credits. As traced in the excellent analysis by Dick Bolling and John Bowles in *America's Competitive Edge*, the formation of the Foreign Agricultural Service within USDA in 1953 and the passing of Public Law 480 the next year were important factors in making this possible.

1. AIDING FOR TRADE: PUBLIC LAW 480

In the early 1950s, as in the 1920s, the United States was confronted with agricultural surpluses. For the first several years after the war, America's aid to war-ravaged countries kept surpluses down to manageable size, but during the early part of the Korean War the United States made the decision to stockpile agricultural produce for emergency war needs. By the latter part of the Korean War, as these stockpiles grew and food relief to Europe and Japan drew to a close, warehouses and elevators overflowed and new surpluses continued to accumulate. One possible solution, the one used in the 1930s, would have been to cut back on production and pay farmers to keep their land idle, but that would have posed serious consequences for all the industries and services that depended on agricultural production, such as farm machinery, cotton and food processing, seeds, and fertilizer. Another alternative was to sell the agricultural produce to foreign nations, but many potential purchasers lacked foreign currency. Yet another option was simply to give away produce, either domestically or internationally. But this in turn could destroy the market, wreck production incentives, and create a worrisome dependence among those aided.

One person who played a key role in forging a creative solution to these problems of surplus was Gwynn Garnett. Thoroughly engrossed in the big questions of agricultural policy, Garnett was a conceptualizer with unrelenting determination. Reared on a farm in Wyoming, Garnett studied agricultural economics at Iowa State and at the end of World War II, he administered food and agricultural programs in Frankfurt under the Marshall Plan. His experience in Europe led to concepts later embodied in PL 480. Garnett had been impressed with how the proceeds of sales of American food brought into Germany had helped the revival of German agriculture by financing research and experimental stations. His views took further shape in 1950 when he visited India. He believed there was a tremendous untapped potential for Indian development, and that proceeds from the sale of American agricultural produce brought into India could help generate the capital to make it possible. While still in India he wrote a draft of possible legislation that several years later became PL 480.

Garnett's vision was far-reaching but intricate, from aid to trade by way of development, but it was incorporated into PL 480 and it worked. The United States would provide food to needy countries at concessionary rates, sales of the food within those countries would generate local currency to be used for economic development, and development would generate exports and the capacity to earn foreign exchange that could be used to purchase, among other things, American agricultural goods. Concessionary grants would thus gradually be replaced by sales at regular prices, and in the meantime American agricultural surpluses would have a continuous outlet. While still serving in Frankfurt, Garnett had talked with Allan B. Kline, director of the American Farm Bureau, who was impressed with his broad vision. In 1950, Kline brought Garnett to Washington as the congressional liaison official for the American Farm Bureau Federation. While in this post, Garnett began to lay the political groundwork for the program embodied in PL 480 several years later.

To build support for his plan, Garnett met with many farm groups. Some organizations like the state farm bureaus worried about the risks of depending on sales to foreign countries and believed that production restraints, as in the 1930s, were a more reliable way to prevent surpluses. Others feared that government involvement would lead to red tape and potentially to price ceilings that would limit their incomes. Yet most farm groups could see that exports would not only dispose of surpluses but perhaps expand sales. Eventually Garnett won the support of the American Farm Bureau Federation, the Farmers Union, the National Association of Farmer Cooperatives, and sectoral associations like the Cotton

Council. Their support, along with that of Secretary of Agriculture Ezra Benson and Assistant Secretary John Davis, and of church groups that believed in the plan's humanitarian purposes and could see a role for themselves in distributing food, enabled Garnett to win the cooperation of farm-state congressmen from both parties.

That, however, was not the end of the battle within the government. The State Department, afraid that the program would depress grain prices and cause trouble to grain-producing allies, resisted. Some officials in the Commerce Department opposed the legislation for fear they might be called on to develop a comparable program. Opposition was not formidable, but it was sufficient to delay passage until 1954, when food surpluses became so large that support was overwhelming. In effect PL 480 formalized and extended the program originally developed for war-torn countries, linking it with the explicit goal of developing long-term agricultural exports.

Title I provided for concessional sales, with long-term loans of up to twenty or more years to "friendly" (i.e., non-Communist) countries, governments or private firms buying American agricultural commodities. Just as Garnett had envisioned, commodities were sold in the recipient countries in local currency and proceeds used to finance internal development projects, thus increasing the capacity of the countries to buy American agricultural commodities. The 1959 revision of PL 480 specified that 5 percent of the proceeds in local currency would be earmarked to develop the market for U.S. agricultural exports.

Title II was designed to meet famine or other extraordinary relief needs, to combat malnutrition, especially in children, and to promote economic and community development in friendly countries. It provided for nonprofit school-lunch programs outside the United States. Many of the commodities were distributed by American welfare associations, such as CARE and Catholic Relief Services, which remained strong political boosters of the program.

The mechanics were relatively easy to work out and went smoothly. Requests for assistance from recipient countries were processed through the American agricultural attachés in those countries and then sent to USDA in Washington (later to an interagency committee that included representatives from the departments of State and Treasury and the Office of Management and Budget). Within the United States, the USDA's Commodity Credit Corporation (CCC) bought the surplus commodities from the farmers and then made them available for export.

The PL 480 program evolved from internal dynamics and from new political forces. In the beginning, the program centered on finding appropriate outlets for accumulated surpluses, but as surpluses became more manageable and countries began to pay for their own purchases, attention turned increasingly to market development and farmers were encouraged to produce goods to meet newly created demand. As a country's economic situation improved, twenty-year credit was phased out and replaced by ten-year credit and later by three-year credit until the country became a cash customer. This process proceeded rapidly in war-torn countries like Japan, Germany, Italy, the United Kingdom, and the Netherlands, and therefore concessionary loans from PL 480 were soon replaced by sales. Officials administering concessionary loans then turned their attention to countries like India, Pakistan, and Chile. In 1961, as the Kennedy administration took more interest in international development, the new Secretary of Agriculture, Orville Freeman, devoted greater attention to the economic development of Third World countries, particularly to transfer of agricultural technology, and the program was more closely tied with the Agency for International Development (AID). In the 1960s, as the international exchange system began working more smoothly and as the United States became more concerned with its balance of payments, payments were no longer tied to local currency, and since 1971 all payments have been made in American dollars.

Despite these modifications through the years, the imaginative program embodied in PL 480 that explicitly linked efforts "to combat hunger and malnutrition" with those "to expand export markets for U.S. agricultural commodities" basically worked very well. To be sure, market demand had created the opportunity, and the large American family farm the potential for meeting the demand, but PL 480 was a creative way to link the two, and two new structures, the Foreign Agricultural Service and agricultural commodity associations, played indispensable roles in seizing the opportunity.

2. PREPARING GLOBAL STRATEGY: THE FOREIGN AGRICULTURAL SERVICE (FAS)

The Foreign Agricultural Service (FAS) of USDA, formed on the eve of the passage of PL 480, illustrates what can be done to develop a tightly knit, well-trained, specialist corps within the federal bureaucracy. From the beginning of the twentieth century, USDA had had an Office of Foreign Agricultural Relations in the Bureau of Agricultural Economics, gathering information from around the world to estimate world food supply and demand and to track programs dealing with agriculture around the world. But in American embassies abroad, the Foreign Service had simply assigned someone to serve as agricultural attaché. Ordinarily the official was a Foreign Service officer—only about half of the agriculture attachés had any background in agriculture—and, after two- or three-year terms, most went on to other assignments unrelated to agriculture. The system made for smooth-running embassies, but it was frustrating for USDA that in its overseas work it had to rely on people not always attuned to agricultural issues.

FAS was officially established as a distinct corps within USDA in March 1953 by a memorandum of the Secretary of Agriculture, and on August 28, 1954, PL 690 was enacted, transferring the position of agricultural attaché from the Department of State to the Department of Agriculture. The State Department's lack of enthusiasm for this move was more than balanced by the enthusiasm of the Department of Agriculture and its supporters, farm organizations and congressmen from rural states. As part of the reorganization, the total number of positions related to foreign agriculture was reduced by about a third, but because USDA used the opportunity to develop a corps of dedicated and talented agriculture specialists, morale immediately shot up. Gwynn Garnett was appointed to head the service, and he remained in that position for four years.

The leaders of the service immediately transferred into FAS a small number of foreign-affairs specialists within USDA, but they then began a campaign to recruit outstanding young officers, particularly recent university graduates with majors in agricultural economics who could handle at least one foreign language. They went to the deans of agriculture schools throughout the country to recruit the ablest of their graduates. Talented young people could identify with their sense of mission and were therefore eager to join. A major effort was made to recruit a small number with special skills, especially knowledge of key foreign countries, of computer programming, and of econometrics. By 1980 about 800 people were employed in the Foreign Agricultural Service, half of them professionals. Of these 800, about 275 were serving overseas in some seventy locations.

Most of the professionals and even many of the nonprofessionals shared a common background that facilitated communication and made it easier to achieve consensus about major goals. Most came from farm backgrounds and instinctively understood the impact that various programs might have on the American farmer and the organizations that represent him, and their esprit was based in part on their sense that they were helping the American farmer. Although not all had farm and agricultural economics backgrounds, those who brought other skills learned to share the dominant intellectual orientation. The group was sufficiently small that all the professionals knew one another, and this provided the basis for institutional and personal loyalty.

USDA is not immune from political pressures, as was made all too clear during 1963–67 when the House Committee on Government Operations launched investigations of alleged "junketing" by some FAS officials and especially their private-sector "cooperators." But success in running a good operation and congressional support from farm states gave FAS much more room for maneuver than that enjoyed by many other parts of the bureaucracy. This freedom enabled the professionals to do what was needed to keep an effective organization, preserve continuity, and maintain a long-range perspective. Ray Iaones, who took over the FAS as Administrator in March 1962, proved so successful in running the organization that he was retained until September 1973 by secretaries of agriculture of both political parties. A dedicated official with a sense of what it takes to run a successful service and maintain effective career development, he looked after talented people under him and, in spite of the resentments it caused, refused to appoint ineffective officers. Iaones was ready to do battle with other agencies like the State Department to defend the people under him. He believed that on matters of import even if FAS did not have explicit authority that its officials should issue statements as if they did, with the result that they were often granted the authority they wished they had. Secretaries of agriculture learned that he could make FAS work well and keep up good relations with Congress.

Iaones and others developed a rationale for rotation and career development. Because there were many single posts in small countries and because people with farm backgrounds could understand many issues that others could not, most of these single posts went to people who had farm backgrounds. In order that the system not be skewed, those who were going overseas were not allowed special promotions. A typical professional career began with three to five years in Washington for basic orientation followed by an overseas post. After another tour of duty in Washington the officer was then ready for a small overseas post where he could assume primary responsibility. Almost no one resigned before retirement, and FAS is one of the few government agencies to have an active alumni association.

FAS officers abroad monitor and report on foreign agricultural developments. Their reports center on the crops of interest to American agriculture: wheat, rice, cotton, corn, soybeans, feed grains, and livestock. In addition to basic information about production levels and demand throughout the world, reports include everything that affects agricultural supply and demand, including changing food tastes, food distribution patterns, and political changes that might affect agriculture, as well as trade and market development information. FAS not only makes its own estimates of supply and demand but follows and analyzes the various estimates made by governments and research institutes around the world.

As such reports are collected from more than seventy countries, the information coming into the Department of Agriculture on world food developments is by far the best in the world, rivaled only by that of the UN's Food and Agriculture Organization, which tends to be one to two years behind and suffers from the inability to make tough judgments that might offend member states. FAS reports provide a solid basis for analyzing supply, demand, and trade and for making price projections—a task that is ably carried out by FAS's Washington analysts and USDA's Economic Research Service.

One of the main tasks of FAS is "market development." This is not the same as marketing, which is done by private companies. Market development is much broader in scope, including all things that make marketing possible. It includes research and study groups to better understand nutrition, food processing, and procedures to ensure health. It includes demonstrations and the use of mass media to introduce new foods, enlarging food habits and tastes. It includes troubleshooting problems of customs inspections, transportation, and storage. It includes educating American farmers and their representatives about the needs of the foreign market. It includes the monitoring of costs and standards at home to increase the competitiveness of goods abroad. It includes the formulation of trade policy and continuous efforts to maximize the openness of foreign agricultural markets. And it includes using the information collected to make assessments of promising potential markets and the development of strategies and plans of action to develop these markets. The provision that 5 percent of PL 480 sales to a given country be used for market development in that country for some years supplemented efforts in Washington, ensuring that financial resources would be available in the consuming country.

The high morale, competence, and sense of mission of the FAS were reinforced by success. For market development, FAS forged triangular relationships with groups in the host countries with whom they shared a common commercial interest and with their American cooperators. The key to market development was the relationship developed with these cooperators.

3. COOPERATING FOR MARKET DEVELOPMENT

Those who helped launch FAS began in 1954 with little experience in developing foreign markets and less than a clear idea of everything needed for market development. Although the U.S. government had been assisting farmers almost from its inception, foreign market development was a completely new function. FAS officials realized they needed advice; they were ready to go outside to get it, and they were eager to learn. They gradually cultivated an able group of retired advertising executives, people with considerable experience like Frank White, who had served as an executive both of ABC and NBC before becoming NBC president. These executives stressed the importance of a marketing plan. For each country where they hoped to sell, they would require an annual statement stating the marketing goals, the activities designed to meet the goals, and an evaluation of the effectiveness of the program. Like the basic reporting system, this program became a new tool of disciplined accountability. Successes and failures could be measured as clearly as profits and losses in a business.

In the early years when they had many different commodities they were trying to introduce into a country, FAS officials used trade fairs, especially in Europe and Japan. To attract attention some were on a grand scale, with accompanying public forums with Arnold Toynbee and other well-known figures. They found that the fairs with the most impact were not those aimed at consumers but those aimed at business people in the food trades, for if these people decided to purchase, products were soon accepted by consumers. FAS quickly adapted its trade fairs accordingly. One of the new services developed to help provide marketing information was Trade Opportunity Referral System (TORS). With the cooperation of state departments of agriculture, TORS developed lists of some 7,000 U.S. suppliers. To match these, it developed lists of some 10,000 potential buyers in fifty-six countries. The lists are linked by each officer abroad, who monitors opportunities as they develop and sends them out by computer to appropriate categories of possible suppliers. In the mid-1980s the weekly mailing is sent to some 2,000 firms and organizations involved in agricultural export. As necessary, similar assistance is available to help groups of foreigners coming to the United States or Americans going abroad.

In deciding how to organize foreign market development on an ongoing basis, FAS considered taking direct operational responsibility itself, but this would have strained its control in activities in which its officers were less than expert. Another alternative would have been to hire consultants and contractors to do the job. Instead, FAS hit upon a more creative solution. It would encourage the private sector to form industry associations to cooperate with FAS for market development. The first model was the National Cotton Council, already in existence. It was relatively well organized, determined to sell abroad, and prepared to use money. The head of its international division, Reid Dunn, had a good sense of what was required in foreign markets but needed financial help and the assistance of FAS in providing the broader information network needed to expand opportunities, formulate strategies, and draw up market-development plans. The cooperation clicked, and it became a model for tobacco and then other commodity associations—wheat, rice, corn, dairy products, soybeans, and other agricultural products.

The commodity associations were the logical extension of market-development activities. They brought their own expertise and that of member firms, all strongly committed to exporting. The associations accepted as "cooperators" had to be nonprofit, represent a broad segment of producers, and deal in commodities with a domestic surplus that could be competitive abroad. They had to indicate willingness to cooperate with FAS for long-term programs, and to have a staff and financial base to assure adequate execution of the programs. USDA agreed to put up a small amount of funds to get the program going, but it insisted that the cooperator, with funds from the producers, provide half or more of the funds to demonstrate commitment. As FAS initially had ample local currency abroad (from the 5 percent of PL 480 sales earmarked for market development), it generally paid expenses abroad while the cooperator paid salaries and other expenses in the United States. Originally, most funds came from the government, but currently about two-thirds of the budget comes from cooperators and about $20 million a year comes from USDA, a small amount compared to the $40 billion of annual exports.

Originally most of the cooperators were existing trade associations, but with the development of FAS some new cooperators were formed specifically to help develop new markets and represent appropriate commodity groups in the United States. Private firms were brought in through cooperators and helped to identify markets, lent technicians for overseas training programs, supplied products for fairs, and contributed financially to the associations. By maintaining close touch with the information flow, these firms were ready to take advantage of new market opportunities. Even existing commodity associations were strengthened by this new role as they reorganized to help develop foreign markets. By the early 1980s more than fifty cooperators were taking part in the program.

When American products first started going abroad, new problems of health and taste had to be confronted. Nonfat dry milk, for example, was perfectly satisfactory, but when mixed with local water it could cause serious health problems and FAS had to find ways to help improve the local water supply. President Jomo Kenyatta of Kenya appeared on local TV in Nairobi eating yellow corn before Kenyans were convinced that it was edible by humans as well as by animals. President Bourguiba of Tunisia had to use soybean oil in public to show that it could be used instead of olive oil.

Cooperators also must convince local people that the United States is an appropriate and reliable source of supply. They must demonstrate the nutritional value of the foods, vouch for their healthfulness, and teach local specialists how to guard against spoilage. FAS and cooperators search out local groups with whom they share commercial interests—cotton spinners and weavers, bakers, feed-grain mixers, soybean crushers, and livestock breeders, as well as wholesalers, retailers, and restaurants. They help introduce cakes and doughnuts that use American wheat and assist in local livestock production that relies on American feed grains. They help promote rice-grading programs on the American side so that foreign rice sellers can assure its acceptability to their customers. And they must work with local government officials to reduce formal barriers, work out mutually satisfactory inspection procedures, and overcome problems in the smooth flow of the commodities.

In Japan, the largest market for American agricultural supplies, nine cooperators have permanent offices. Japanese consumers as well as government bureaucrats are very nutrition-conscious. Some of the large breakthroughs in sales to Japan have come through school-lunch programs with surplus foods provided through PL 480, but they were facilitated by nutrition specialists hired by the cooperators who worked closely with educational administrators defining the nutritive values of wheat, soybeans, and other products.

Through a variety of mechanisms, from tariffs to informal arrangements, the Japanese have made it difficult or impossible for many finished food products to enter Japan. It is Japanese national strategy to have as much value-added work as possible done in Japan, and that makes it easier for bulk commodities to enter. Even the extent of penetration of basic commodities is by no means a foregone conclusion. U.S. cooperators have made great progress in expanding their markets in Japan, which went from being over 90 percent self-sufficient in food in 1960 to being about 70 percent self-sufficient in 1980. By then more than $6 billion worth of American agricultural products, about 40 percent of Japan's food imports, came from the United States. In the course of this, Japanese learned new food habits, like the switch from rice to bread in school lunches. FAS and the cooperators were often imaginative in opening up new channels for sales. Having trouble convincing Japanese of the potential for pork, they helped arrange for Iowa's governor to give hogs to the governor of Iowa's sister prefecture, Yamanashi. To feed the hogs they then sent free carloads of corn for demonstration purposes. The experiment worked. Farmers raising hogs in Japan found opportunities for profit, and producers of feed grain and corn in the United States found new outlets for their products.

Much of the success in penetrating the Japanese market came from assisting with technology transfers that had the effect of increasing demand for American agricultural products. The wheat cooperators assisted in developing flour milling and bakeries, and Japan now claims one of the most modern milling and baking industries in the world, with a steady demand for American wheat. Cotton cooperators helped supply technology to spinners, who bought large amounts of American cotton.

There is room for more market growth, but the potential for growth in agricultural sales to Japan are limited because of Japan's protectionist policies. Imported wheat, for example, cannot be sold directly to Japanese wholesale or retail dealers but must be sold in restricted quantities at international prices to the Food Agency, a state food monopoly that in turn sells it within Japan at much higher prices so wheat will not cut too deeply into rice consumption. In the late 1970s, when Japan had a big surplus in rice, it encouraged some rice producers to go into wheat production, even though wheat had to be subsidized even more than rice. This also cut into American wheat sales. Although tariffs on soybeans were abolished, bean processors maintained a cartel-like arrangement whereby they would process only an agreed amount of beans in order to maintain a price at a certain level, and thus American export opportunities were limited. Quarantines, delays in inspection, and unpredictable rules delay the expansion of fresh produce into Japan. Yet, despite these problems, American agricultural exports as a whole have constantly increased in value.

FAS and its cooperators have, of course, continuously used political as well as administrative channels to try to reduce formal and informal import barriers in Japan, but they have also learned to search out markets where there is less political resistance. Of course, Japanese farmers and farm associations resist the entry of products that compete with theirs, but about 75 percent of American agricultural goods imported into Japan, including feed grains and other products, are actually used by Japanese farmers.

The role of the cooperators in making this kind of growth possible may be illustrated by the role of the American Soybean Association in penetrating the Japanese market. In 1956, when George Strayer first went to Japan to represent them in developing the soybean market, he began developing relationships with potential Japanese users. Within a year he had helped establish a joint United States–Japan Soybean Study Group, with five Japanese associations, associations for makers of soy sauce, miso, tofu, edible oil, and soybean meal. The American Soybean Association set up its own internal inspection procedures to ensure that products going to Japan would meet Japanese standards and helped develop types of soybean products most appropriate for the Japanese market. As early as 1958 it sponsored a ten-month American tour for two Japanese food chemists to help Americans develop beans appropriate for making miso and tofu. One of the earliest members of its Tokyo staff, Yoshiko Kojima, got trained in nutrition and then worked with Japanese school systems, illustrating how soybean products could be used in school lunches. In 1961 it sponsored a group of nutrition specialists, Kojima and three others, on a study mission to the United States, where they studied edible oils, and by 1961 a margarine composed entirely of soybean oil was successfully introduced into Japan. It assisted in setting up oil-producing plants in Japan. Since oil uses only about 20 percent of the soybean product, the key issue is to make use of the other 80 percent, and here the use of soybean meal as feed for chickens, hogs, and cattle was critical. It sponsored visits of American specialist teams to Japan and Japanese specialist teams to America, and hired animal nutrition specialists to help devise optimal mixes for animal feeds.

The highly successful American penetration led to efforts by Japanese soybean producers to eliminate or reduce American sales, but FAS and its Japanese allies who had a vested interest in American soybeans were able to resist this. In 1973 when U.S. Secretary of Commerce Frederick B. Dent held up soybean shipments from the United States for several weeks, Japanese who wanted to reduce reliance on American soybeans and other commodities made good use of the incident. Despite these problems, Japanese imports of soybeans rose from 717,000 tons in

1956, when the United States supplied less than 75 percent, to 4.4 million tons in 1980, of which the United States supplied 96 percent.

The importance of American bureaucrats maintaining a solid base of political support was illustrated by an issue that preoccupied FAS for several years. In 1960, in response to complaints from cooperators about the red tape of requiring prior FAS approval for overseas trips and other expenditures, FAS relaxed its control. An energetic and politically motivated staff member of the House Government Operations Committee, Arthur Perlman, led an extensive investigation of extravagances of FAS and cooperator officials on junkets around the world. Eventually FAS was able to convince congressional committees that it had used its funds modestly and wisely, but at such times support of key congressmen is essential in preserving the activities and freedom of both the Service and the cooperators to respond effectively to market opportunities.

Perhaps the most difficult problem for FAS is mediating between cooperators who have conflicting interests. One of the most common problems is that between the feed-grains sector, which is often willing to help the livestock industry in another country, and American livestock interests, which oppose it. One FAS ground rule to avoid unfair favoritism while still taking an activist role is not to initiate programs that displace American commodities. However, if a foreign country is already developing a livestock industry, the FAS will work with American cooperators selling to that industry. At times, the FAS has made geographic trade-offs, offering, for example, to support a poultry program in one country if the American poultry cooperator would drop objections to an American feed-grain program in another country. A similar kind of problem exists between, for example, American soy processors and producers who want to sell raw soybeans abroad. FAS made an effort to assist American soy processors where possible and to seek their understanding when other countries made this impossible rather than forfeit the market entirely. In 1969, however, the soy processors left the program, objecting to the encouragement of sales of raw soybeans abroad.

A related kind of problem is the disagreement between the pork and beef industries over the appropriate share of financial support coming to each from FAS. In such a case FAS officials endeavor to bring the groups together so both can concentrate their energies on market development.

In the early years, when the FAS cooperator budget was growing, the conflicts over budget allocation were easier to resolve because FAS could expand into new areas without sacrificing old sectors. Also in the past the fact that most American farmers grew a number of commodities and could shift production made FAS's task of mediating much easier. Unfortunately, budgets have leveled off and American farmers are becoming more specialized, making the task of mediating conflicts much more difficult for FAS.

Another difficult issue within U.S. agriculture concerns those agricultural commodities like sugar, dairy products, tobacco, and peanuts that are less inter-nationally competitive. The success of American producers in creating protec-tionist barriers makes it more difficult for FAS to make the case for knocking down foreign barriers to American products overseas. Because the vast majority of commodity associations have very competitive products, the thrust of FAS is, of course, vigorous support of free trade.

In the early 1980s an Agricultural Export Development Council was created consisting of all the cooperators, and this council, which meets twice annually, also helps the FAS in arriving at positions good for the group as a whole. This makes it easier for FAS to avoid political pressures on a particular commodity group and to rally broad support for efforts to keep international markets open.

In the early 1960s, as Eastern Europe and Russia began to show more interest in higher quality food products, FAS began to follow their tastes very closely. The decision to purchase American food supplies on a large scale was very risky, for Russian and Eastern European officials realized that once they began purchas-ing American goods it would be very difficult to face their populations with a decision to cut them off. It was therefore ultimately a political decision made by the Russians, and it followed years of careful behind-the-scenes contacts and negotiations by FAS officials, who learned to adapt to the commissars' bureau-cratic procedures and give them a feeling of the reliability of American supply. President Johnson agreed to sell grain to the Russians, and in 1971 President Nixon lifted the requirement that half the transport be in U.S. ships, for Russians could not easily afford to use American ships. The sudden increases in sales to the USSR in the early 1970s not only greatly increased American exports but led to a rapid rise of prices on the international market, and FAS was positioned to help American agriculture take advantage of the opportunity.

In 1956, when PL 480 began operating, about $1 billion worth of American agricultural products was exported as part of that program. Although the value of the dollar declined thereafter in current dollars the value of the agricultural produce being exported under PL 480 remained roughly the same through the 1970s, when humanitarian purposes became more prominent. By then, however, FAS and the cooperators had been highly successful in moving from aid to trade. In 1956, exports under PL 480 constituted about 30 percent of American agri-cultural exports, but by 1980 it was less than 3 percent. The cooperators had proved to be an excellent link between the private sector and the bureaucracy, bringing together private firms and producers, devising creative programs in keep-ing with their common interests, and interacting with the government not as adversaries but as partners pursuing the same objectives.

The experience of FAS and the cooperators working together accomplished far more than the immediate development of foreign markets. It developed new networks of information and new alliances that enabled groups of farmers to think through the implications of their situation and political position. FAS developed its own publications that went directly to cattlemen associations, to port authorities, to land-grant universities, and to cooperators. FAS sent out its own speakers and cultivated a series of informed writers for national newspapers and magazines. After programs developed, congressmen, state officials, deans of agricultural schools, and other influential people were informed about them and invited to visit facilities overseas, establishing a broader political base of understanding that helped ensure continuity. President Reagan's Secretary of Agriculture, John Block, for example, did not continue all his predecessors' support programs, but he had been familiar with FAS and cooperators programs from years before and supported their efforts. Robert Dole led the fight for the Chinese textile agreement because he realized it was necessary to get their cooperation to sell them more agricultural products.

These alliances enabled FAS and the cooperators to anticipate developments. FAS officials worked with Russian agricultural specialists for years before trade began and with Chinese officials in Ottawa long before Secretary of State Henry Kissinger's first visit to China. The network of alliances enabled FAS to work with farmers' groups and prepare them for opportunities that eventually came their way. These new alliances thus greatly raised the level of awareness of farmers and their supporters and established a basis for further effective programs on their behalf.

4. PRODUCING FOR GROWTH: THE FARMER AND THE RESEARCHER

Unlike American industrial production, American farm production is still largely in the hands of individual producers and yet the 2.5 million farms are able to respond quickly to changing world markets. Their ability to respond so effectively draws on a century of infrastructure that began with the land-grant colleges and includes state universities and state departments of agriculture. It includes an extensive agricultural extension service and agricultural research stations. It includes a system of establishing quality standards and inspections for agricultural crops, and an elaborate network of information channels that keeps the farmer well informed on new technology as well as changing markets. FAS was able to draw on this infrastructure in adapting research and production to meet the needs of the foreign market. This enabled the states to undertake research into varieties of crops and seeds to meet foreign demand and the kinds of fertilizers necessary to expand production. It led to new ways of cutting meat and new ways of processing foods to adapt them to foreign tastes.

The effort through PL 480 to provide adequate nutrition to countries suffering from malnutrition led to the commercialization of new research and new products such as nonfat dry milk, corn soya milk, and other fortified foods that greatly raised standards of nutrition around the world. As poor countries increasingly try to rationalize their food and agricultural policies in terms of nutritional intake, it ensures that American agriculture will be ready to assist in the effort.

FAS officials, like MITI officials pushing Japanese industries forward, are constantly dissatisfied that farmers and their organizations are too conservative, too slow in responding to opportunities and to the changes they see around the world. Yet American agriculture is often in a different league from many American small businesses not even aware of international developments in their sectors. The creative tension of FAS bureaucrats—acutely aware of foreign opportunities—and farmers serves to help drive forward agricultural practice and research even if FAS is not fully satisfied with the results.

5. ADJUSTING TO NEW PROBLEMS: MARKET FLUCTUATIONS, INFLATION, EMBARGOES, PRESSURE GROUPS, CHANGING MARKETS, SOIL DEPLETION

Increased U.S. dependence on world markets has created or intensified a whole host of new problems that confront the Department of Agriculture, FAS, their cooperators, and the American farmer:

1. Market fluctuations. Consumer countries are highly sensitive to their dependence on world food markets. Bureaucrats and politicians in these countries, responsible for ensuring a stable food supply, endeavor to make long-term contracts and diversify their food sources. Some seeking food security insist on long-term contracts and government-to-government agreements that in turn limit the flexibility and the size of the open market. In producer countries, farmers and their supporters seek insulation from sudden changes in world politics and world markets while leaving themselves maximally free to take advantage of new market opportunities. The problems for the United Sates are how to help provide security to countries purchasing its goods, provide security to its own producers, find some mechanisms to provide enough price stability to enhance the basis for this security, and yet maintain a relatively free market. In the early 1970s, for example, with the decision of the USSR to purchase substantial amounts of grain abroad, worldwide food shortages led to quintupling of the price of wheat. The problem then was not only to provide some price stability for consumers but to ensure adequate supplies for the home market and for the poorer countries. However, the situation changed sharply after 1979 with a constricted world economy, and the key question for American policymakers became how to contain protectionist pressures and ensure adequate income to farmers.

2. *Inflation and the squeeze on farmers.* In the mid-1970s, with the world food shortage, American farmers acquired more equipment, and the price of farm land quickly escalated. Young farmers or speculators were willing to go into debt and pay high interest with the expectation, based on the best advice at the time, that these forces would continue. With the world recession beginning in 1979, prices fell, interest rates rose, and ambitious farmers who had borrowed in the 1970s were unable to generate the income to meet their payments. By mid-1981 a third of the loans from the Farmer's Home Administration were delinquent, and by mid-1982 farm indebtedness was twelve times farm income. Farmers were caught in the worst squeeze since the Great Depression.

Temporarily, crop subsidies through the Commodity Credit Corporation (CCC) eased the adjustment, but CCC was under pressure on the one hand from federal budget-cutters and on the other from particularly strong commodity groups that made it difficult to maintain a balanced program.

3. *Embargoes.* As agricultural goods become more subject to unpredictable market forces, and as nations become more dependent on agriculture imports for their food supply, the temptation increases for the United States to use embargoes, either to adjust to market crises or as a political weapon. The most striking case was, of course, the restriction on grain exports to the Soviet Union in 1980 in response to the Soviet invasion of Afghanistan. The cutting off of food supplies creates such anxieties and arouses such hostilities that the effects are longer lasting and deeper than politicians, who assume that markets can easily be reclaimed, imagine. The embargo of the Soviet Union affected not only Russian attitudes. Even countries like Mexico became much more cautious in buying from the United States. At a minimum, it makes the job of all United States sellers much more difficult. Even if the world market operated so smoothly that other countries would supply the USSR, leaving equal opportunity for America to sell abroad, the replacement would require arrangements with a much more diversified group of countries, greatly increasing costs of sales, promotion, and transport. At worst, it means that when grain supplies are ample the United States becomes the residual supplier, selling only if all other world supplies are exhausted.

The temporary soybean embargo in 1973 was designed not for political purposes but because there was concern that some buyers were trying to corner the market and that the supply of soybeans would not be adequate to meet the demand. Although the embargo lasted only a few weeks, countries like Japan used the incident to strengthen protectionist policies and diversify sources of supply. Japan helped Brazil develop a soybean crop and, within a decade, Brazil, which had been producing less that 2 million tons of soybeans per year at the time of the embargo, was producing some 15 million tons. Although the United States eventually recovered a considerable amount of lost sales in soybeans because of its extraordinary competitiveness, it has lost sales in soybean meal and soybean oil to Brazil, which has had a program of subsidies and incentives for its domestic soybean-processing industry. At best, embargoes greatly complicate the work of American representatives trying to persuade other countries of the reliability of American exports.

4. *Controlling pressure groups.* With heightened international competition, pressure groups concerned with commodities like sugar, tobacco, dairy products, and cotton, which are not always competitive, are sufficiently strong that they can obtain protectionist measures or subsidies that go beyond temporary adjustment to changing conditions of supply and demand. Given the difficulties in countering world protectionism at times of oversupply on world markets, as in the early 1980s, the question is whether these protectionist pressures can be contained for the good of American agriculture as a whole.

5. *Changing markets.* In the late 1970s and early 1980s the greatest growth in world markets was in high-value-added products (HVP), such as meats, dairy products, beverages, cereal preparations, flour, corn oil, and soybean oil, rather than in low-value-added products (LVP), such as grain, corn, and soybeans. Some of the biggest changes in food consumption are in developing countries, where the diet is continuing to improve rapidly. Their demand for HVP is therefore increasing very rapidly while patterns of food consumption in developed countries is more stable. USDA therefore estimates that in the 1980s HVP trade is likely to grow at 10–14 percent (about $13 billion to $20 billion) per year, much more rapidly than LVP trade.

In recent years, as countries have become more conscious of trade balances, they try harder to maximize the amount of value-added work done at home. Because they see more market opportunities in HVP, they tend to be far more protective of these products and to exert themselves to export much more of them. Traditionally, America's greatest strength has been in LVP, and most American cooperators have worked in the LVP area. The U.S. global market share of HVP has remained fairly stable at about 10 percent, but because most U.S. exports are in LVP and most of the export expansion is in HVP, America's agricultural exports in the late 1970s and early 1980s were not keeping pace with world expansion. FAS early recognized the problem but, whether because the United States has had difficulty in pushing allies to open more to HVP or whether as some FAS critics charge it has been slow to develop new organizational patterns and find new cooperators to exploit the HVP market, it has not been as successful in the HVP market as it was earlier in the LVP market. This area is clearly at the center of FAS strategy for the 1980s.

6. *Depletion.* With the great expansion of American agricultural production

to keep up with export demand, some land otherwise marginal was brought into use. Critics charged that this lowered water tables and mortgaged future scarce water resources for marginal current financial gain. Some farmers, anxious to take advantage of new opportunities, have exploited their land for quick production and have not done enough to maintain the quality of nutrients in the soil. Controversy surrounding these topics temporarily eased in the early 1980s with the decline of demand, but if world agricultural demand again rises rapidly the questions of soil nutrients and water tables will become serious problems for FAS to manage while meeting international demand.

Several of these problems (embargoes, pressure groups, and inflation) involve policy questions and require political decisions beyond the power of agricultural specialists. But even in these areas, the new network of relationships between FAS, cooperators, and farmers provides a framework for rapid identification of the issues, collection and analysis of relevant data, and effective response. The success of FAS, like that of MITI, derives not so much from a particular policy as from a sense of direction and from a framework that permits rapid adaptation to the new problems through ongoing analysis and cooperative efforts to solve them. Agricultural specialists are keenly aware of agricultural sectors that could have done better, but in contrast to American industry, which has fallen seriously behind in world competition, American agriculture remains at the forefront. Even political barriers throughout the world cannot entirely keep out its competitive products, which reflect its ability to adapt to changing world markets.

6. INDUSTRY LEARNING FROM AGRICULTURE?

It is immeasurably more difficult for the United States to develop a framework of cooperation between government and industry than between government and agriculture. Agriculture has a history of government-private cooperation going back to the nineteenth century providing a base of trust and mutual respect rarely found in relations with industry. The American public is more disposed to provide help to private farmers, whom they respect, than to large corporations, which in their view evade social responsibility, harm the environment, tolerate poor quality and poor safety standards, and provide inadequate service. The higher levels of support given to agriculture by the government in turn give bureaucrats more leverage in working with the private sector. Commerce Department officials come from more heterogeneous backgrounds, and able officials have more opportunities in the private sector where salaries are higher than in government, making it difficult to develop a unified core of talented and dedicated officials such as those in FAS. The Commerce Department supervises such a broad range of products that it cannot keep informed on all of them, as FAS does on its small range of key commodities. Large American enterprises with their own information and marketing networks feel they can operate without the government and are reluctant to support government services for all American firms which in effect would reduce the gaps between them and their less powerful competitors. Agricultural officials have become accustomed to working harder to look out for their sector, protecting, for example, farmers in downswings, for farmers cannot so easily abandon and buy farms in cycles as businesses can hire and fire workers. The privately owned large American farm is a highly competitive unit more effective in responding to outside guidance than many large corporations, tied down as they are by bureaucratic, accounting, and legal procedures.

There is no way a Foreign Commercial Service could become really effective overnight. It would take at best several years to develop a core of able officials and to develop the relationships of trust with the private sector to make it effective. But the intersectoral advisory committees developed during the Tokyo Round of trade negotiations in 1973 illustrate how private sectoral groups even in industry can work effectively with government bureaucrats. Unfortunately, there has not been the political will to extend these successes to other areas. There was only a half-hearted and abortive effort in the early 1980s to establish a Foreign Commercial Service. The effort was consciously inspired by the success of FAS, but there was not enough high-level support to overcome bureaucratic resistance. The State Department was more reluctant to give up positions to commercial specialists than it had been to agricultural specialists, and OMB refused to create new positions, requiring the Commerce Department to give up other positions. High officials within the Commerce Department did not support the new Foreign Commercial Service, and other parts of the Commerce Department asked to give up positions to the Foreign Commercial Service were hostile from the beginning. It would take a much greater sense of urgency and a much broader commitment than at present to create an effective framework for cooperation in industry.

As America's competitive position continues to deteriorate, we would be wise to apply to industry and commerce several lessons from agriculture:

1. *The United States needs a body of talented, knowledgeable, and committed professionals* with a sufficient base of support to develop a framework of cooperation with the private sector to work for American industrial competitiveness. These experts must have sufficient understanding of international competitive dynamics to gain the respect of the business community, and they must be committed to professional careers in government, working with business to explore programs of benefit to American business in the long run. We must develop a large group of specialists who, with the knowledge of foreign countries and

languages and of industrial sectors, would together provide the expertise needed for such a service. Given the complexities of the industrial fields, it is difficult to imagine how this cadre could be smaller than that of the FAS, and it would undoubtedly take several years to select and train an appropriate staff.

2. *The United States needs to develop sectoral associations* like the agricultural cooperators and the intersectoral advisory committees of the Tokyo Round. Representatives in a sector must be able to meet and discuss problems of their sector as a whole without fear of antitrust proceedings. Given the disparity of interests, especially between large and small firms, it may be necessary to have several associations and perhaps occasional ad hoc groups within a single sector. The focus of these associations should be research, marketing, financial, and tax needs of the companies within the sector. It would undoubtedly take time for representatives of different companies to develop the relationships of trust and the frame of mind to allow them to focus on issues where they share common interests. Some leverage from a Foreign Commercial Service, such as FAS had in providing funds for common market development, would be desirable for maintaining the framework of effective cooperation.

3. *The United States must develop vastly expanded programs of research, information, and overseas marketing* that would give content to a new framework of government-business cooperation. It must draw in specialists who can assist companies in thinking through their common interests, as in the case of agriculture, who can develop forward-looking approaches to anticipate change.

A number of large multinational companies based in America are already able to handle many of these research, information, and marketing programs by themselves. But their interests are not the same as national interests, and their lack of enthusiasm for broader-based sectoral cooperation should not be allowed to block efforts on behalf of American industry as a whole. There is no reason they should not be given wholehearted national support in adapting to international market conditions at the same time that the mass of American companies could be helped by cooperative efforts such as those that have helped make American agriculture preeminent.

9

Private Housing, 1945–65: Facilitating Finance

by Ezra F. Vogel and Karen DeVol

It is commonly said that the U.S. government does not favor certain
sectors, that it does not pick winners and losers but leaves such decisions
to the marketplace. Yet in fact, throughout U.S. history, the government has
often given special encouragement to certain sectors while neglecting others.
One example is home building in the decades immediately after World War II.
Government housing policies evolved over a period of years and resulted less
from long-range planning than from responses to crises. Yet they represented a
forward-looking effort to provide the conditions for a healthy private-sector
home-building industry. After World War II these policies facilitated an extraordinary growth of home building by minimizing risk at every critical stage. They
constituted a uniquely American solution, with the basic initiatives in the hands
of the private sector, making possible the growth of private housing in little more
than two decades from a marginally adequate level to what was arguably the
highest level in the world.

On the eve of the Great Depression, the American housing stock was supris-
ingly backward. Nearly half of existing housing units lacked a private bath or
shower. Although the bank crisis led President Roosevelt to provide government
support for housing finance, the Depression was too severe for housing demand
to increase significantly before war broke out. During the war, with priorities
directed elsewhere, the housing problem grew worse. At the end of the war, the
pent-up demand for better housing led to a national consensus to give it special
attention. In the 1949 Housing Act, Congress committed itself to work for a
"decent home and a suitable living environment for every American family." It

continued and even extended the programs begun during the Depression to ensure an adequate and stable source of funds for home building.

Government policy has rightly been faulted for its failure to give sufficient attention to the housing problems of lower-income groups, problems given more attention in housing policy after 1965 but still not solved. Yet in the two decades immediately after the war, the housing industry made extraordinary progress in improving living conditions for a broad range of middle-income Americans. In 1940 some 44 percent of housing units were owner-occupied. By 1950 the figure had grown to 55 percent, by 1960 to 62 percent, by 1970 to 63 percent, by 1980 to 66 percent. When the Bureau of the Census first collected data on housing quality in 1940, 45 percent of existing units lacked some plumbing facilities. By 1950, this had fallen to 34 percent, by 1960 to 15 percent, by 1970 to 5 percent, and by 1980 to 3 percent. Overcrowding, as measured by the percentage of units with more than one person per room, fell from 20 percent in 1940 to 15 percent in 1950, to 11 percent in 1960, to 8 percent in 1970, to 4 percent in 1980. This dramatic improvement in housing quality would not have been possible without a bold program by the U.S. government to provide the financial underpinnings. The framework that made possible this achievement began as a response to the crisis of the Depression.

1. RESPONDING TO THE DEPRESSION CRISIS

In Japan, the bureaucracy is constantly surveying the entire social landscape, trying to anticipate new developments. In the United States, individuals or think tanks may think in these terms but we generally make major departures in response to crises. The new departures in housing stem from the crisis of 1932, when there were 240,000 home foreclosures, almost twice the number of new housing starts that year. Toward the end of the year, home foreclosures were occurring at the rate of 1,000 per day. This threatened not only to dispossess millions of families but to destroy construction companies and the banks, savings and loan associations, and insurance companies that held the mortgages.

The crisis resulted in part from the shaky system of housing finance in the 1920s. Because there was no mortgage insurance and because many bankers expected that the prices of homes would come down substantially, banks considered it very risky to lend to home buyers. They required large down payments and issued short-term, high-interest mortgages. Families unable to make the high payments tried to take out second and third mortgages, which, if available at all, entailed exorbitant interest rates. With the Depression, more people unable to make payments desperately tried for second and third mortgages, and when they could not make payments the whole system was in danger. The system also restricted home ownership mostly to the top one-third in income. Housing production peaked in 1925, and because demand among high-income groups was quickly saturated, little new housing was produced in the late 1920s and early 1930s. Among advanced Western nations, the United States was alone in having no government support for housing for the lower and lower-middle classes.

In the last days of his administration, President Hoover acknowledged the seriousness of the housing finance crisis and took emergency action. The Reconstruction Finance Corporation was provided with funds to make self-liquidating loans for the construction of low-income housing. The Federal Home Loan Bank System, modeled after the Federal Reserve System, created twelve regional banks authorized to lend money to savings and loan banks and other mortgage lenders with the aim of reviving the home construction industry. Because these institutions were slow in getting started, little progress was made before Roosevelt came into office.

The most urgent problem confronting Roosevelt was mortgage default, then threatening millions of households with loss of ownership and thousands of financial institutions with bankruptcy. Beyond that were questions of reviving home construction to deal with both the housing shortage and unemployment. Among the programs Roosevelt devised to deal with these problems were the following:

1. *The Home Owners Loan Corporation (HOLC), 1933.* This corporation, financed by federal funds, purchased defaulted home mortgages and replaced them by new loans that were fully amortized (repayable in regular installments over a period of years until fully repaid). During the course of HOLC's first year some 1 million loans, worth $3.1 billion and constituting one-fifth of all mortgages on nonfarm owner-occupied homes, were refinanced. The average mortgagor thus refinanced had already been two years delinquent in mortgage payments and three years delinquent in tax payments. The refinancing not only helped those homeowners, but lending institutions thus refinanced could use funds formerly tied up in bad mortgages to issue new mortgages.

HOLC was not designed to deal with long-range housing problems but simply to handle the emergency, the breakdown that had destroyed confidence in the American financial system. As the emergency began to ease, however, Roosevelt created new institutions to encourage housing construction.

2. *The Federal Housing Administration (FHA), 1934.* This new agency came into being with the Housing Act of 1934. To stimulate housing construction and create new jobs in the construction industry, FHA needed to restore the confidence of lenders in the housing market, and it did this by insuring mortgages. This led to banks being willing to issue mortgages with lower down payments and at less interest. Prior to FHA insurance, a typical home mortgage required a 35 percent down payment, with a repayment period of less than ten years. The FHA

guaranteed loans if the down payment was as little as 20 percent and permitted twenty-year loans that were fully amortized. The FHA did not require that mortgages be issued on these liberal terms, but the 20 percent down, twenty-year fully amortized loan quickly became the standard. In the 1930s, however, it took some time for bankers to amass the necessary capital and to acknowledge the wisdom of making many such long-term loans. And with wages still depressed, few families could afford the down payments. Hence the real effects of FHA mortgage insurance were not felt until after the war.

To process applications for insurance, the FHA created field offices to review plans for new houses, inspect existing structures, and appraise property. This review process simplified mortgage lending because FHA approval provided an objective national criterion for evaluating properties and removed much of the risk from the lending decision. The resulting standardization of the mortgage instrument thus facilitated the development of a national housing market, one in which bankers in one area financed homes on the basis of information supplied elsewhere.

3. *Federal National Mortgage Association (FNMA, "Fannie Mae"), 1938.* One reason a potential lender was reluctant to respond to the new mortgage insurance program was his fear of being stuck for twenty years holding a mortgage when he needed cash. By establishing a secondary mortgage market (a market where the original mortgages could be bought and sold), Fannie Mae reduced the original lender's fear of illiquidity. A potential lender was therefore much more prepared to extend a twenty-year loan to finance housing construction. This also greatly increased funds available for mortgage lending because it brought new financial institutions, ones that did not have the range of services necessary to decide on original loans, into housing finance. The original lender who sold a mortgage in the secondary market was then free to use the proceeds to make another loan.

Fannie Mae is also a balance wheel. It both reduces the impact of economic cycles on housing construction and helps distribute funds to localities where demand for new housing is greatest. The countercyclical effect of the secondary mortgage market is needed because when the economy heats up short-term interest rates rise above those on long-term housing mortgages, and money therefore flows into short-term loans. As the economy cools down and short-term interest rates decline, investors return to long-term mortgages. In effect, long-term housing borrowers are in competition for capital with short-term borrowers. By design, Fannie Mae buys mortgages from lenders when mortgage money is scarce—that is, when short-term interest rates are higher than long-term rates—thus making money available in the primary market. It sells mortgages back to the primary lenders when there is an oversupply of capital available for mortgages.

Also by removing primary lenders, such as savings and loan associations, from total dependence on their immediate depositors for capital, Fannie Mae assists in developing a national mortgage market. This, combined with the standardization of loans, makes it easier for money to flow into new geographical areas of rapid growth where the incoming population needs new housing.

Roosevelt introduced other programs affecting housing. Public works programs provided employment opportunities, and the U.S. Housing Act of 1937 provided federal subsidies for public housing for the poor. However, these programs were not developed on a major scale, and in the postwar period they played a minor role in terms of the overall availability of housing. It was FHA, Fannie Mae, and, later, Veterans Administration mortgage guarantees that were to make possible the great improvement in America's private housing.

2. HELPING THE VETERANS

At the end of World War II, the public was prepared to help servicemen return to civilian life. Some 9 million veterans returned to civilian life in 1945 and 1946, and housing, along with jobs, was at the top of their needs. The housing market, long neglected, became tighter on their return. Even those who had homes waiting often required larger dwellings, and many were ready to start families. Even before the end of the war, the Servicemen's Readjustment Act of 1944 provided guaranteed home loans for veterans. The program was similar to the FHA program but the terms were even more favorable. When it started, the VA guaranteed loans at 4 percent interest with twenty-five-year amortization and virtually no down payment. Originally the maximum guarantee was for $7,500, but this was later raised and interest rates were adjusted.

In the immediate postwar period, many feared that shortages would lead to runaway inflation, reducing the availability of materials and supplies needed for veterans' housing. In January 1946, President Truman therefore appointed Wilson W. Wyatt to a new position of Housing Expediter to see that housing materials were available for veterans. By 1947, as the political mood of the country forced the end of wartime controls, these special programs were ended, but they had provided special temporary help to veterans during the early period of critical shortages, enabling the housing industry to get started quickly with veterans' housing.

3. BUILDING A POSTWAR POLITICAL BASE

The political consensus that jelled in 1949 to support postwar housing growth was a product of the acute housing shortage, of the guidance of the National

Housing Agency under John Blandford, Jr., and of the leadership of President Truman and key Republicans like Senator Robert Taft.

During the 1920s U.S. builders started some 7 million housing units, but in the sixteen years from 1930 through 1945 they started only 4.7 million units, two-thirds as many as were produced during the 1920s. Between 1940 and 1946 alone some 5 million new households were formed, and with the return of veterans, between 1947 and 1950 another 5 million new households were created. During the war, to fill the needs of defense-related industries, many Americans had migrated to the cities, but few of them returned to the countryside after the war. Most veterans who had originally come from rural areas chose to look for new work in urban ones. In addition, as agricultural efficiences grew, more rural dwellers moved to towns and cities, placing further pressure on urban housing.

During World War II, with materials shortages, rationing, and price controls, people had little on which to spend their money, and the personal savings rate grew unusually high. In 1944 households saved 25 percent of disposable income, a rate as high as any achieved in postwar Japan. The availability of savings and the vast increase of new households created a tremendous effective demand and a strong political base for effective mechanisms to make new housing accessible.

In 1944, before a gathering that brought together leaders in the housing field, John Blandford, Jr., made a statement on the basic philosophy for postwar housing policy. Housing construction was primarily the responsibility of the private sector, but the federal government played a supplementary role in providing assistance to cover those sectors of the housing market that the private sector could not reach. Furthermore, the federal government had a role in facilitating the financing of private housing.

Although Blandford's statement won widespread support, debate on the size and nature of the government's supplementary role continued. At the end of World War II, many Americans worried that the Depression might return. Many bankers and government administrators feared that, after immediate housing needs were met, houses might decline in value. Many liberals therefore argued that the government, as in many European countries, should take a greater direct role in administering housing, thereby frightening businessmen, who denounced the dangers of socialism. Although the term "urban coalition" was not yet used, in fact there was a proto-urban coalition composed mostly of northern liberal urban democrats, with a smattering of Southern Democrats like Senator John Sparkman and of Republicans like Senator Robert Taft. These congressmen favored a greater role for the federal government in making available financing to local areas to assist in slum clearance and construction of lower-income housing. Organized labor and local government officials, governors and mayors, also wanted the federal government to play a larger role in devising a comprehensive national housing policy.

At the time, the housing construction industry, though terribly fragmented and diverse, opposed a large government role. Rarely in the postwar period was any single firm close to having as much as 1 percent of the national home-construction market. In the late 1940s the vast majority of firms built fewer than 100 homes per year. These firms were hardly united or sophisticated, but many felt a deep suspicion of government, a suspicion shared by many of the small thrift institutions (mutual savings banks and loan associations) that held the majority of mortgages. Some even had questions about FHA and Fannie Mae until they could see how immensely useful these agencies would become. Small businessmen channeled their views through organizations like the National Association of Real Estate Boards, the U.S. Savings and Loan League, the National Association of Retail Lumber Dealers, and local chambers of commerce. They became a very effective housing lobby, countering the proto-urban coalition. They even opposed a special government program for lower-income groups for fear that it might be an opening wedge for governmental control. And large numbers of middle-class Americans who would acknowledge the need for special housing help for the poor by the 1960s then believed that, if housing was available, it was up to individuals to take advantage of it. Few could foresee clearly the seriousness of the housing problem for the urban poor that was to develop in the next decades.

After heated debate, in June 1948 Congress passed a housing bill, but it was a great disappointment to the proto-urban coalition, which dubbed it "the teeny weeny" housing bill. It reaffirmed government support for VA loans and for the government purchase of FHA mortgages, but it included almost nothing to help lower-income groups. These housing issues were again debated by candidates Truman and Dewey during the 1948 presidential race. Truman campaigned against a "do nothing Eightieth Congress," and he made housing a central issue, urging a greater government role. When Truman won, he moved forward with a bigger and broader housing bill, and in the summer of 1949, with a new election mandate, Congress passed the Housing Act of 1949, which formally accepted the national commitment to a "decent home and a suitable environment for every American family."

Although the Housing Act of 1949 supported public housing, the national consensus on that issue was too weak to sustain a consistent long-term program. The real estate lobby failed to block support for public housing in the Housing Act, but it waged a determined and ultimately successful campaign to derail it. At the local level it succeeded in creating or utilizing controversies on site selection for new public housing projects and other issues to arouse public opposition and prevent a substantial public housing program. The urban poor and their advocates were not yet well-organized, as they would be after the late 1960s, and therefore unfortunately public housing made at best uneven progress.

However, in the case of private housing, the veterans and substantial numbers of middle-class families wanting housing provided a political base for a program that in effect subsidized homeowners. Economists who felt it desirable to stimulate the postwar economy could rightly argue that housing was an engine of growth. Bankers, home builders, and suppliers, who gradually realized how fortunate they were, could argue that it supported private enterprise. The 1949 election jelled the support of these groups and the Housing Act embodied this consensus, supporting the framework of VA loans, FHA loans, Fannie Mae, and the secondary mortgage market. This framework, reinforced by success, thus acquired a basis of political support that made it unassailable for three decades. This ensured long-term continuity, allowing home builders to go to work at unprecedented speed.

4. CHANNELING FUNDS FOR HOUSING GROWTH

As with NASA, housing administrators were creative in devising mechanisms that built on this stable consensus in a way suited to America's political and economic systems. The lack of new housing built within the previous fifteen years, the high levels of new household formation, the relocation of population in cities and in Western states, and substantial personal savings created tremendous demand for new housing. In the years after World War II new housing starts occurred at more than twice the rate of the 1920s and more than six times the rate of the 1930s. How did the VA, FHA, and Fannie Mae operate to make possible the construction to meet these demands so effectively?

1. *Guarantees from VA and FHA made it possible for banks, especially savings and loan associations, to offer more long-term loans at low interest rates not possible previously.* Ceilings set by VA and FHA assured home buyers of reasonable rates of interest. Although there were some loopholes allowing for additional charges, they were of a minor order and provided some adjustment for market conditions. Some lenders and builders did not consider it profitable to lend at such low rates of interest, but the vast majority were more than happy to cooperate.

2. *More favorable terms made it possible for a much larger portion of American families to purchase their own homes.* During the 1920s savings and loan associations, which held about half of home mortgages, on the average made loans of 58 percent of property value, leaving the homeowner with the responsibility of coming up with the other 42 percent. On the average, their loans were for eleven

years. About 30 percent of mortgages were held by life insurance companies and commercial banks. Life insurance companies on the average required repayment in six years, commercial banks in two to four years. Their loans averaged about half of estimated property value, and only one-fifth were fully amortized. The change to fully amortized loans spread over twenty years or more and requiring only a 20-percent down payment, and at much lower rates of interest, constituted an enormous change.

Because housing is by far the largest single investment for most families and a difference of even 1 percent makes an enormous difference in the amount of money they must repay, even moderate changes in the interest rate have a large impact on the availability of buyers. For example, the difference of 1 percent in the interest rate of a $40,000 twenty-five-year mortgage (a not unusual mortgage by the 1960s) is more than $30 per month and more than $9,000 over the life of the mortgage. Indeed, minor changes in the interest rate have great impact on affordability. As the change from before the war sometimes amounted to several percentage points in interest rate, a vast new group of middle-class and lower-middle-class Americans could for the first time afford home ownership.

3. *The stability of the new system, with inspections and guarantees, attracted other primary lenders and the secondary mortgage market attracted other secondary lenders.* In the 1950s about a quarter to a half of new houses were financed by FHA or VA mortgages. But the stable system of inspections and appraisals built up by FHA and VA provided more security to the market, so lenders were more willing to lend on non-FHA- and non-VA-backed homes than had these institutions not existed. Although a potential home buyer might be able to avoid red tape by not going through VA or FHA, the commercial bank could not depart too far from FHA-backed rates for the buyer had the option of going for FHA-backed homes. This system made possible the sound expansion of home mortgages. In 1950 there was some $45 billion worth of credit outstanding; by 1960 this had risen to $141 billion, 40 percent of it in VA- and FHA-guaranteed loans.

The government gave tax advantages to savings and loan associations and allowed them to pay slightly more interest than commercial banks to attract depositors in exchange for requiring that a vast majority of their funds be used for home mortgages. This provided the backbone of the funds for the construction of new homes. These savings and loan associations and banks that might have been worried about lending money for as long as twenty or twenty-five years were given the option of selling their mortgages to Fannie Mae in the secondary mortgage market, and this increased their willingness to lend and thus the stability of the whole system. This stability in turn attracted institutional investors like life insurance companies looking for investments, and this created a financial market for secondary mortgages. Because thrift institutions were local institutions, with knowledge of local neighborhoods and local tastes and trends, they and the FHA and VA inspectors could provide the know-how to make appropriate evaluations on the homes and then sell mortgages to institutional investors. New mortgage companies also grew up to originate mortgages with the aim of passing them on to institutional investors. In the 1950s more than a fifth of the mortgage loans on residential housing were held by life insurance companies, and with some fluctuations about the same amount was held by commercial banks. All this greatly increased the amount of money available for residential housing construction.

These institutions continued to evolve and were modified after 1965. Although VA insurance remained important, and veterans were even allowed to pass on VA mortgages to nonveterans, by 1962 the amount of FHA-insured mortgage debt had surpassed that of VA mortgage debt and VA became progressively less important. The role of Fannie Mae was occasionally changed by Congress. In 1968 during the Vietnam War, when there was a shortage of federal funds, to eliminate Fannie Mae's reliance on the federal budget it was made a private company, owned by stockholders. Fannie Mae was permitted to sell its stock publicly, and in order to be attractive to private purchasers it was allowed to withdraw from granting subsidies for low-income housing and providing countercyclical adjustments for the economy as a whole. After Fannie Mae became a private corporation, a smaller corporation, Government National Mortgage (GNM, or "Ginnie Mae") was newly established on a smaller scale to take over the subsidy role formerly filled by Fannie Mae. In 1970 a Federal Home Loan Mortgage Corporation (FHLMC, or "Freddie Mac") was created to establish a secondary mortgage market exclusively for savings and loan associations. Yet the basic institutional structure and the basic role of the government or quasi-government institutions remained much the same until the early 1980s, when the Carter and Reagan administrations moved toward deregulation.

5. MOVING TO THE SUBURBS

A number of factors, partly fortuitous, directed the vast mass of new housing away from small towns and central cities to the suburbs of large metropolitan areas, but officials at both the national and local level provided the support and infrastructure to make this flow smoothly.

After World War II as cities became more crowded with the influx of new population, limited land and rising prices made it impossible for most families to achieve the American ideal of a separate home with ample space and privacy within the central core of cities. Movement away from central cities had begun early in the century as motorized transport replaced ships and horses, and movement to nearby suburbs had begun by the 1920s. In the postwar period the growth of the car and highway construction made accessible vast amounts of inexpensive land and brought suburban growth to entirely new levels.

In 1920 some 9 million people owned cars, by 1950 some 49 million. The percentage of families owning a car grew from 54 percent in 1948 to 82 percent in 1970. Paved roads had greatly accelerated with the National Defense Highway Act of 1941, and the federal government continued to play a role in the financing of these roads after the war. In 1945 there were 450,000 miles of paved roads under state control; by 1965 this had increased to 650,000. In addition, Eisenhower created the Interstate Highway System, greatly increasing the distances that could be covered within reasonable commuting time. He drew on the widespread support for more highways, but provided excellent leadership, effectively molding that support into a consensus for a long-range integrated nationwide program. He launched the program in 1956, with the goal of completing some 42,000 miles by 1969. By 1960 some 10,000 miles were open to traffic and another 14,000 were under construction. By 1965 more than 21,000 miles were open to traffic and an additional 17,000 were under construction. As soon as highway locations were designated, nearby land became attractive, and home builders hastened to purchase tracts of land and develop it.

By and large local communities during these two decades were cooperative in providing the infrastructure of water, electricity, gas, roads, schools, and other services, and the federal government was also cooperative in assisting with this infrastructure. There was, of course, wide variation among states and local communities in the degree of cooperation. However, knowing that development would expand the tax base, most communities were prepared to invest in the infrastructure, in effect subsidizing part of the cost of home construction. Retail and other services followed quickly. In 1946 there were eight shopping centers in the United States, by 1960 some 3,800, virtually all accessible to major roads.

6. MODERNIZING HOME BUILDING, PARTLY: MERCHANT BUILDERS

The idea of building houses the way one builds cars has been a recurring vision for home builders since long before World War II. During the war, with urgent housing needs for troops and for workers at war-related plants, some progress was made in achieving economies of scale for certain standardized, usually inexpensive units, and after the war mobile-home makers (since 1980 commonly referred to as one kind of "manufactured home") began to approach assembly-line methods. But the vision proved elusive. The costs of transporting modules or even mobile homes long distances, the wide variations of local building codes, the rigidities of the crafts unions, and the fluctuations in demand for housing locally and nationally make it difficult to develop a large stable market to justify the investment in equipment required for anything like mass production. Furthermore, the housing construction business is so complex, involving so many different tasks—financing, site selection, planning with local government, site development, design, foundation laying, construction layout, finishing, and marketing—with so many unpredictables, including weather, local government decisions, availability of subcontractors, and many complex managerial problems of coordination, that it has sometimes been called a service industry rather than a manufacturing one.

One can easily imagine that new technologies, increased cost of conventional home building, and the threat of foreign competition in home building might someday propel the United States to break through the institutional barriers of varying local standards and limited base of demand that have thus far made the vision of producing assembly-line housing so elusive. Yet in the decades since World War II the combination of increased demand and entrepreneurial creativity have permitted great productivity increases in home building. A study of home building productivity commissioned by the President's Committee on Urban Housing in 1968 concluded that between 1929 and 1947 the construction industry was technologically stagnant, but that between 1947 and 1965 output per employee grew at an annual rate of 2.3 percent. This was made possible in part because of the increase in the proportion of homes built in batches. Before the war, most houses were custom-built, one at a time. In 1949, firms that built more than 100 houses per year accounted for about a fourth of housing starts, but by 1960 they accounted for about three-fourths. A new type of firm grew up after World War II, one that purchased large tracts of land and developed many homes, getting economies of scale and producing a house, according to Ned Eichler's estimates, for about 50 percent less than a single house using the same model. This new type of firm came to be known as the "merchant builder."

There were no university programs to train merchant builders. Merchant builders came from diverse backgrounds and evolved very different approaches to design, financing, construction, and marketing. Yet they all coordinated the different tasks needed for acquiring and developing land, house construction, and marketing. They varied greatly in how much they delegated these various tasks to others and how much of the work they tried to do within their own organizations. Generally they began with little capital and devised arrangements to limit the amount of capital required. Many did not buy a whole tract at once but took out options, developed a small part with a few model homes, took deposits from those who wished to move in, and then, depending on demand, exercised their options and undertook construction. Often they arranged to make small down payments on the land with full payment when homes were sold. Because they could purchase materials and supplies in quantity, they could often obtain them more quickly and at lower cost than could small builders.

Merchant builders commonly developed staffs of employees, usually more than 100, who among themselves possessed all the requisite skills for building houses. Builders could therefore rationalize the building process, increasing the degree of specialization of workers and reducing wasted time. For many the ideal was to have new projects within commuting distance for their workers, with a tightly organized schedule so that workers of any given specialty would be continually kept busy and not held up by delays. Increased demand led more suppliers to prepare precut materials and preassembled parts in factories where they could be produced more cheaply than by workers on site. Although houses were still built singly ("stick built"), design was simplified. Builders eliminated basements and reduced the number of exterior corners. Large equipment like power tools was purchased to save on heavy labor. In short, with stable demand and financing, it was American private enterprise at its best. A great deal of entrepreneurial ingenuity went into the work, and until the mid-1960s merchant builders made many advances in productivity.

There seemed to be limits on how large these firms could become and still remain effective. Levitt, which achieved the greatest economies of scale and the highest level of specialization among workers, could not find new sites with as many promising customers to follow up its success in Levittown, New York. Others like Eichler, which found a niche with a certain kind of home in a certain geographic area, sometimes satiated so much of the market that they could no longer produce on the same scale in that area. To move to a new community and develop relations with local officials and hire new workers was almost like starting over again. Some who expanded to do several large projects in different localities found that they lost the crisp control that they could exercise as a small company in one metropolitan area. Many who bought equipment and hired their own employees to rationalize their work found they were too vulnerable in the downturns. Few of the firms that had been most successful through the mid-1960s remained strong independent companies through the early 1970s, and few advances in technology and productivity have been made since the mid-1960s.

7. NEW EFFORTS IN MODERNIZING MANUFACTURING AFTER 1965

We will not trace here all major housing developments since 1965, but it is necessary to consider two developments after 1965 relevant to the programs discussed above: modernizing manufacture and changes in financing. One of the efforts to modernize manufacture was spearheaded by the government.

1. *Operation Breakthrough.* By 1969 it was clear that a new housing shortage was developing. Housing starts in the late 1960s had fallen off sharply with the decline of available funds and the rapid rise in construction costs. Shortages of skilled labor led to increased wage bills, and the decline and unpredictability of housing demand made it difficult for the housing construction industry to maintain control over efficient operations. In 1969, therefore, when George Romney became Housing and Urban Development Secretary, he tried to devise a scheme for giving government encouragement to increase housing starts, and he sought the answer in productivity increases that would compensate for the increases in cost. As the former head of American Motors, he found the idea of increasing efficiencies as in automobile production a natural. It was a rare case of the government taking an interest in the efficiency of an industry.

Romney's program, Operation Breakthrough, included a modest $15 million budget to finance promising innovations that might be used in mass production of housing. His request for proposals elicited great interest, and twenty promising ones were selected. Romney also attacked the problem of varying standards in local governments that had made economies of scale so difficult, and the new atmosphere led to considerable relaxation of local standards and a willingness to accept some kind of national standards. Operation Breakthrough created a great deal of interest, and it was widely acknowledged that many of the ideas had a great deal of merit. However, Romney had not enlisted the cooperation of firms in the housing industry, and most of the innovations supported were made by firms from other industries not overly familiar with the needs of the housing industry. The result was that most of the innovations did not produce the expected cost savings, and the program lost political support. The program's premature end doomed the government and industry to existing technological levels while other countries like Japan were beginning to make rapid technological progress in the construction industry.

2. *"Manufactured homes."* After 1955, when the first ten-foot-wide trailer was produced and "mobile homes" became less mobile, they found a much wider market among people who wanted stationary housing. Most interesting developments took place after 1965, when labor costs in stick-built housing increased without comparable increases in productivity. By finding ways to use less-skilled workers in a single enclosed setting where they were not subject to weather delays, mobile-home builders achieved economies, finding a niche in the lower-price range virtually unchallenged by ordinary housing. Some 100,000 mobile homes were sold in 1955 but the number rose rapidly in the late 1960s, peaking in 1972 at 576,000, about one-third of all new housing. They then seemed to

approach a limit of people willing to live in such modest dwellings, and sales declined to 276,000 in 1978.

In the late 1970s mobile-home makers began to change their sales target, producing larger homes and linking two or three widths on a permanent foundation. This led to a very different way of conceiving their product, symbolized in 1980 by their changing the name of their product from "mobile home" to "manufactured home." Until that time, mobile homes were not generally treated as regular homes and were commonly located in trailer parks. Though they were in fact rarely moved, they were not taxed by the local community as housing, and they were not eligible for FHA-backed mortgages. Because the consumer had to use higher-priced commercial loans, even if the price of the home was 20–30 percent lower than that of a conventional home the higher costs of financing meant that down payments and monthly payments might be the same. Through the early 1970s mobile-home companies had used much cheaper materials to build a product that cost significantly less than a conventional home. In the late 1970s these builders began making something more like a conventional home. Other companies, including some merchant builders like Ryan Homes, the Ryland Group, and Fleetwood Enterprises, also began moving into manufactured homes, and the distinction between those making mobile homes, delivered on wheels, and those making modules, not delivered on wheels, became almost meaningless. Manufactured homes are now being placed in regular neighborhoods or tract developments very different from trailer parks, and courts have ruled that local communities cannot discriminate against them. Manufactured homes are now eligible for FHA loans, and more are now receiving loans essentially on the same terms as other housing. In 1980, Fannie Mae began including mortgages from "manufactured homes" in the secondary mortgage market.

Although manufactured homes are considered to have growth potential, transport costs beyond 300 miles are still considered prohibitive, companies remain relatively small, and the economies of scale over what other merchant builders can achieve with precut and preassembled materials still give them only marginal advantages. Producers of manufactured homes are making productivity advances, but thus far these are at modest levels.

8. CHANGES IN HOUSING FINANCE AFTER 1965

After 1965 government changes in the economy and in macroeconomic policy not primarily concerned with housing had a profound effect on the financing of housing. Some institutional investors left housing finance beginning in the late 1960s to earn higher returns in short-term loans, but finance for housing remained strong in the 1970s. The big change in housing finance began as a result of the Federal Reserve's tight-money policy to control inflation and Carter's and Reagan's deregulation of financial institutions. These changes initially led to severe difficulties for housing construction and the thrift institutions, but by the mid-1980s the government, the housing industry, thrift institutions, and home buyers seemed to be reaching a new modus vivendi.

However, toward the end of the 1970s, as short-term interest rates increased, thrift institutions were still not allowed to offer depositors more than a modest fixed rate of interest. As depositors realized they could earn higher interest in money-market funds, they reduced their deposits in savings and loan institutions, which consequently had less capital to finance housing construction. By 1980 a decision was made to free the savings and loan institutions from regulation and to let them bid for deposits like other institutions. Some of these thrift institutions already suffered badly from large portfolios of low-interest fixed loans and the role they had been encouraged to play by the government at a time of high interest rates. Some were so badly affected they could not survive and adapt to the new, less regulated environment. By 1983, the government, through the Federal Home Loan Bank Board and Freddie Mac, made clear that thrift institutions would still have a specialized role for making loans to housing after deregulation, supported by Freddie Mac. To adjust to the new uncertain situation thrift institutions began making variable-interest loans rather than fixed-interest loans, giving them the ability to survive fluctuations of the market, and house buyers also began adjusting to this new, more flexible system.

These new uncertainties that began in the late 1960s and became greater after the oil shock, with inflation, tight money policy, and deregulation, forced home builders to give much more attention to finance. Estimates of inflation rate, new sources of funds, financial management, and tax considerations all became more important. The economic cycles and especially the tightening of funds by the Federal Reserve led to wider swings of boom and bust in the housing industry. Although builders could often diversify, moving into repair and restoration during bad years, this was more difficult for suppliers of building materials. In boom years like 1971–73 and 1977–79, some companies could make extraordinary profits, but in the bust years of 1966–67, 1974–75, and 1980–82 more companies went bankrupt. Increased fluctuations in the cost of capital and in housing demand made business less predictable, and many companies that had invested in equipment and had hired regular employees to gain efficiencies did less well than companies with fewer efficiencies poised to adjust to swings in the economy. As in many manufacturing industries at the same time, the fluctuations and concentration on issues of finance and taxation at the expense of efficiency helped retard advances in technology and productivity, which essentially came to a standstill. Although by 1983 housing construction had begun to revive, the long-range impact of fluctuations and variable interest rates was not yet clear.

9. LIMITS OF SUCCESS

Despite the enormous success of the housing program in improving housing for a substantial number of Americans in the two decades after the war, at least two serious deficiencies of policy in this period should be acknowledged. There is no inherent reason why the government could not have done more to deal with these issues without in any way interfering with its other housing successes. Both problems remain as challenges for the future.

1. *Lack of housing for lower-income groups, especially minorities.* Although home ownership was extended to almost two-thirds of American households by the mid-1960s, housing for the other third, especially the urban poor, remained seriously unsatisfactory. The process of filtering, of passing on homes from those who moved to the suburbs to those who remained behind, did not always provide satisfactory housing. Despite some successes, as in turnkey apartment projects, the issue of housing for the poor was plagued with problems—political controversy, lack of clear direction, and maladministration. Incentives for builders to provide modest-priced urban housing as efficiently as possible or for recipients to take great pride in and support the well-being of their dwellings proved inadequate. Even poor people who received the benefits of subsidized housing did not always take pride in their dwelling, and arguably many poor who did not receive subsidies were in fact helping to subsidize the two-thirds of the population owning their own homes. Henry Aaron calculated that in 1966, for example, homeowners paid $7 billion less in taxes than they would have if governed by rules applicable to investors in other assets.

Until 1950, FHA loans explicitly favored economic and racial homogeneity as a basis for neighborhood stability, and until the 1960s, when discrimination was explicitly outlawed, it was common practice for developers to refuse to sell new homes to blacks. Clearly the United States should have dealt with these problems throughout the postwar period.

Since the cost of housing has since risen relative to the consumer price index, housing problems for lower and lower-middle income groups have become more severe since that time. In the 1960s the cost of housing tended to be 30 percent or less of income, but by the early 1980s it had risen to more than 40 percent. Furthermore, because of increases in divorce and in single-person households, the current housing stock includes more large houses than needed and fewer dwellings than needed for small households. The lack of national consensus was reflected in starts and stops, but by the mid-1970s better incentive systems were in place, especially for condominiums and redevelopment.

2. *Inattention to modernization for international competition.* Unlike the Japa-

nese Construction Ministry, which continuously tried to prod and upgrade the efficiency of construction, the U.S. government essentially played no role in this effort except for the ill-fated Operation Breakthrough. The government has done little to encourage research on housing construction that might have increased productivity. Its educational programs to inform people in home construction on advances in technology and organization cannot compare with what the Department of Agriculture does for farmers.

The American home-building industry has assumed that the complexities of financing, buying land, site development, meeting local standards, building, and marketing in addition to ocean transport costs has made them immune from foreign competition, just as auto makers had assumed that they were immune from foreign competition in the early 1970s. It is quite possible that Japanese house suppliers will export parts for houses like windows, doors, bathroom parts, plumbing, and other supplies much as they manufacture other products. Although Japan home manufacturers also developed slowly in the 1970s, by the early 1980s home builders like Sekisui and Misawa, partially with government support, had far larger and more systematic research and development facilities than any American home manufacturer. One cannot rule out the possibility that once they develop new materials and new systems of house construction, and as they accumulate experience in the American market, they might choose certain strategic locations for the manufacture of homes in the United States. One might wonder if similar developments in the United States might be advisable both to cut spiraling costs of home building and to help maintain a competitive domestic home-building industry.

Yet in spite of these problems, in terms of improving the quality of housing for the American people, the two decades after World War II constitute an extraordinary success story. Although latent demand was there, the latent demand had not been translated into new housing in the 1930s. Without the role of the U.S. government in backing VA and FHA loans, in creating a secondary mortgage market, in distributing money around the country, in lessening the impact of economic cycles and in directing funds through savings and loan associations, the record of success would not have been possible. Initiative was left in the hands of private enterprise, but the government played the role of facilitator, providing the context that enabled private enterprise to do its job well. These successes were achieved at a time when other world and national conditions permitted the government to provide a relatively stable economic environment, which further undergirded the government's institutional efforts.

The combination of housing and the Interstate Highway System created an engine of growth that had enormous spillover into other parts of the economy during these two decades. Housing is unlikely to be an engine of growth in the late 1980s and in the 1990s, but housing construction remains an important sector, second only to agriculture in its contribution to the economy, and proper housing remains central to the ambitions of the average household. The problem is to devise a new mechanism that can achieve the successes of the postwar period while adapting to the needs of smaller households and a broader range of income groups.

The lesson from housing is that we do have the capability of finding creative mechanisms for helping to finance crucial areas of growth even without special development banks. There is no reason that in areas like communication systems, the rapid diffusion of home information systems, the development and rapid application of new kinds of materials, biotechnology, availability of new kinds of health systems the government could not play a role similar to what it provided in housing if there is a political consensus that it is desirable.

10

North Carolina's Research Triangle: State Modernization

by Ezra F. Vogel and Andrea Larson

In our American system of decentralized government, states will play a major role in any effort to compete in world trade. Because unemployment so keenly affects local areas, states' political sensitivity to issues of competitiveness will often lead them to respond with greater speed than the nation as a whole. The question is how to use this sensitivity so that it does not lead to wasteful competition among states outbidding one another to attract industry, to no national benefit, but rather helps build on local resources and talents to create something otherwise impossible.

In an era of global competitiveness, the Japanese system of strong central leadership has certain advantages, advantages that were consciously developed only late in the nineteenth century as part of the drive to catch up. Until 1868, Japan's clans were perhaps as independent as American states, but out of fear of domination by foreign powers Japan then established a strong central government, abolished former clans, and redistricted national land so that new prefectural boundaries no longer coincided with clan boundaries. The national government then established unified systems of education, banking, transportation, health, and criminal justice and provided advice and training to ensure that local officials were well trained and informed. By Japanese standards, American state government seems haphazard, uneven, and often amateurish. In Japan, the Home Affairs Ministry has overall responsibility for local government. It ensures and sometimes helps provide high standards of professional training for regional administrators in virtually every field of endeavor. "Equalization grants" to poorer prefectures, ensure that they have at least a minimum of funds for education, health, and infrastructure, while prefectures have considerable flexibility in how they use them. National standards and rules, unlike the morass of conflicting and overlapping rules found among American states, facilitate commerce in Japan. While some American state governments have superb leadership, Tokyo ensures a minimum quality everywhere in Japan and links prefectures to outside information more quickly and systematically than Washington does for American states.

Now that we in the United States are in a new global competitive era, we face new questions. How can we build on America's traditions of state initiative to match the success of Japan in achieving high minimal standards of education and information? How can the natural interest of states in revitalizing their economies be combined with an understanding of international competitive facts of life so that their efforts can be successful? How can they work out new relations with the private sector and national networks of information, government and private, to achieve this?

One state that pioneered a highly successful effort to modernize industry is North Carolina. The focus of the effort was a gigantic Research Triangle Park that provided the critical leverage for bringing research and modern industry to a state that had been among the nation's most economically backward. As with NASA and the housing industry, the origin of this innovation stemmed from a crisis. After World War II, North Carolina, already backward, confronted the prospect of rapid economic decline in all of its three key industries: tobacco, textiles, and furniture.

Tobacco's prospects dimmed as it was identified as a cause of cancer. Also, other countries with cheaper labor costs began to improve the quality of tobacco, threatening to affect the incomes of both the cultivator and the processor. Furthermore, it was not clear that national government support for tobacco growers, which had sustained the industry since the 1930s, would be continued. The New Deal had provided aid to tobacco by restraining tobacco production and allotting rights to production. Over time, as holders of these rights left production, the ownership of the rights became increasingly distinct from production, and the system became increasingly anachronistic as financial institutions traded in the rights while producers benefited from the system only marginally. Nonetheless, tampering with the system might easily lead to loss of federal support. A high proportion of the state's farmers were involved in tobacco, and since tobacco could be profitable on a very small plot of land, the average size of tobacco farms was under fifteen acres, making North Carolina's average farm size the smallest in the nation. If North Carolina's small independent farmers gave up tobacco, they would have difficulty finding other crops to sustain them. Prospects were for continued decline in the tobacco industry.

North Carolina's textile plants had grown rapidly in the 1920s and 1930s as spinning and textile plants from New England and apparel manufacturers from New York moved south to take advantage of lower wages. By the early 1950s, the emerging countries of East and Southeast Asia, at first Japan and then Hong Kong, Taiwan, Korea, Thailand, and Malaysia, had begun to develop textile and apparel manufacturing and were paying their workers far less. Import protection was precarious at best, requiring constant efforts to get political support from the national government, and even with protection the prospect was for continued decline of North Carolina's textile and apparel industries.

The forests of North Carolina, on which the furniture industry depended, had already been badly depleted. Walnut stocks were among the most serious problem, for they were being exhausted and could not be replaced for 200 years. North Carolina had moved quickly to modernize its furniture industry in the early years after World War II, but states like Pennsylvania, New York, and Illinois were developing their industry as well, to say nothing of the Northwest, which was near larger timber reserves. In addition, with reduced costs of ocean transport, foreign countries could expand furniture exports to the United States.

In the early 1950s, leaders in North Carolina could see the handwriting on the wall. Industrial wages were virtually the lowest of any state in the country and were under pressure from foreign competition to remain low or decline. Farm land could barely support the half of North Carolina's population living in rural areas, but cities provided no opportunities for those who wished to leave. In 1959, North Carolina's median income was forty-fifth among the fifty states. The problem was especially acute for the 20 percent of the state's families that were black. Their income level was about half of the state's average, about a third of the national average.

The idea of attracting outside industry had a long history in North Carolina. At the end of the Civil War, Southerners, like developing countries many decades later, decided that they did not want to be only the suppliers of food and raw materials to an industrial North. They wanted to have industry themselves. North Carolina had fewer plantations than most of the Southern states, and in the rolling Piedmont area of central and western North Carolina, along the river valleys, it was easy to develop water power for textile mills. Hundreds of small towns set out to attract textile mills, collecting funds from local citizens and elsewhere to make this possible. The process continued in the 1920s and 1930s. In the 1950s, the new kind of industry that seemed to be the wave of the future called for higher technology. With the examples of Massachusetts and California, it seemed obvious that a good research environment was needed to attract modern industry, and therefore the question before North Carolina's leaders was how to develop that research environment.

North Carolina may have a weak labor movement and a weak civil rights movement, but it does have a large group of leaders prepared to work for whatever the state needs. State leaders were sufficiently secure that they erected no clubs or other barriers holding back others who aspired to positions of state leadership, and their sense of responsibility for the state gave them broad social support. Just as North Carolinians, with no single large urban area, centered their philanthropy on the state, establishing the first state symphony in the 1930s and the first state art museum in the 1950s, so the modernizers thought of the state as a whole. Until the early part of the twentieth century there was a sharp cleavage between the plantations in the eastern part of the state and the small industrial and mountain towns of the Piedmont and the west, but by the midtwentieth century people thought of the entire state. The great unifier was the University of North Carolina. In many states the elites were divided among several universities, but even after Duke University was built in the 1930s those who aspired to state leadership, whether business, political, or academic, overwhelmingly went to the University of North Carolina. Most of the people active in the development of the Triangle—Bob Hanes, Archie Davis, Terry Sanford, Bill Friday, George Simpson—had studied there. Another, a student leader at the university, Luther Hodges, was to draw on these relationships when he became governor and helped launch the Research Triangle.

1. ESTABLISHING THE RESEARCH TRIANGLE

If there is a secret to North Carolina's success it is in the ready cooperation of leaders in various circles and their persistence over decades, especially through difficult times when, at the brink of failure, they had to develop entirely new approaches.

The seeds of the idea of linking research and regional economic development go back at least to the 1920s. No state in the South had been more studied than North Carolina, and no one in the South played a larger role in promoting these studies than the longtime chairman of the Sociology Department at the University of North Carolina, Howard W. Odum, who is widely acknowledged as the spiritual godfather of the Research Triangle. His monumental work, *Southern Regions of the United States*, published in 1936, was a classic in the field.

Originally from Georgia, Odum had taken part in TVA, which helped convince him of the potential of public programs in promoting regional development. He was similarly impressed with the potential of coordinated research efforts of universities and technical institutes like those he observed during World War II. He played a major role in the Social Science Research Council's efforts to promote research on the South and in the Ford Foundation's efforts to develop regional research centers to promote industrial development. Odum had specifically proposed an institute to integrate the work of North Carolina's three major universities. The institute was to be located near the Raleigh-Durham airport, the location eventually chosen for the Research Triangle Park. Although Odum died in the early 1950s when his ideas were still on the drawing board, a favorite student, George L. Simpson, Jr., became executive director of the Research Triangle Committee that was to make possible the realization of Odum's vision: an institute to provide intellectual leadership, linking research and economic development, thereby improving the livelihood of ordinary people.

North Carolina's leaders in business, government, and academe were all caught up in a passionate desire to erase their state's backwardness, low level of education, and poverty and to catch up with other parts of the United States. Their goals and methods were not totally different from those of developing countries trying to catch up with the West. In the 1950s, North Carolina, like Japan at the same time, sent missions to study Massachusetts's Route 128 area and California's Silicon Valley. Leaders from North Carolina, together with numerous Japanese, were studying the experiences of successful research institutes like Stanford Research Institute and Battelle in forming think tanks. Like leaders in developing countries, leaders in North Carolina realized they could not accomplish their goals without close cooperation between government, businesses, and the universities.

In the early 1950s a small committee, led by State Treasurer Brandon P. Hodges (no relation to the governor) and State Representative Walter W. Harper, took the lead in trying to develop industry for the state. In 1954, one member of the group, Romeo H. Guest, presented the idea of a huge research park development to be bounded roughly by three university communities (Duke in Durham, University of North Carolina in Chapel Hill, and North Carolina State University in the state capital of Raleigh) and gave it the name "Research Triangle." Guest was a private real estate developer with a business interest in the project, for he had helped develop textile facilities and was concerned that the migration of textile plants had come to a halt. But he also had a vision that went beyond his personal interests. A graduate of MIT, he had been particularly impressed with the Route 128 research area and wanted to help create a research center in North Carolina to stimulate industry.

Guest consulted with a broad range of state leaders, including Robert M. Hanes, president of Wachovia Bank in Winston-Salem and chairman of the Committee on Industry of the State Board of Conservation and Development. Hanes, whose family owned the Hanes Knitting and Hanes Hosiery Mills and played a prominent public-spirited role in the state, was to play a critical though unanticipated role in the project.

A few months after Guest's initial proposal, in November 1954, Governor William B. Umstead suddenly died after a brief illness, and Lieutenant Governor Luther Hodges succeeded to the governorship. Not long before that, Hodges, in his mid-fifties, buoyed by his broad-ranging activities in Rotary International, had decided to give up a highly successful business career as a leading Marshall Field executive to devote the rest of his life to public service. He had previously been a textile mill owner and had sold his mill to Marshall Field, but he had also served a brief stint as an administrator for the Marshall Plan in Europe, and there he had been involved in the process of remaking an area and planning for economic revival.

Unlike other political leaders in North Carolina, Hodges had no background in politics and when he decided to run for lieutenant governor most observers gave him little chance. He toured every county in North Carolina, drawing on the support of friends from his student leadership days at the University of North Carolina and from local Rotary clubs. Although Hodges was elected lieutenant governor in his first run for public office, Governor Umstead considered him too inexperienced in political affairs to consult him. When Hodges succeeded to the governorship, he had to be briefed on various matters. When briefed on the idea of the Research Triangle, he took to it immediately. The Research Triangle was a private project, and Hodges was careful not to interfere with the decision making of the private planners. But Hodges was a man of great enthusiasm, the Research Triangle became the favorite object of his enthusiasm, and under his leadership the state gave it strong support.

Governor Hodges soon commissioned a report, "A Proposal for the Development of an Industrial Research Center in North Carolina." In early 1955 he met with administrators of the key universities to discuss the possibility of cooperation for a Research Triangle, and in late spring 1955 he appointed a group of business and education leaders to be members of a Research Triangle Committee, with Robert Hanes as chairman. The committee served informally for more than a year.

By September 25, 1956, the committee members had made sufficient progress in defining their goals that they decided to enter a program and fund-raising stage. They hired two employees, Elizabeth Aycock and George Simpson, chartered the committee, and opened their offices on October 1, 1956. Aycock, whose husband had worked under Hanes at the Wachovia Bank, was to be a pillar of the Triangle for three decades, later serving as secretary-treasurer of the Research Triangle Foundation. Simpson had served in the office of President Gray at the University of North Carolina and was selected by Gray's newly appointed successor, William Friday, because of his excellent contacts in the academic community and with leaders throughout the state, because of his informed vision of regional development, and because of his practical bent of mind. Simpson in short order raised some $60,000 to cover expenses for the office and the two salaries, for publicizing the program, and for organizing a major fund-raising effort.

The Research Triangle Committee's strategy was to find companies that wanted to expand research efforts in areas where the three universities had great strengths. Simpson organized an inventory of relevant faculty activity. On the basis of this inventory and consultation with key people, the committee concluded that the universities could claim three relevant areas of special strength: chemistry, electronics, and pharmaceuticals. Simpson then helped assemble a team of academic salesmen representing these fields, such as William F. Little of the University of North Carolina's Chemistry Department, who during the 1957–58 academic year traveled to some 200 firms and government agencies to explore the possibility of their locating in the Triangle area. The academic salesmen soon discovered that their best leverage for seeing companies was the desire of companies to attract recent graduates in a time of shortage of good research scientists. All company doors were open, but they also found that attracting firms would at best be a long, slow process.

In the meantime others were attacking the problem of real estate. With the cooperation of the committee, Guest had continued his efforts to develop a research park on a commercial basis. He had identified Karl Robbins, for whom he had developed a number of textile plant sites, as a potential sponsor of the project. On April 12, 1957, Robbins was invited to the governor's mansion for breakfast to meet with the governor and with Simpson, and there he indicated his willingness to back the project financially. Robbins asked Guest to take charge of the negotiations concerning land, and Guest and Simpson in turn asked a land consultant to survey land and begin buying it up, discreetly, since most of the area was scrub pine land of very low value and they did not want news to drive up its price. Guest acquired the first 994 acres in June 1957 from nine heirs who agreed to sell the whole plot. By August 1957 he had options on almost 4,000 acres. In September, with considerable fanfare, a new commercial corporation, Pinelands, was announced, with Guest as president and Robbins chairman of the board. (Over the years, various spots in the area were gradually acquired to round out the property to 5,800 acres.)

Thereafter, however, the project stalled, and by the summer of 1958 it was close to collapse. Negotiations with the city of Durham to supply water bogged down. Economic prospects were dampened by a recession, and Pinelands had difficulty selling stock. Many people saw the park idea as too visionary, too much of an economic risk. Some Northern firms still feared the South would be a battleground of racial violence and, before air conditioning was widespread, many Northern families were not eager to move. Companies were skeptical as to whether it made business sense.

Even Robbins began to lose confidence in the project. At first he had anticipated investing $1 million but, seeing the lack of progress after his first installment of $275,000, he declared he would invest no more until other North

Carolinians matched his purchases. Guest and three others invested a total of $64,000, but the project was still some $700,000 short. A number of people tried to push the project but without success.

In mid-1958, when he discovered that he had cancer and only a few months to live, Hanes decided that the project would be the focus of his efforts in his remaining days but that he would immediately enlist someone else to carry on. In August 1958 he and Governor Hodges invited Archie K. Davis, who formerly worked under Hanes at Wachovia Bank, to breakfast with the thought of enlisting Davis's support in selling Pinelands stock. Davis was then chairman of the board of Wachovia Bank and a state senator. Wachovia Bank, though slightly smaller than the North Carolina National Bank in size, has been rated by *Forbes* as second to Morgan as the best-run bank in America and enjoys great respect in North Carolina. Davis, thoroughly steeped in the tradition of Old Salem, North Carolina, settled by his Moravian ancestors in the eighteenth century, was a history buff who was to begin working on a history Ph.D. at the University of North Carolina after retirement from the bank. He was also totally dedicated to philanthropic causes throughout the state and had many loyal friends. He realized that action was required soon if the project was to go forward, but he asked for a little time to think it over.

Within a few weeks, Davis returned with an entirely different approach. Davis could see that business people regarded the venture as commercially risky and he doubted that he could persuade them otherwise. Also he doubted that they could get the wholehearted support of university faculty and of state politicians in a project in which some people might benefit commercially. Simpson, too, had been troubled by the lack of enthusiasm of academics in a commercial project. Davis proposed that, instead of selling stock, they make an appeal to public-spirited citizens to donate the necessary funds to buy the land and erect the first building. The proposal was accepted.

The new public corporation first had to buy out Pinelands. Robbins, Guest, and others agreed to accept payment at cost plus a modest interest charge of 4 percent. Davis calculated that it would take $1 million to purchase the land and some $250,000 to erect the first building and that the funds would have to be raised before the end of the year (1958). He then personally visited public-spirited citizens he knew and appealed to them on the basis of what was good for the future of the state. On that basis, he found that none of them could refuse and that it was surprisingly easy to raise the necessary funds. Davis had promised that if the total amount necessary to make the project go was not raised by the end of a year, the funds would be returned to the donors. He began his effort at the end of September and two months later had in hand pledges of $1.4 million. In addition to the substantial pledges he collected, large numbers of individuals throughout the state volunteered small contributions.

A considerable portion of the funds came from the family and friends of Robert M. Hanes. On January 9, 1959, Governor Hodges gave a luncheon to celebrate the founding of the Triangle Park, in good part a tribute to Hanes. It was announced that the first building would be named in Hanes's honor, and Hanes responded that it was perhaps a good thing that he was being honored "in the late afternoon or early evening of my life" since he would no longer have the opportunity to tarnish the honor. Two months later he died.

There was room for considerable doubt as to whether the Internal Revenue Service would grant tax-exempt status to the new enterprise when it bought out a commercial firm. Davis decided that taking the matter to court and employing lawyers would be out of keeping with the spirit of the effort, and he went to discuss the matter with Thad Eure, North Carolina's secretary of state for almost fifty years. Eure went through the proposals to establish the Triangle and gave his personal opinion that all that was necessary to be tax exempt was to change the name of the charter. It was not possible to get an answer from the Internal Revenue Service before some time the following year, which would be too slow to move ahead. Davis consulted with IRS officials in Greensboro, who went over the documents carefully and reported that, though their views were unofficial and they could not make any guarantees, they personally thought there was no problem. On the basis of this advice, Davis and others were willing to move ahead, but they were much relieved when some months later the IRS granted them tax-exempt status.

While Davis was raising the funds in the fall of 1958, Simpson was carrying on consultations to determine the organizational structure. On the basis of these consultations, Simpson proposed three separate but related organizations, a foundation, a park, and an institute. The foundation, chartered as a nonprofit corporation, was to be owned by the three universities, and any profits would revert to the universities to support joint research ventures. The foundation would purchase the Pinelands Company, taking over its debts, and organize the Research Triangle Park, which was to become a profit-making subsidiary of the foundation to handle the rental and sale of land to the prospective corporations, with proceeds going to the foundation. The Research Triangle Institute was to be an independent nonprofit research organization conducting contract research as well as basic research. Simpson's proposal was accepted, and these three institutions, the foundation, park, and institute, came into being officially on December 29, 1958.

2. LAUNCHING THE RESEARCH TRIANGLE INSTITUTE (RTI)

The Triangle leaders, like those in NASA, embodied American creativity and pragmatism in shaping organizations to meet clearly defined goals. The troika they created—the nonprofit foundation, a profit-making subsidiary to handle real estate, and the nonprofit institute—was a one-of-a-kind combination. After sweating out the potential tax problems of the transition, the organizers faced another big question, that of the institute. For, despite many faculty supporters, many others, observing that virtually no new nonprofit institutes had been established since 1948, when there were only nine such institutes in the country (including Battelle, Mellon, and Armour), doubted that such institutes had much future.

As with other matters, the question of the institute received very thorough and professional review, in this case by a faculty study group which, beginning in 1957, sent representatives for study visits to the leading institutes and invited in staff from other research institutes for consultations. In the end, the faculty group decided that, to provide an intellectual core for the Triangle and to keep the wholehearted cooperation of the three universities, the nonprofit research institute fit their needs. The faculty study committee noted that generally an institute goes about $500,000 in debt before it emerges in the black. Because of this, in December 1958, when it was established, the institute was given $500,000 by the foundation. The Hanes Building was completed by New Year's 1961, but the institute was off to a running start in 1959.

One of the outside consultants brought in, George Herbert, a resourceful executive in the Stanford Research Institute, seemed so knowledgeable and to have such a clear vision of what was required, that he was chosen to become the first president when the institute was formed in December 1958. At the Stanford Research Institute, from 1948 to 1956, Herbert had seen a small institute with close relations with Stanford University grow large and lose its intimate ties to the faculty. Herbert and the faculty at the Triangle were determined that this not happen at RTI, and they therefore included faculty from the three universities directly on the governing board of the institute and gave them key responsibility in selecting personnel for the institute. These efforts succeeded in keeping close links between the institute and the universities, and about a fifth of new professionals selected for the institute have adjunct appointments at one of the universities. Basically, the faculties at the three universities believe in "their" institute, for it helps them in recruiting first-class faculty, it offers opportunities for outside consulting, and it has built joint research facilities that none of the three universities could have afforded on its own.

Of course, the institute was prepared to carry on research for local businesses and local government, but Herbert was willing to come only because RTI planners accepted the fact that research was a national effort. To be successful, they would have to achieve national levels of competence and serve business and government clients throughout the country. In analyzing broad research trends in the country, they concluded that fields like health, education, environment, and pharmacology were areas of growing interest. They decided, therefore, to build up expertise in these fields rather than compete with existing institutes in areas like defense research. Many institutes had originally been set up with the goal of serving small business, for it was assumed that large companies could afford their own research. Although RTI aimed to service small companies, it realized from the beginning what most institutes found only later—that most institute business is with large companies and the federal government, since small businesses either cannot or choose not to sponsor much research.

The institute's careful professional definition of its work paid off. It grew steadily but soundly until it peaked in size with some 1,100 employees in the early 1980s. The new buildings reflect the growth of its interests. Aside from the Hanes Building, used for administration, the second building, the Camille Dreyfus Lab, was built for polymer research. The third building was for solid-state research, chemistry, and life sciences. The fourth, the William Trent Ragland Building, was used for operations research and economic and statistical research. A fifth building was used for measurement and controls and a radiation system laboratory, and a sixth for public health pharmacology and toxology laboratories.

Although the institute got off to a good running start, companies took a while to decide to locate in Triangle Park, and in the early 1960s when the public, which had developed great expectations for the Triangle, felt let down, the institute had a considerable burden of public attention to keep up interest in the park development. Only in the mid-1960s was the park on a sufficiently sound footing that RTI could begin concentrating wholeheartedly on its own research mission. Thereafter it remained the part of the park with the most university involvement, a nerve center with a broader mission and broader activities than the more specialized research centers that companies were to build in the park.

3. EXPANDING RESEARCH IN TEXTILE FIBERS

The research organizations North Carolina attracted are an excellent example of building on what the state had to offer in universities, industry, and potentially attractive residential areas. The state's successes were the result of a systematic examination of areas of strength and opportunities for expansion.

In tobacco research, North Carolina was well served before the Research

Triangle started. North Carolina State University, the U.S. Department of Agriculture station at Oxford, and the large tobacco companies all had their own research facilities. North Carolina State University also had a research program in forestry and had recently established a pioneering program in furniture manufacturing and management. The greatest new demand for research in areas of North Carolina industrial strength was in textiles. North Carolina State had the nation's strongest research and teaching program in textiles, and the explosive success of nylon and orlon shortly before the park opened made fiber research potentially very lucrative, the most promising area for park development.

Fiber research drew on the universities' strengths in chemistry, and Professor Bill Little of the Chemistry Department at the University of North Carolina, a loyal North Carolinian originally from Hickory, proved to be a talented recruiter who used every possible angle, including working through recruiters who visited the campus to attract able new graduates. A former textile executive himself, Governor Hodges also met with top textile executives to encourage them to locate in the park.

The first company to decide to locate in the park was Chemstrand, a wholly owned subsidiary of Monsanto. A forward-looking president had already decided the company ought to be engaged in long-term research and it was already far along in its search for a new research site at the time the park opened. Chemstrand then had a research facility in Decatur, Alabama, with a staff of some 400, but Decatur was not a stimulating environment and it was difficult to attract new researchers of quality to that site. Chemstrand had already narrowed its choices to five locations, and the final choice was left to David Chaney, head of the Alabama facility. He investigated the Triangle area thoroughly, liked the enthusiasm of the local people in solving logistic problems, the academic environment of the nearby universities, and the potential of the park. Agreements were reached in May 1959 and the facilities were completed the following year. The Chemstrand lab engaged in applied research in artificial fibers and polymers and by the mid-1960s had some 500 employees, although for several years it was the only major research lab in the park.

The negotiations with Chemstrand forced the managers of the park to become more explicit about park policies. In order to preserve the parklike atmosphere, they decided that 3,000 acres of the park would have research facilities with no manufacturing facilities, and a tenant could cover no more than 10 percent of the land it purchased with buildings. These rules were so strict that no other large tenants came for four years, when the rules were eased to permit 15 percent of the land to be used for buildings and to expand the area allotted for "research application," that is, production.

The early difficulties in getting water to the Pinelands led to the formation of a Research Triangle Regional Planning Commission to ensure the smooth development of park infrastructure and effective coordination between the park and municipal and county governments in the Triangle area. The commission includes the mayors of Raleigh, Durham, and Chapel Hill, the county board chairmen from the three corresponding counties, Wake, Durham, and Orange, and three members appointed by the governor, ensuring that the needs of the communities as well as the park are well represented.

The second facility to be located in the park, also engaged in textile-related polymer research, was part of the institute. George Herbert had worked through Robert T. Armstrong, vice-president for research of the Celanese Corporation, to submit a proposal to the Camille and Henry Dreyfus Foundation. Governor Hodges was actively involved in the effort, and in October 1959 he announced a grant to the institute of $2.5 million for the Camille Dreyfus Laboratory. Planners originally hoped this facility would attract research from many companies, but it met with limited success, in part because many companies were less than enthusiastic about funding research in a facility named for the founder of a competitor.

Once the center of the American textile industry had moved to North Carolina from New England, it was logical that national textile associations should be located there as well, and the establishment of the park provided the stimulus for the American Association of Textile Chemists and Colorists, founded in 1921 and previously located in Lowell, Maine, to relocate on a small lot in the park. Its relocation, of course, helped strengthen the critical mass of researchers on chemical fibers.

Beaunit Corporation, which in the mid-1960s had plants in seven North Carolina communities, decided that one of its divisions, Beaunit Fibers, would locate a new research and development center in the park. And in 1966, Hercules, Inc. located a fibers and film department on a forty-four-acre site in the Research Triangle to carry out experimental work on its "Herculon" olefin fibers.

One problem with research programs is that they are perishable, for success may lead to termination. The great advances of the 1950s and 1960s seemed to make new lucrative breakthroughs in the 1970s less likely. Furthermore, the move into textile manufacturing by Asian countries had cut into the profits of some of the large textile firms, which therefore had less to spend on research. In the late 1970s and early 1980s many of these companies reduced or eliminated their park facilities. But by then they had fulfilled their role of supporting the park during its early critical development and, of providing the base for developing a healthy, more diversified research capacity.

From 1959 until 1962 no new company located in the park, and once again the very existence of the park was in doubt. A New York recruitment office was established in 1962, but it was closed eighteen months later without a single success. After Karl Robbins died in 1960, the Pinelands Company, then a subsidiary of the foundation, was forced to buy out his shares from his executors. Since no new companies had located in the park, by 1963 the park was more than $1.3 million in debt, and Archie Davis was again called in. He arranged to borrow this sum from some eight banks and eight insurance companies, with the park land as mortgage. It was at this point that rules were changed to allow companies to use as much as 15 percent of their land for buildings and to permit more research-oriented production in a "Research Application District," a plan of action that George Simpson had proposed as early as 1957. During these early years, leaders in all circles—academics, bankers, governors, and state administrators—joined in the effort to attract companies to the park. The state was very aggressive in recruiting and in advertising that it had a convenient airport, a new highway, an adequate labor force accustomed to modest wages, a relaxed atmosphere, nearby universities, and an uncrowded environment. Yet as difficult as it was to recruit companies, park officials insisted on maintaining a spacious woodsy setting, and the state never offered special tax advantages to new companies. It wanted corporate citizens who would pay their share of state expenses, and eventually it found them.

4. EXPANDING TO MODERN SECTORS

For North Carolinians who wished to make their state as modern as the most advanced states in the country, high technology posed new risks and new opportunities. The gap in advanced work between North Carolina and states like Massachusetts, California, and Texas was hard to bridge, and at best the effort was expensive and success uncertain. Yet the enormous expansion of high technology beyond a few centers gave new opportunities for other states prepared to take advantage of them. The state governments of Massachusetts and California did not need to take great initiatives to develop high technology. The scientific communities around MIT and Harvard and around the California Institute of Technology, Stanford, and the University of California at Berkeley were well established and obviously attractive. North Carolina had universities sufficiently distinguished in high technology to be potentially attractive to industry in that area if government and university leaders acted wisely, but it required special efforts to ensure that the potential was realized.

The push to modern technology and particularly the manufacture of high-technology products was not attractive to everyone in North Carolina. Leaders in traditional industries feared that the state's use of resources to build an infrastructure for high technology might be at their expense. Even more disturbing was the possibility that high-tech manufacturing could offer higher wages than they could offer, driving up wages and attracting away some of their best workers when they were struggling to stay competitive with foreign imports. North Carolina had one of the lowest rates of unionization in the country, but there had been some bitter strikes. To many workers who wanted better pay and working conditions, and to their intellectual defenders, the coming of new industry provided new opportunities for improving working conditions and possibly expanding union activity.

Businessmen in the service sectors, intellectuals associated with the Triangle, and their supporters in North Carolina government tended to see things very differently from textile executives. Bankers, the utilities companies, developers, retailers, and other service businesses would benefit from growth. Government officials tended to see it the same way and, like the academics, were generally more concerned about a clean environment and the expansion of cultural activities. Academics and some government officials tended to be more sympathetic with unions, with blacks, and with poor whites than the service industry leaders, but they could all agree about the desirability of attracting modern industry to keep a clean environment and provide a base for expanding cultural activities.

After the financial crisis of 1963, efforts to attract high-tech companies were stepped up and by 1964 they had scored their first success. Technitrol, a manufacturer of computer components, moved into an existing building in February 1965 and by the summer employed a staff of 200.

The great breakthrough came in 1965, when IBM, after some seven years of negotiation, decided to locate in the park. As part of its expansion program, IBM was looking for new facilities to manufacture equipment for its 1050 data communications system and its 360 computer systems. Its purchase of 421 acres of land was an enormous boon to the park. The size of IBM's operations dwarfed other operations up to that time. The IBM unit opened in 1966 and within a year had more than 2,500 employees. After another great expansion from 1978 to 1980, it had some 5,500 employees in the park and some 2,000 additional employees just outside. Within months after IBM purchased its first huge tract of land, the park was able to pay off its $1.3 million mortgage and it has been in the black ever since. By 1970 the park had sixteen facilities, and by 1980 thirty-two, with about half the park land assigned.

In 1970 Burroughs Wellcome Company, a major pharmaceutical research and manufacturing company, moved its headquarters into the park and located a major manufacturing facility nearby in Greenville. In 1973 Becton Dickinson, manufacturer of medical instrumentation and health-care products, dedicated a major research center in the park.

Given the large role of the federal government in supporting research, the park sought from the beginning to attract federal research funds and research facilities. In 1960, when Terry Sanford succeeded Luther Hodges as governor, he became the first major Southern politician to throw his support to Kennedy.

Kennedy was clearly in his debt, and Sanford, after consulting broadly about realistic possibilities, was ready with one single request: that the National Environmental Health Sciences Center be located in the Research Triangle Park. Although it took some years of negotiation, in January 1965 it was announced that this center would be reorganized as the National Institute of Environmental Health Sciences, the only institute of the National Institutes of Health not located in Bethesda, Maryland. The federal government required a show of state commitment, and the General Assembly of North Carolina was ready to oblige, appropriating some $750,000 to the Research Triangle Foundation for the transfer of some 500 acres to provide a home for the institute.

The Triangle really began to take off in the mid-1970s, roughly doubling its size in five years. By 1981 the park included five federal labs, one state lab, three nonprofit institutes, four university facilities, two national trade associations, and twenty industrial labs. Among other companies locating in the park were Airco Industrial Gases, Data General (computers), General Electric's Microelectronics Center, Northern Telecom (communications), Northrop Services (environment), J. E. Sirrine (engineering design), Troxler Electronics Laboratories, and TRW's Environmental Engineering Division. In 1982 Union Carbide Agricultural Products Company opened its first facility in the park, some twenty-five years after it was originally contacted by George Simpson—although Simpson had by then long since departed, first to NASA to work with fellow North Carolinian James Webb and then to the University of Georgia where he became chancellor.

5. PROVIDING SKILLED MANPOWER

Because education and training are in America primarily the responsibility of the states, states have a great but largely unrealized opportunity to upgrade skill levels to meet the potential manpower needs of their enterprises. North Carolina's experience in trying to recruit high-tech companies to a state with low educational standards and a shortage of skilled manpower led state leaders in the early 1950s to focus on training. Hodges took the lead in establishing industrial training centers, and when he prodded the General Assembly to pass a Community College Act, he had one aim in mind: to attract industries and provide for their needs. In part this effort was for the park area, for the park required not only many Ph.D.'s but a still larger technical support staff. However, the new community colleges were also for the industries growing up around the park and elsewhere in the state. The clarity of their goals—meeting the needs of industry —gave their work a sharp focus and provided clear measures of success and failure.

After scouring the country examining technical education programs, North Carolina decided that by far the best state training program was led by Joe Nerden, head of the Commercial Vocational Education Program in Connecticut. Nerden was brought to North Carolina to advise on the new program. Until then, commercial education had been largely remedial education, but Nerden's goal was to create strong collegiate-level courses. North Carolina moved quickly to implement, and once the program was in place, it became a recruiting tool to assure companies that the state would train manpower to meet the needs of companies ready to locate in the area.

When Sanford became governor in 1960, his commitment to education went much further. He was a bright lawyer who attracted a highly talented staff. Sanford until then had no professional experience as an educator, but his mother had been a school teacher and he had traveled around the state visiting schools. He wanted to upgrade public education and had the courage to bring back a sales tax to finance its improvement. But he also aimed to upgrade community colleges and the university system, and in 1961 he set up the Carlyle Commission on Education Beyond the High School Level. In line with the commission's recommendations, in 1963 the General Assembly established a Department of Community Colleges under the State Board of Education, integrating the industrial education centers begun under Hodges into the community college system in one unified administration while greatly expanding the entire effort. To ensure that community colleges meet local economic needs, each community college has a local advisory committee that includes local businessmen.

By 1982 there were fifty-eight community colleges in the system, located in every major community in the state. Over 99 percent of the state population lives within thirty miles of a community college. In many towns the community college has in effect become the local culture center, but vocational training has remained the center of the curriculum, with some 75 percent of the courses designed for vocational and technical training. While integrated into a single system, the four state programs for upgrading skill levels are:

1. *The New and Expanding Industry Program.* This program caters to the one-time need for a locating firm to get trained workers. The president of the community college system has pledged: "The day you break ground, we'll start training. The day you open your business, we'll deliver them to your doorstep at little or no cost to you." The North Carolina Industrial Developers Association, which includes representatives from industrial head hunters, the Department of Commerce, the Chamber of Commerce, the power companies, and half of the community college and technical institute presidents, is designed to ensure that courses meet the needs of companies considering locating in the state. The

community college training people are involved from the beginning in the recruitment effort, and manpower needs are considered along with other needs of the plant. The community college in the area where the plant is to be located is ordinarily assigned responsibility for ensuring that an appropriate pool of manpower is available to the plant when it is ready to open. Generally, companies select their personnel before sending them to the training program but they may also use the training program as a final screening device, requiring satisfactory completion of the course as a precondition for employment.

The largest companies, such as IBM, often have their own training programs so the state offers them only supplementary programs, but many middle-sized and smaller companies have little experience in running training programs and therefore rely entirely on the state. Programs commonly last two to three months, but the state has also developed programs as brief as an intensive one-week, forty-hour training course.

In selecting instructors, the state goes for competence, not certification. Some instructors are university faculty or high school teachers, but ordinary company employees may instruct part-time, and the state often makes arrangements for compensating a company for an instructor teaching on company time. The policy is that ordinarily maximum faculty salaries are two and one-half times the average manufacturing wage. In the early 1980s, the average manufacturing wage was $6 per hour and the average instructor was thus paid about $15 per hour. A hard-to-find specialist, such as a good tool and dye instructor, may be offered special financial inducements. Because of the flexible and changing nature of these "commando" programs, faculty are overwhelmingly part-time.

2. *The Preemployment Training Program.* This is designed for growing companies with a continuing need to train new people. Training programs are offered for some 230 occupational categories. In the early 1980s, approximately 110,000 students were enrolled each year. At that time, for example, some 160 electronic manufacturing firms in the state shared some thirty-eight electronic engineering training programs offered through these community colleges. Even companies that are not growing may request specialized programs when they introduce new equipment like, for example, power sewing.

3. *The In-Service and Upgrading Training Program.* This program is offered to keep people employed when skills become obsolete through modernization or retrenchment as well as to improve training for people currently employed. As in other programs, the goal is to develop skills appropriate to industrial needs. Courses may be offered inside the plants as well as on the community college grounds. Approximately 275,000 people per year enroll in these courses.

4. *The Human Resources Development Program.* This program is geared for the chronically unemployed and people on welfare. It is a relatively small program

(in 1980–81, for example, there were 4,633 participants), with some forty-five of the community colleges offering eight-week programs focusing on minimal "coping" skills necessary for acquiring and keeping a job.

Since the critical test for these programs is industry success, each year the community college system polls graduates on the success of the program, but it also polls employers. Programs are thus changed rapidly to meet changing needs and to respond to course evaluations. In 1970 some 60 percent of the training was connected with the textiles and furniture industries. By 1980 this was reduced to 20 percent, and over 60 percent of technical training was in high tech.

6. EXTENDING THE COOPERATIVE RELATIONSHIPS

As in many other localities, success in revival led to new spin-offs. The cooperative relations that developed as government, business, and academic officials worked together in the Triangle were gradually extended to new areas. Shortly after taking office in 1960, Governor Sanford held a series of small informal dinners with business and academic leaders in the state to discuss possible future scientific programs for the state. In 1963 these beginnings were formalized in the North Carolina Board of Science and Technology, with offices in the park and with the dual function of strengthening the state's research base and monitoring scientific developments that might be useful to the state's industry. North Carolina was the second state in the nation to establish such a science board and the first to undertake a program with significant funding.

The effort to strengthen the state's research base represented in essence a state-level National Science Foundation to provide grants for the state's scientists. Grants were established in four categories: starter grants to help faculty become competitive for national awards, equipment grants to strengthen academic departments, grants for projects especially relevant to North Carolina problems and grants to "seed" new major facilities for multi-institutional shared use.

After Sanford left the governorship, interest in science waned locally as it did nationally, but when James L. Hunt, Jr., became governor in 1976, he brought renewed interest in science policy, and appropriations for science and technology again began to increase. Hunt had previously served in Nepal, working on economic development, and in his term of office he concentrated on training for high tech as Sanford had concentrated on public education.

Within the park itself a number of cooperative ventures have been established that would not otherwise have been possible: The Triangle Universities Computation Center (TUCC) permitted the installation of state-of-the-art computer facilities with time-shared services for all the Triangle universities and research institutes and later to all other colleges and universities in the state, public and private. Seed money from the Science Board also led to the Triangle Universities Nuclear Lab (TUNL) on the Duke campus, and the board provided a grant for an accelerator along with offices for faculty from the three universities. The Research Triangle Mass Spectrometry Center is operated by the institute for the three universities to permit materials analysis. In 1975 the foundation gave the universities land to create a Triangle Universities Center for Advanced Studies (TUCASI). It in turn voted to grant land for the establishment of the National Humanities Center of the American Academy of Arts and Sciences, parallel to the Institute for Advanced Studies at Princeton and the Center for Advanced Studies in the Behavioral Sciences at Palo Alto. In addition to seed money from the foundation, the universities provided a one-time grant, and Archie Davis raised substantial funds from North Carolinians to make the center possible.

In the early 1980s, under Governor Hunt's leadership, the state committed itself to move in two areas of technology of obvious future importance: microelectronics and biotechnology.

In 1980, when General Electric began considering North Carolina as a possible site for its $100 million microelectronics research, development and production plant, Governor Hunt used this as a spur to attract university and government support for a research and education center in the park next to the GE facility. Until this time, the state had provided infrastructure support but, except for the grant of park land to the federal government to secure the National Institute of Environmental Health Sciences, the state had not been asked to make direct contributions to the park. However, as this was for the state, the General Assembly voted some $24.4 million to establish the Microelectronics Center of North Carolina (MCNC). This new research and training center is coordinated and managed by Duke University, North Carolina State University, the University of North Carolina at Chapel Hill, North Carolina A&T, North Carolina at Charlotte and the park's Research Triangle Institute. George Herbert serves as chairman of the board of directors. The Microelectronics Center is the first of its kind in the nation to be established with strong state support. It was established about the time that GE decided to locate in the park and has worked closely with GE in assuring properly trained manpower to meet GE's needs.

In a related development, the Semiconductor Institute of America opened a new research facility in the park to provide for joint research into semiconductors for its member companies that would be too expensive for them to fund separately, and it is a matter of some regret that the University of Texas was able to outbid North Carolina in attracting MCC (Microelectronics and Computer Technology Corp.), a new joint computer research effort.

After a series of discussions among faculty at the three universities dealing with such issues as topics for research and patent and royalty rights, the state moved to establish a North Carolina Biotechnology Center in the park in late 1981. The center sponsors work on agriculture, medicine, forestry and biology. President Friday of the State University System established a University Biotechnology Council to coordinate activities among the various campuses in the North Carolina university system and this new center.

Cooperative activity in microelectronics and biotechnology was much easier for North Carolina to undertake because of the working relationships between universities, government, and industry developed through the Research Triangle. This pattern of relationships was extended not only within the triangle area but in other parts of the state as well. In Charlotte, for example, a smaller-scale research park was developed, and in Wilmington new cooperative relationships were established between academics and business, both drawing on the positive lessons from the original Research Triangle Park.

7. LEARNING FROM NORTH CAROLINA

By most measures, the cooperative government, business, and academic efforts in North Carolina were an unquestioned success. A state that formerly had only low-income workers in traditional industries now has a modern sector with higher-paying jobs which sustains a substantial population. By the early 1980s, some twenty-five years after its founding, the park alone supported some 20,000 employees with annual salaries of almost half a billion dollars. The flow of educated scientific and technical personnel away from North Carolina was reversed. A new area was developed that the participants judge to provide a high quality of life. The project brought pride to the state, to the universities, and to North Carolina business leaders. It benefited the universities, whose faculties had enhanced facilities for work in new areas, companies which had access to new technology and trained manpower, and workers and families seeking better jobs and a higher standard of living.

Thus far, however, the Triangle has grown largely by attracting outside firms and government labs rather than by generating its own. The area has not yet witnessed the internal expansiveness, the explosive growth of new high-tech firms, found in Massachusetts's Route 128 or California's Silicon Valley. Perhaps it is the lack of local venture capital stemming from the lack of technological sophistication of local people of wealth, for when some outside firms were first considering locating in North Carolina and some local people made investments that turned out badly, they became cautious about further investments. Perhaps it is the lack of cross-fertilization between engineering and business administration at the university level, for the business school at the University of North

Carolina is so far from the engineering school at North Carolina State that contact between faculty and students is almost nonexistent. Perhaps it is the small number of staff at the cutting edge of new commercially viable technology.

Thus far, the Triangle has also had only a modest impact on the state as a whole. State levels of literacy remain low, and the average manufacturing wage in North Carolina rose only from 68 percent of the national average in 1960 to 74 percent in 1980. Per capita income in the state has remained at only slightly more than 80 percent of the national average. Although places like Durham have witnessed a substantial increase of middle-class blacks, the vast majority of the state's blacks have not significantly benefited, even indirectly, from the Triangle. In a sense, the very strenuous efforts of people connected with the park helped produce macroeconomic results that on a statewide basis only slightly more than compensated for the natural forces of decline in textiles and tobacco. Considering the natural decline in traditional sectors, the ability to achieve net growth is no mean accomplishment, but it highlights the toughness of the problem.

To slightly overstate the case, the Research Triangle and its immediate surroundings constitute an island of growth while the rest of the state is still waiting for the ripple effects. It is true that some companies (Burroughs Wellcome, Glaxo, and IBM) have located facilities elsewhere in North Carolina because they had moved certain facilities to the park, but thus far this has had only minor impact. It is an open issue whether, as some parts of the state charge, state industrial recruiters could have done more to encourage corporations to distribute themselves in other parts of the state instead of the more attractive Triangle area. It is still conceivable that, as Governor Hunt and many other politicians hope, the explosive growth of electronics and biotechnology in the 1980s will create new jobs that will have an impact on the state as a whole. There are signs that venture capitalists are now being attracted to high-tech firms outside the immediate Triangle area. New training programs in microelectronics, biotechnology, and other areas will undoubtedly have ripple effects in the next quarter-century, but it is clear that other programs are needed to deal with the overall quality of public education and the economic opportunities for poorer citizens of the state.

Yet within the Triangle area, the success has been sufficiently spectacular not only in employment but in training, the development of a professional class, and the creation of attractive surrounding communities that many other states have sent missions to study how they too might emulate a neighbor state's success. The success in vocational training was sufficiently impressive that other Southern states—South Carolina, Tennessee, Virginia, Kentucky, Georgia, Alabama, and Florida—sent missions to study North Carolina's experiences and several fashioned new programs on the North Carolina model.

Other states drawing on North Carolina's experience will, of course, fashion different programs. From the national perspective, it would be unfortunate if

11

American Patterns of Successful Cooperation

America's experience in NASA, private housing, agriculture, and the Research Triangle shows that its public and private sectors can work well together and achieve impressive results when we have:

1. *Committed imaginative leaders.* In each case, a purpose, a compelling vision was clearly articulated by public and private leaders. Success in each case required going beyond existing procedures and structures to conceive new goals, new frameworks for achieving them, and a consensus built around the new moves. In all these cases political and bureaucratic leaders rose to the occasion.

For manned space flight John F. Kennedy and Lyndon Johnson mobilized the nation and NASA administrator James Webb, a bold visionary, deftly gained the support of Congress, scientists, businessmen, and the public. In agriculture, the original visions came from bureaucrats like Gwynn Garnett and Ray Iaones, but FAS received creative help from both Republican and Democratic administrations and secretaries of agriculture like Betz and Freeman. Housing programs were pushed by Presidents Roosevelt and Truman as well as by housing administrators but would not have succeeded without Eisenhower's imaginative leadership in shaping the interstate highway program. In North Carolina, in addition to active leadership by governors like Luther Hodges and Terry Sanford, such public-spirited philanthropists as Bob Hanes and Archie Davis and research administrators Bill Friday, George Simpson, and George Herbert played indispensable public entrepreneurial roles.

2. *Long-term bipartisan support.* Concern with Russian advances in space

caused Americans to bear willingly the costs of putting an American on the moon. Belief in the humanitarian goal of feeding the world's needy and respect for American farmers led to public support for donating and then selling agricultural products abroad. The shortage of housing and the widespread desire for home ownership after World War II created a consensus for financial programs to make this possible. In North Carolina, widespread recognition that the state desperately needed modern industry paved the way for the Research Triangle.

Not only were most people attracted to the compelling visions, but adjustments were made to the interests of those most negatively affected by change. In each of the four cases, some people doubted whether the effort was in their interests. Scientists not concerned with space feared that their research budgets would suffer at the expense of space research. Some nonfarm groups objected to the high level of support going to agriculture, some industrialists worried that the financial resources going into housing would be at their expense, and some North Carolinians in geographical and industrial areas far from the Research Triangle feared that they would indirectly pay for the Triangle. But efforts were made to accommodate them so that they did not suffer seriously. Opposition was therefore minor.

Each of these programs required a decade or more to succeed, and in each case the public gave the leaders the continuing support necessary to sustain their commitment. In many cases leaders remained in office to see the results but when they did not, their successors saw the programs through to the end.

Although the program to place a man on the moon required only eight years once Kennedy had made the commitment, the expanded space program had begun five years earlier. The Foreign Agriculture Service had some successes within a few years after it began in 1953, but the really impressive successes came almost two decades later. Government programs to backstop private housing finance began in 1934, a secondary mortgage market was established in 1938, and renewed commitment with some modifications in these programs after World War II made possible successes that continued for decades. The length of the mortgages, twenty and thirty years, scarcely supports the view that Americans can think only of the short term. The leaders in North Carolina originally estimated that it would take a quarter of a century to make a Research Triangle work, and most of the original leaders remained that long to see it happen.

3. *Mutual respect between public- and private-sector representatives.* In each case private and public representatives understood that the other had an essential contribution to make to a successful outcome, and they came together not as adversaries but as partners in solving a common problem. Government officials and business representatives did not have identical interests, but they worked together where they shared common ground.

Some of the nation's most talented scientists and businessmen became NASA administrators, and they gained the wholehearted cooperation of business and the research community. In the Foreign Agricultural Service, most officials came from farm backgrounds and were thoroughgoing professionals who enjoyed easy relationships with farmers and farm organizations. In housing, officials of organizations like Fannie Mae had strong backgrounds in finance and enjoyed the respect of bankers and others in the financial community. In North Carolina, Governor Hodges had been himself a leading businessman, and the private sector organizers recruited by state officials were sufficiently respected that they could even obtain financial contributions from private-sector leaders. In both the public and private sphere, professionals (whether businessmen, lawyers, economists, scientists, or technicians) shared with their counterparts a basic approach to solving problems that transcended the organizations they represented.

4. *Coordinating mechanisms.* In each case leaders found ways to ensure that the mutual respect existing at high levels was translated into effective coordination among government branches and between the government and the private sector. NASA used scientific and business advisory councils. FAS used the "cooperators" as the link to farm commodity sectors. Housing officials had broad consultations with associations of builders and bankers. In North Carolina, the Research Triangle Foundation, the park, and the institute all had committees that included representatives from government, business, and the academic community. But, in addition, all made ample use of ad hoc meetings and groupings to ensure that all major actors were in step as the programs developed.

5. *Involvement at the national level.* The development of the Research Triangle illustrates what can be done with state initiatives, but it also shows that the role of the national government and national corporations is so large that major state projects cannot succeed without their close cooperation. Even the extraordinary efforts of North Carolina leaders in all circles did not succeed until they obtained the cooperation of national corporations and branches of the federal government.

Part Four

AMERICAN RESPONSE

12

Competitive Strategy, American Style

From the early days of our national existence when we began catching up with England in textile production until the 1980s, we Americans did not have a serious trade imbalance. Accustomed to spectacular economic success since World War II, we have been slow to recognize how dependent we have become on international trade and how ill-prepared we are to respond to the most serious competitive challenge in our national history.

Of late we have begun to realize how many Japanese products are competitive, but we have not yet acknowledged the depth of our problem or the scope of change required to respond effectively. Many Americans want to believe that with correct monetary and fiscal policies, lower interest rates, a balanced budget, and a revalued yen, the problem would go away. Many want to believe that if the government got rid of some regulations and American managers did their jobs properly there would be nothing to worry about. Many want to believe that the Japanese will lose their competitive edge as they become affluent, as their industries mature, or as they move to original research. Many want to believe that Japan succeeded largely because of unfair practices, by copying, dumping, protecting, and stealing, and that if the playing field were level, Americans would win again. Many want to believe that our economy can continue to do well indefinitely despite huge trade imbalances.

Though there is more than a kernel of truth to many of these beliefs, it is an illusion to think that America would automatically respond better if we balance our budget and adopt "correct" monetary and fiscal policies. The confidence that we can be competitive without a national strategy corresponds to past experience, but it no longer accords with present reality.

First, it ignores the superior flexibility of Japanese institutions, coordinated by government, to adapt more quickly to new opportunities. The complexity of contemporary life requires national coordination, and the Japanese have fashioned a system to get the cooperation of sectors that enables companies to perform more effectively. With a smaller percentage of GNP going to civilian government services than in the United States, they have devised a system that obtains superior information and analysis and is more flexible and faster in providing a broad range of possible solutions for companies to adapt to the international marketplace.

Second, it ignores the critical nature of strategic and sometimes irreversible changes in competitive advantage that is not reflected in company balance sheets or aggregate statistics until much later. Japanese organizations have done a superior job in positioning themselves in organization, information, research, and education to prepare for tomorrow's opportunities.

As Japan acquires higher levels of capital and research know-how, in areas in which America once enjoyed preeminence, Japan's advantages are likely to become more rather than less pronounced. Trade gaps with Japan are likely to increase substantially despite upward revaluation of the yen, just as they did in the 1970s.

America needs to find its own way to adapt to the rapid changes in the world competitive environment. An effective national system is delicate, for it rests on the wholehearted support of the people and must fit our traditions and predilections. We cannot and should not attempt to copy the Japanese. Our private companies will not tolerate elite interventionist bureaucrats with the power they have in Japan. America could not mount a comprehensive industrial policy in every sector for, unlike Japan, we lack the sense of vulnerability, homogeneity, and consensus needed to support strong central direction and to counter political pressures. Yet there is a great deal we can and should do to improve our system, and there is much we can learn from Japan as we endeavor to match its competitiveness.

What difference does it make if America fails to respond effectively to the competitive challenge? Our standard of living would continue to decline relative to those of Japan and other countries, but Americans have a sufficiently high average standard of living that this need not cause great pain. Even if Americans were less able to afford products made abroad as trade deficits become more serious, this would not necessarily produce great economic strain on the average American family.

A more serious danger is that failure to adapt effectively could cause disastrous difficulties for millions of affected householders and could deepen the cleavages between the affected regions and the rest of the country. Even more serious is the vicious cycle of defeatism and protectionism. Workers afraid of losing their jobs would resist the modernization needed to keep their companies competitive. Managers who lost hope of maintaining competitive facilities in the United States would push for quick profit-taking and personal benefits while preparing to close plants, yielding to foreign companies or building new facilities abroad. Noncompetitive sectors would go to Washington for protection, wreaking even more havoc with free trade and creating strains with the country's trading partners. Increased American protectionism may well spark a collapse of the world trading system, as did the Smoot-Hawley Tariff of 1931. Within America, relations between workers and management, government and business could become even more filled with mutual recriminations and bitterness.

Our ability to respond to the new international competitive environment is the paramount problem of our generation, and a successful response may well provide the paramount opportunity for national renaissance. A successful response could involve Americans in the process of raising educational standards, improving relations between workers and management, hastening technological innovation, and speeding adjustment to changing economic circumstances. Except for a national emergency, when issues of security take precedence, no issue is as likely to have such an impact on Americans' daily lives and the national spirit. We would be unwise not to give it the sustained public attention it deserves.

The issue is how to increase our awareness so that competitiveness receives sustained attention and priority on the national agenda. How many more industries must America lose to convince those who believe that yen revaluation and correct monetary and fiscal policies are enough to solve our problems? How large does the trade imbalance have to become? How much of the high-tech market and service sector must America lose before it gives up the ideological pretense that the private sector is able to respond effectively if just left alone? What could leaders do to increase public awareness of the underlying problems?

1. GUIDELINES FOR A SELECTIVE INDUSTRIAL STRATEGY

Competitiveness is the combined result of all the national qualities and policies that help people and companies perform at more effective levels. Success will not come primarily from legislation or reorganization but from wholehearted efforts of government, business, and labor working towards common goals. Better national competitiveness draws on better educational standards, more dedicated workers, and more successful management. It is helped by a predictable economic environment and the lower cost of capital that gives companies greater leeway to consider long-range results. It is therefore affected by savings rates and budget deficits and requires effective monetary and fiscal policy. It is helped by strong companies led by effective managers. But to deal with complex issues that require national coordination, there is no alternative to developing a selective industrial strategy. The government is already involved because public interests are at stake; the only question is how to improve that involvement.

The fact is that the United States does have a competitive policy. That policy is to give competitiveness lower priority than security and regulatory policy. The U.S. government delays or stops the export of equipment for security reasons, not only putting American companies at a disadvantage vis-à-vis foreign competitors but creating doubts in the minds of many foreign purchasers about the reliability of American supply. We deregulate our banking and communications industries, opening them to foreign companies, without considering the impact on our competitive position. In both banking and communications, Japan is prepared to enter deregulated U.S. markets, and our pressure on Japan to open its markets is less effective than if the United States had used access to its markets for negotiating leverage.

The United States does have de facto industrial targeting for in the mid-1980s we give over $100 billion in various kinds of aids to defense-related industries, airplanes, agriculture, housing, and other industries. Our de facto industrial targeting policy gives special protection and help to declining sectors that are no longer competitive but have political clout. We could once afford a de facto industrial policy that gave no attention to issues of international competitiveness, but we can do so no longer. America now needs a conscious strategy that imposes no greater burden on our budget while providing as guidelines for government decisions that affect the changing competitiveness of specific sectors.

Most citizens support the following goals, which could serve as aims of an improved strategy: (1) Preserve industries essential to national security and national economic health and provide stimuli to make these industries as competitive as possible. (2) Assist in the smooth transition of workers from manufacturing areas no longer competitive into other areas. (3) Encourage research, development, and rapid commercialization of new technology in areas acknowledged to be important for the future.

There are no magical ways to achieve these goals and to ensure that America remains competitive, but we do have mechanisms well within our experience to move in this direction. We cannot attempt to help all sectors, but the government is already involved in four areas where consideration of competitive issues would make a very large difference, and to achieve these aims we would do well to concentrate our efforts in these areas:

1. *Strategic national industries.* The U.S. Department of Defense already stimulates production of supplies acknowledged as important for national defense. From World War II until recently, it could be assumed that virtually all supplies needed could be produced in the United States, but with the deterioration of the American industrial base this can no longer be assumed. It is advisable to specify what industries are vital to the American defense effort. Aid to these sectors could be coupled with consideration of how government procurement could enhance the competitive position of these key sectors.

2. *Injured industries.* The International Trade Commission now has a legalistic procedure for determining when industries are considered to be injured by imports. Under the present system, if sectors like machine tools, steel, footwear, flatware, and copper are given special relief, no quid pro quo is required. Injured companies can accept and profit from the relief without making any effort to remain competitive. Those industries given relief by the government could be required to submit a plan to remain internationally competitive, and continued relief would be contingent on reasonable adherence to the plan of action.

3. *Trade policy.* American pressure for opening other markets and decisions about whether to open American markets are responses to pressures from various American sectoral groups. Trade policy could give more weight to the significance of the areas protected or opened for the long-range competitiveness of American industry.

4. *Research, development, and the commercialization of new technology.* Although the U.S. government supports a very substantial amount of research considered to be in the national interest, until recently the question of the impact of the research on the competitiveness of American industry has not received serious consideration. In addition to support for basic research, the government should encourage the rapid commercialization and diffusion of important new technologies.

The measures America chooses to achieve this competitiveness must have broad bipartisan support to survive changes of administrations. The idea of a Development Bank, for example, is unlikely to gain such support from the American public or to provide sufficient funds to make a major difference in our overall competitiveness. Rather, tax incentives, guaranteed loans as used in private housing finance, and public tax-exempt bonds, methods already in use, are likely to achieve a much broader base of support.

In the end, final decisions in these areas can only be made by elected political leaders. Only they can gain the broad public support to make these programs work. Our real challenge is to build a basis of consensus and strong bipartisan support that political leaders will want to back wholeheartedly.

To ensure objective information on all aspects of the country's competitive position, the U.S. government needs data and analysis on each industrial sector, performed by a group independent of political pressure. The analysis must draw on data derived from all relevant branches of the government and it must include the work of the best analysts in the private sector.

With this kind of analysis available, many parts of the government would make use of it in carrying out their regular responsibilities. The Antitrust Division of the Justice Department, for example, is now willing to consider the impact of international competition in making its determinations, but it often lacks relevant objective data and analysis. The data and analysis thus gathered are likely to be used widely by many government agencies.

The approach for realizing the above aims can be divided conveniently between defensive and offensive strategies.

2. DEFENSIVE STRATEGY: MAINTAINING STRATEGIC INDUSTRIES

America needs a better system for determining which industrial sectors are vital for national security and economic health. These issues are too important to be determined as they are now by happenstance or political pressures alone. Once we select a sector we also need a better system for providing assistance to companies and workers adversely affected so as to speed adjustment and ease the transition.

For the moment, for better or worse, the United States has determined through its political process that several sectors, notably textiles, footwear, TV, steel, and autos, deserve special protection. Other sectors like machine tools and semiconductors may soon be added. The questions are: How can we anticipate global changes so as to reduce the chances that other sectors will become noncompetitive? How can we improve the process for selecting industries to receive special help? What can we do to increase the likelihood that the industries selected will become more competitive?

The issues can be illustrated by what happened to the steel industry. Despite ideology to the contrary, the American government has in fact for some decades given the steel industry substantial aid in tax benefits and special protection. The aid helped sustain profitability in the steel industry, satisfying stockholders and lifting salaries of steel executives and the wages of workers far above average levels in manufacturing. The aid was given without any strings attached. Despite this special aid, American steel companies did not invest in modern plant and equipment to keep up with international competition. The federal government had inadequate mechanisms for tracking and reporting on international competition and failed to recognize how much our steel industry had fallen behind.

When it became obvious how far behind Japan's large integrated steel plants

American steel companies were, the latter responded by diversifying their hold-ings, closing plants, and cutting their work force. From the perspective of the firm, the response was not unreasonable and the firms survived perfectly well. They maintained profitability for a considerable time and moved to new sectors after they lost profitability. But the policy was not in the long-range interest of the workers and was not in the long-range national interest, for it has not only cost the nation a modern integrated steel industry and many jobs but related industries and their jobs as well, including high-tech jobs.

In retrospect, the lesson seems quite clear: When the government gives spe-cial aid to a sector, it has an opportunity to look out for national interests. As in the Chrysler bailout, it could have given aid to the steel industry in exchange for agreements to invest in modern facilities and control runaway wage increases and other costs that would have made it possible to maintain a viable American industry. To do this successfully requires that the government collect relevant data and make timely analysis and have a clear picture of the long-range national interest.

A slightly more complicated opportunity was similarly lost in the auto indus-try. By 1980 the U.S. Department of Transportation had excellent information on the international competitive problems of our auto industry. The auto com-panies made strenuous efforts to cut costs and made some progress. In 1983, when the government was considering working with Japanese officials to get a voluntary agreement limiting the number of cars coming into the United States, some auto officials urged the government to require auto company management and labor to make certain concessions in exchange for the protection from imports, as it had in the Chrysler bailout. Though many government leaders could see the wisdom of such a requirement, they responded that it was not their particular responsibility. Officials within the companies and unions trying to restrain exec-utive salaries and other wages felt their efforts were undercut. Not surprisingly, once the voluntary restraint agreement was reached, salaries of high officials and auto workers went out of control. Then the government officials who had pres-sured Japan for "voluntary restraints" criticized the auto companies for their selfish behavior and threatened the end of "voluntary restraints."

Would it not have been better when "voluntary restraints" were negotiated to couple them with an agreement restraining company wage increases and re-quiring new investment, as in the Chrysler bailout? America now has an auto industry increasingly unable to match the costs of Japanese competitors. Instead, it has mutual recriminations among government, business executives, and labor when it could have had an agreement that would have made its auto companies far more competitive.

Now it is doubtful that American steel and autos can ever regain competi-tiveness on a large scale, and the new issue is whether the national interest requires the rebuilding of these industries. In the case of steel it is also unclear how much demand will be affected by the development of new composite materials.

One can always argue that any particular industry is not necessary for national economic survival and that goods can be imported in a tradeoff for services. But letting industry after industry move out of the United States will have a profound impact on the country's high-tech industries and software and other services, and no one has adequate methods of measuring this impact until it is too late.

It is clear that certain kinds of microprocessors are developing more rapidly in Japan because of their close link with consumer electronics, and we do know that there are strong vertical linkages between Japanese firms in different sectors that make foreign penetration difficult simply on the basis of market competitiveness. It is known that when Britain abandoned manufacturing industries to concentrate on finance, insurance, and other services, it took some years before London began losing services to New York. A comparable switch from New York to Tokyo in financial services is already beginning and with further liberalization in Tokyo could proceed faster because of the tight vertical linkages between Japanese manufacturing and service sectors. Europe, affected earlier by declining competitiveness in manufacturing, was not able to increase service-sector jobs in the 1970s. Although America increased service-sector jobs in the 1970s, with the loss of competitiveness in many manufacturing sectors in the late 1970s and early 1980s it is difficult to see how its service sector could continue expanding into the early 1990s without a strong industrial line.

How then does the country speed up the process of selecting sectors like steel and autos, and companies like Chrysler and Harley Davidson, to which to give national relief before it is too late, and what can Americans do to ensure that our relief efforts are in keeping with the national interest?

1. Improve information for early warning. We need much better information and analysis to permit our government to make independent assessments. In the case of autos, the Department of Transportation's Transportation Systems Center provided that information by 1980 and is a model of how timely data and analysis can be made available to government officials. The analysts had a measure of independence from political officials, patiently collected and analyzed relevant data, and worked with the private sector to arrive at reliable results. Even without formal government action this information pushed our auto industry to a much more rapid response to its competitive problems than would have been otherwise possible. Given the immense size of the federal government and the importance of these issues, it is shocking that the country does not have comparable data and analysis for other important industrial sectors.

The question of how to make use of the data is, of course, more complicated.

At the very least, it makes possible a more timely granting of relief than in the case of the Chrysler bailout and the relief given to Harley Davidson although the quid pro quo required of Chrysler and the plan submitted by Harley Davidson for modernization provide good models of what the government should require in exchange for special aid.

2. *Provide individual incentives for finding new work.* America needs a system of incentives to speed up readjustment and to encourage the unemployed to return for retraining in areas identified as having employment opportunities. Training vouchers that provide partial government support to pay for an unemployed person to be trained by a company that has a vacancy is one program that would provide such incentives. We also need a placement system with a professional staff that understands the individual qualities and backgrounds of the people being placed as well as the demands of the organization hiring.

3. *Encourage retraining in areas of labor shortage.* It has been estimated that between 500,000 and 1 million people have lost or will lose jobs in the industrial areas between Pittsburgh, Detroit, and Chicago as a result of the decline of the steel and auto industries. Some may have to relocate, and others may find new work at far lower salaries in growing service-sector positions that require relatively little retraining. But other sectors in growing fields are still short of properly trained manpower and, as the number of people becoming old enough to enter the work force will decline during the next few years, retraining in areas of short supply also accords with demographic trends. As in North Carolina's program, retraining should be geared to the needs of local business.

4. *Establish a framework of shared responsibility for the structurally unemployed.* Some companies have been willing to consider programs to help with the readjustment of former employees adversely affected by structural change. However, retraining and new employment cannot be provided entirely within a declining sector, and the solution to these problems therefore requires the brokering by state and, in areas beyond state borders, by the national government. Unemployment insurance in the United States was designed to deal with cyclical problems of the economy, to tide workers over until a new cycle provided more opportunities. The system encourages unemployed workers receiving benefits to wait for something to turn up, thus slowing readjustment even for the structurally unemployed and imposing a heavy drain on the national budget. We therefore need a broader framework for specifying and sharing responsibility for structural change, and only the federal government can convene the parties needed to work out an appropriate sharing of responsibility.

3. OFFENSIVE STRATEGY: FACILITATING GROWTH INDUSTRIES

All Americans agree about the desirability of encouraging sectors of future competitive importance, and the only question is how best to achieve this. Some believe that it can be best accomplished by leaving everything to the market, but they are stymied by the question of how to respond to other countries that "target" certain industries.

The unpleasant fact is that America can do nothing to deter other countries from successful targeting. If a country uses direct financial subsidy to help in targeting, America can provide a countersubsidy, although by the time it is granted the foreign product may already have won an irreversible battle in the marketplace. But the greatest impact of targeting comes not from financial subsidy but from the sharing of information and technology, government reorganization to interface effectively with the private sector, removal of obstacles to rapid development, the availability of long-term capital at low rates, specialization and cooperation among companies to speed up the experience curve, timely standardization and compatibility of products, and assurance of sales. All these things can be done legally without special subsidies or tax advantages and can provide a decisive competitive advantage.

It is difficult to imagine international agreements that would prevent such assistance. American companies are correct that "the playing field is not level," and it is unrealistic to assume that our companies have such overwhelming advantages that they can compete effectively against companies in countries that provide a more favorable environment. The only meaningful American response is to find American ways to encourage American companies. Notwithstanding current ideology to the contrary, the American government has long played a major role in paving the way for economic growth, especially in areas like construction, defense, and health. In transportation, our national government played a critical role in promoting canals, railways, interstate highways, and air travel.

Loss of competitiveness in areas the Japanese have targeted for the future, like computers, communications, satellites, new materials, and biotechnology would create far more serious problems than any we have yet faced. Although these fields may lack the concreteness of railways and roads, they will play the same role in opening new development in the future that railways and roads did in the past. In the past the government helped build the transportation infrastructure to promote economic development, and it could do the same for communications, health systems, pharmaceuticals, and other sectors that are likely to be the engines of growth in the future as private housing and highways were engines of growth in the early years after World War II.

In addition to appropriate monetary and fiscal policies that would balance the budget, control inflation and encourage savings, among the most important roles the national government could play that would be perfectly in keeping with American customs and predilections are the following:

1. *Evaluate competitive impact.* In shaping major policies such as taxation, antitrust policy, monetary policy, defense spending, and trade policy, political leaders should give much more weight to the size and strategic nature of the long-run impact on competitiveness.

2. *Provide incentives for rapid application of new technology in manufacturing.* We should continue to promote research and development but give more weight to priority areas that are strategically important in key competitive areas. Because America is much slower than Japan in applying new technology, rather than in research itself, Americans should speed the application process by the timely setting of standards for promising developments, providing tax incentives both for the producer and the purchaser of the product to increase demand as well as producing key goods..

3. *Upgrade research facilities in key areas.* The country should improve research facilities in universities and other national labs in key areas of technology where facilities have fallen behind world levels.

4. *Encourage joint research and marketing.* In critical areas, the government can take the lead in encouraging cooperation between firms and in clearing away antitrust risks to carry out joint research projects like those already begun on computers and semiconductors. Universities with special strengths could be enlisted in research consortia.

5. *Promote defense-related research and procurement.* Planning in defense should consider what industries and economic bases in America are necessary for supporting military efforts in emergency situations. It should also consider the impact of procurement on the commercial competitiveness of American firms in key sectors, including technology developments, pressure for cost-effectiveness, and manpower supply.

6. *Facilitate bureaucratic processes.* Given the many government agencies involved in large projects of research, technology, modernization of new plants, and foreign projects, the timely solution to competitive problems for American industrial sectors requires commitment of high-level political leaders to provide coordination and cut through blockages wherever they may be.

7. *Support trade negotiations.* U.S. trade policy should reflect an evaluation of which sectors are critically important for national competitiveness, and Ameri-

cans should broker internal agreements that enable them to leverage access to parts of the American market so as to achieve critically important access to foreign markets.

8. *Improve educational quality.* The national government ought to help set higher standards in national education, especially in science and mathematics. The country should take nonelite education much more seriously, providing rigorous courses of study for specialized skills that upgrade the quality of training and provide a basis for pride and better performance.

9. *Train manpower in key areas.* The government should monitor manpower needs in critical areas and develop programs to produce and sustain needed specialists. Areas like electrical engineering in which America has been producing about 50 percent fewer university graduates than Japan for over a decade and technical, scientific, and commercial specialists able to follow research and other relevant publications in foreign languages are especially critical. The country ought, for example, to have thousands of people able to follow the diverse technical research in Japan and thousands of others able to work in Japan within a range of public relations, information gathering, trouble shooting, cooperation, and lobbying activities comparable to those of Japanese now in Washington and New York.

As obvious as these goals may seem, the United States has not yet made a national commitment to achieve them. Until recently, reasonable people could have argued that these problems were not sufficiently serious to require special government effort. This is no longer the case, for dealing successfully with these issues requires national government leadership as well as deliberation by business leaders working within a framework of cooperation between government and business.

Skeptics may reply that the federal government is incapable of dealing with such issues or that political pressures from regional and sectoral interests will make rational policy impossible. The fact is the federal government is dealing with all these issues already. The issue is not whether to deal with them but how to improve the quality of government action to cope with international competition. The four American case studies suggest that the United States can deal effectively with these tough issues when its people believe it necessary to do so.

4. MECHANISMS FOR COORDINATION

Our experience in space exploration, agricultural marketing, and housing finance shows that Americans have a great capacity to develop innovative and creative organizational mechanisms when there is a will to do so. If we develop a strong national consensus about the importance of improving our international competitiveness and about how to achieve the goal, we have every reason to expect that appropriate mechanisms will follow. Nonetheless, selecting the mechanisms for coordination and getting them to work effectively is a complex task that deserves careful attention.

There are two major possibilities: reorganize an existing structure, as the Department of Agriculture did to form the Foreign Agricultural Service, or establish a new organization, as was done for NASA. Assuming we wish to work basically through our present political structure and give competitiveness very high priority, we have the option of a structure within the White House or a new one outside the White House, or some combination of the two. In either case the staff would be relatively small, as the goal is to provide overall policy and give critical input on certain crucial cases, not to give detailed guidance for the entire economy. One promising approach that would reorganize two existing structures and create one new structure would be as follows:

1. *The National Competitiveness Council.* The existing White House staff could be reorganized to include a new subunit parallel to the National Security Council. This small council would review major domestic policy issues for their impact on international competitiveness. It would monitor information and analyses about competitiveness to provide: a. early warnings about important sectors of the economy in danger of being adversely affected by international competition; b. an analysis of the consequences of major actions on competitiveness; c. guidelines for overall directions to achieve a healthy competitive economy.

Staff members should collectively have a broad base of experience and know-how in dealing with business, labor, Congress, the budget, the media, and the academic community. The staff would include people able to monitor studies in these various sectors, but it would draw on the work of the Council of Economic Advisers and other parts of the government rather than undertake its own research. It would help heighten national awareness of competitive problems and coordinate both offensive and defensive strategies. The Council would report directly to the President.

2. *The National Economic Cooperation Council.* A new semi-independent organization could be created outside existing institutions bringing together labor, business, and academe as well as government representatives to forge agreements to respond to competitive problems. It would deliberate on issues related to competitiveness and attempt to build a consensus among key groups and then submit proposals through the regular political process. It could help broker the quid pro quo required of "injured industries" once the issue of injury was decided by the International Trade Commission. It could also broker the arrangements with industries designated as essential for national security to ensure that they would modernize and remain as competitive as possible.

The advantage of locating a council in the White House is to link it closely with the great locus of power, the presidency, and the danger is, of course, that it may be subject to undue political influence. The advantage of locating a council outside the White House is that it could have a measure of independence from political pressures. These two organizations could be combined either inside or outside the White House, but it may well be that it would work better to have a small National Competitiveness Council in the White House to provide timely overall coordination and a National Economic Cooperation Council outside to build consensus among major groups about desirable lines of policy.

3. *Office of Trade.* Whether the council is located inside or outside the White House, a new organization is needed to better link trade negotiations, currently under the Special Trade Representative's Office within the White House, with commercial work currently performed in the Commerce Department to ensure that in trade negotiations America speaks with a single voice and concentrates its efforts in areas of greatest long-range national interest. An Office of Trade could be located within the Commerce Department or outside as an independent institution.

The Office of Trade would have primary responsibility within the government for analysis of America's competitive problems. The government already collects and analyzes massive amounts of data, and units like Congress's Office of Technology Assessment and parts of the Commerce Department provide excellent analytic studies. Yet not all the relevant information required for competitive analysis is currently being collected; data collected by various parts of the government are often never brought together, and many studies relevant to competitive analysis have never been commissioned. The Office of Trade would not duplicate existing studies and few studies would be conducted within the Office. Rather, it would keep track of the major relevant studies throughout the world, amassing data to be used in competitive analysis and commissioning the collection of further data and studies as needed. The analysis would include not only macroeconomic trends but assessments of technology, of strategic factors affecting the health of firms in key sectors, and, where relevant, of broader social trends and public attitudes. Central to this work is an analysis of industrial sectors, and this requires the leadership of the Office of Trade and cooperation from the private sector.

The Foreign Agricultural Service and the industry sectoral advisory committees of the Tokyo Round of trade negotiations in 1973 provide excellent examples of sectoral cooperation. They are models to build on, but the new sectoral associations need to consider broader topics, such as research, technology, manufacturing facilities, overseas marketing, availability of low-cost capital, trained manpower needs, and negotiating positions. Their role is primarily advisory but to guard against the dangers of cartel-like arrangements not in the national interest, the government needs a strong independent analytic capability.

Two subunits under the Office of Trade are also desirable:

a. Science and Technology Advisory Council. This council, composed of scientists and business leaders dealing with high technology, would be concerned with research and development as it affects the country's competitiveness. The council would provide analyses of long-range scientific and technological needs of American industry with a view to providing incentives to supply the manpower, training, and research programs required to keep American industry abreast of international developments. The council would be, in effect, America's answer to Japan's AIST (Agency for Industrial Science and Technology). The United States does not need an elaborate structure like AIST because it already has strong academic and industrial research centers and strong organizations like the National Academy of Sciences. It could therefore develop advisory boards of individuals from these various organizations but with an emphasis on commercial application rather than basic science.

b. Capital Resources Advisory Council. This council would monitor the financial needs of key sectors of American business in capital equipment, infrastructure, and research and development. It would also monitor the cost of capital as it affects the American competitive position.

These mechanisms are modest adaptations of existing organizations, well within America's capability and within the range of its tradition and political inclinations. They are minimalist in the sense that they do not attempt to achieve comprehensive industrial strategy. Assuming there is a political consensus that accords competitiveness high priority, they provide the vehicle to make strategic inputs to ensure that competitive issues are properly considered.

5. PROSPECTS

History is filled with stories of successful people who became self-satisfied and were then pushed aside by others with greater ambition. It is not hard to imagine that a nation of homogeneous, highly disciplined people with a sense of urgency and a well-honed competitive strategy may displace a nation of individualists reluctant to acknowledge the need for national cooperation.

Unfortunately the United States has been so successful that, like China in the nineteenth century or GM in the 1970s, it is slow to acknowledge that problems are serious enough to require basic rethinking. Many American businessmen try to avoid contact with the government until they are no longer competitive. Many economists who defend the free market believe in monetary and fiscal policies but show little interest in strategic factors that affect business advantage until they are reflected in aggregate quantifiable data, when it is too late. Many private citizens, relatively satisfied with their current lot in life, do not want to be bothered. Many who follow quarterly reports are sufficiently cheered by an ephemeral upturn in the economy to dismiss "apostles of doom" who talk of long-run difficulties. Many citizens are eager to rally behind politicians who gloss over underlying difficulties.

Even many who recognize that the nation faces serious long-term problems despair of trying to get effective national action. Therefore, despite the valiant efforts of some wonderfully dedicated leaders in government, the private sector, and universities, the prospect of achieving the level of national consensus needed to improve America's competitive position in the near future is not good. In the short term more American industries are likely to go the way of ships, watches, motorbikes, machine tools, steel, autos, and consumer electronics.

Yet it is too early to count America out. Public opinion polls show that the American public is increasingly concerned with the seriousness of our competitive problems and increasingly aware that a structural transition is taking place from heavy industry to information and high technology. The Public Policy Analysis Poll, using national samples, found in 1984 that almost three-fourths of Americans agreed that America was undergoing not merely an economic downturn but a basic change in the economy. Three-fourths also acknowledged that America's economic position was seriously declining around the world. More than half believed that competitive imports from Japan would take away America's technological lead in the same way they hurt the auto industry. Over three-fourths believed it would take at least several years for America to deal with these problems.

In 1984 about one-fourth of American households were thinking of buying computers, and about half expected that within the next five years they would be using new technologies like shopping or banking by computer, electronic mail, and two-way communication through cable television. Over 90 percent said it was important for children today to take a course at school using computers.

Three-fourths believed that more cooperation among government, business, and labor is needed to deal with America's economic problems. A substantial majority believed that economic matters cannot be left entirely to private enterprise but that bipartisan cooperation among government leaders is required to balance the budget and encourage economic growth. More than two-thirds of respondents favored a National Economic Cooperation Council with representatives from government, business, and labor to establish national goals and work out strategies to achieve them. An equal number favored federal guarantees for banks to provide low-interest long-term industrial loans to small and medium-sized businesses modernizing plant and equipment. To be sure, the proportion of the public supporting any particular solution was smaller than the proportion recognizing the problems, reflecting the need for leadership and consensus building.

Forward-looking business leaders are beginning to meet together to work toward a consensus, and many able congressmen and bureaucrats are searching for solutions to long-term economic problems. Despite their affluence, Americans are, as shown by Public Policy Analysis polls, very concerned about the American economy and prepared to sacrifice to put it on solid ground for the long term.

Many of America's best programs, including NASA, foreign agricultural marketing, private housing finance, and interstate highways were products of years of careful thought and consensus building. The developments in NASA after 1957 made possible the dramatic decision to move ahead in 1961. As urgent as our problems are, perhaps we should be thankful we are not moving immediately to a national competitive strategy for we still have a great deal of work to do in forging the consensus that will make it work. A new downturn in the economy may well galvanize us into action, and with careful preparation we can make good use of the opportunity. At best, it will take years to chart our new course. If we succeed, Japan and other countries should be thankful that a major pillar of world trade is again securely in place, and we should be thankful to the Japanese for prodding us to launch our comeback.

POSTSCRIPT

By Ezra F. Vogel

This book was inspired by John Bowles, who patiently taught a "fuzzy academic" Japan specialist about the realities of American business and politics. Since the issues in this book go far beyond the competence of any one specialist, I could not have written it without many colleagues who have been wise in their counsel and generous with their time, especially Robert Reich, George Lodge, Bruce Scott, Dick Johns, Bill Givens, Bill Spring, Tom Hout, Joe Bower, Frank Weil, Harvey Brooks, Ray Vernon, Phil Jones, Dick Finn, Rick Dyck, Ron Napier, Chalmers Johnson, Hiroshi Ogawa, Kozo Yamamoto, Heizo Takenaka, Masutaro Urata, Dan Okimoto. In America, at various stages I have profited from the able research assistance of Kathaleen Kelly, Sally Solo, Anna Laura Rosow, Mary Ellen Hoke, and Peter Rubin.

In Japan, I have benefited especially from the long years of friendship and guidance from Kazuo Noda and members of the Amagi Kaigi. During 1982–83 when I was conducting research in Japan, I was ably assisted by Nagayo Sawa, a brilliant researcher, and Katsuhiko Sakuma, a brilliant teacher. Naotada Kurakake and Toshio Sanuki graciously arranged a series of background briefings. Many people were extraordinarily hospitable, generous with their time, and far more open than most Americans could imagine.

For each case study, I found one or two people who shared their profound expertise, patiently educating me in the early stages of my research and guiding me throughout: Kiyohide Terai on shipbuilding; John Long, Andy Ashburn, and Shinshichi Abe on machine tools; Masahiro Sugio on Kyushu; George Lindamood, Hiroshi Ando, Junji Tsuji, John Alic, and Bill Finan on the information revolution; Bernard Frieden and James Brown on housing; Ray Goldberg on agriculture; and Elizabeth Aycock on North Carolina.

Among those I interviewed on shipbuilding were: Hisashi Shindo, Masao Yoshiki, Isamu Yamashita, Masaaki Kanayama, Masao Mizushina, Masao Yamashita, Ryoichi Sasakawa, Misao Noguchi, Kumashi Kakehashi, Tatsuo Sato,

Takumi Yamamoto, Yasuro Kita, Kanesada Sufu, Hisashi Yamashita, Yoshiyuki Kawai, and Shosuke Idemitsu.

On machine tools, Seiuemon Inaba, Shoichiro Toyota, Seiichi Ishizaka, Kotaro Shimo, Toshio Shishido, Minoru Kanai, Teruyuki Yamazaki, Takeo Okuma, Takeshi Asada, Katsuhiko Ueno, Motoki Yoshida, Shuhei Aida, Taizo Ueda, Michihiko Nishida, Robert Neff, Naoaki Usui, Kouitsu Tsuchiya, Yoshihiko Takeoka, James Gray, Jessie Maffuid, Jim Geier, Fred Searby, and Carl Green.

On Kyushu, Kiyoshi Kawarabayashi, Hiromi Arisawa, Keiji Yasukawa, Morihiko Hiramatsu, Tsukasa Shijima, Daijiro Tsuru, Masao Hama, Taiichi Sato, Noboru Niwa, Toyokazu Abe, Yoshiaki Goto, Yoichi Enbutsu, Akio Imamura, Yoshiyuki Kawai, Nobushige Kiso, Minoru Kubo, Akira Mogi, Saburo Nagakura, Tsukumo Nagasue, Shinji Nakatsu, Yoshitaka Oki, Hideo Suzuki, Tatsuo Yoshida.

On the information revolution, Norman Achilles, Hideo Aiso, Vincent Bastioni, Justin Bloom, Edmund G. Brown, Jr., Michael Connors, Ian Dennis, Max Donnor, Ed Feigenbaum, Kazuhiro Fuchi, Makoto Hattori, Jerry Helfrich, Toshio Hiraguri, Katsusada Hirose, Kenichi Imai, Osamu Ishii, Kazuro Ito, Yutaka Kanayama, Fumihiko Kato, Masahito Kawahata, Peter Kelly, Yasusada Kitahara, Hisashi Kobayashi, Tsutomu Kobayashi, Seisuke Komatsuzaki, Chikara Kuranari, Michio Maruta, Yasuhiro Mori, Masasuke Morita, Ichiro Nakajima, Hiroji Nishino, Kenjiro Nitta, Hiroshi Ogawa, Andrew Osterman, James Otis, Rolf Library, Steve Schwartz, Osamu Seki, Takeo Shiina, Junichi Shimada, Kotaro Shimo, Hisashi Shindo, James Shinn, Reikichi Shirane, Berkley Tague, Korenobu Takahashi, Shigeru Takahashi, Nozomu Takasaki, Toshihiko Tanabe, Tsuguo Yagi, David Yancey, Kiyomi Yukihiro, Tom Zengage.

On Japanese business and economy in general, Toshio Doko, Haruo Maekawa, Hosai Hyuga, Sohei Nakayama, Haruo Suzuki, Naohiro Amaya, Hiromi Arisawa, Shigeya Yoshise, Nihachiro Hanamura, Tadashi Hosomi, Kazuo Iwata, Masaki Nakajima, Atsushi Shimokoobe, Tatsuo Suzuki, Mitsuhiko Yamada, Hajime Ota, Toshio Sanuki, Masaya Miyoshi, Yoshihiko Morozumi, Kazuo Nukazawa, Shoichi Akazawa, Tomiji Yamazaki, Nagahide Shiota, Lawrence Snowdon, Bill Dizer, Gary Flint, Yoshimasa Uchiyama, Bill Piez, Tait Ratcliffe, Koichiro Ejiri, Susumu Kajita, Sei Shirane. On Japanese politics, Yasuhiro Nakasone, Yasuhisa Shiozaki, Jun Shiozaki, Tadashi Kuranari, Masayoshi Ito, Tatsuo Murayama, Soichiro Ito, Koichi Kato, Kiichi Saeki, Seizaburo Sato, Masataka Kosaka, Hideo Sato, Gerald Curtis, Bob Immerman, Bill Clark, Yoichi Funahashi, Yoichi Miyazawa, Keizo Takemi, Tatsuo Arima, Hiroaki Fujii, Yonnosuke Nagai, Hisahiko Okazaki, Sam Jameson, Terry MacDougall.

Among the facilities visited are those of Koyagi (Mitsubishi Heavy Industries), Sasebo Heavy Industries, Miike (Mitsui Mining), Omuta, Takashima (Mitsubishi Mining), Tagawa, Iizuka, Okuma Tekko, Fanuc, Yamazaki, Murata,

Fujitsu (Kamakura, Numazu), Toyoda Koki, Toyoda Motors, Nissan, Sony (At-sugi), Brother, Nippon Steel (Oita, Yawata), NEC (Kumamoto), Honda (Ku-mamoto), Toshiba (Oita), Osaka Machine Tool Fair, Electrotechnical Lab, Mechanical Engineering Lab, Agency for Industrial Science and Technology.

On NASA, James Webb, Harvey Brooks, Brainard Holmes, Donald Hornig. On agriculture, Suzanne Hale, John Child, Bill Davis, Orville Freeman, Ray Iaones, Gwynn Garnett, Erland Higgonbotham, Jimmy Howard, Gunnar Lynum, Jimmy Minyard, John Baize, Burleigh Leonard, Bob Paalberg, Michael Reich, Peter Timmer, Yasuo Endo, John Langwick, Nelson Denlinger. On housing, Paul Barru, Ronald Gebhardt, Arthur Solomon, Herb Colton, Henry Schechter, Joseph Burstein, Ray Stryk, Louis Winnick, Robert Wood, Donald Lawson, Franklin Wright, Michael Sumichrist, Dale Riordan, Duane McGough, and Ed Silverman. On North Carolina, Elizabeth Aycock, Tony Bevacqua, Joe Sturdi-vant, David Chaney, Archie Davis, Joel Fleishman, Henry Foscue, Linda Fran-kel, Ken Freidlein, Bill Friday, George Herbert, Tom Lambeth, Quentin Lindsay, Bill Little, Ida Simpson, Larry Blake, Bob Brinkley, George Watts Hill, Ned Huffman, Michael Prandich, Terry Sanford, and Ed Tiryakian.

In addition to those listed above, I have benefited from comments on drafts of various chapters by Clyde Prestowitz, Anthony Oettinger, Oswald Ganley, Ithiel Poole, Tom Lifson, Don Klein, Peter Fuchs, Ed Whatley, C. T. Chen, Robert Silin, Andrew Gordon, Mark Fruin, Pierre Defraigne, Dan Sharp, and Dick Finn.

BIBLIOGRAPHY

The works I have found most useful in preparing this report are as follows:

Chapter 2. SHIPBUILDING

1. Cohen, Jerome Bernard. *The Japanese War Economy, 1937–1945.* Minneapolis: The University of Minnesota Press, 1949.
2. *The Financial Times* (London), passim.
3. International Business Information, Inc. *The Japanese Shipbuilding Industry.* Economic Reporting Service, vol. V, no. 24. December 1979. Tokyo.
4. International Business Information, Inc. *The Japanese Shipbuilding Industry: Prospects and Interim Policies, 1976–1980.* Tokyo.
5. Ito, Mitsuharu, and Ekonomisuto Editorial Department. *Sengo Sangyoshi e no Shozen.* Mainichi Newspapers, 1977.
6. Katayama, Noboru. *Nihon no Zosen Kogyo.* Tokyo: Nihon Kogyo Shuppan, 1970.
7. Nihon Zosen Gakkai, ed. *Showa Zosenshi,* vol 2. Tokyo: Genshobo, 1971.
8. *Nihon Zosen Kogyokai 30 Nenshi.* 1980.
9. Seiji Keizai Kenkyujo, ed. *Nihon no Zosengyo.* Tokyo: Toyo Keizai Shinhosha, 1959.
10. The Shipbuilders' Association of Japan. *Shipbuilding in Japan, 1980–1981.* Tokyo, October 1981.
11. Totten, George C. "The Reconstruction of the Japanese Shipbuilding Industry." Unpublished paper, 1978–79.
12. Unyusho, *Unyusho 30 Nenshi.* 1978.
13. Yoshiki, Masao. "Kinnen ni okeru Nihon Zosenkai no Hattatsu." Unpublished paper. Tokyo, 1976.

Chapter 3. MACHINE TOOLS AND ROBOTS

1. AIST. *Agency of Industrial Science and Technology.* MITI, 1982.
2. *American Machinist.* passim.
3. Aron, Paul. "Robotics in Japan." Report #22. Daiwa Securities America Inc., 1980.
4. Aron, Paul. "Robots Revisited: One Year Later." Report #25. Daiwa Securities America Inc., 1981.
5. Committee on the Machine Tool Industry, National Research Council. *The U.S. Machine Tool Industry and the Defense Industrial Base.* National Academy Press, 1983.

6. Covington and Burling (attorneys for Houdaille Industries). *Petition to the U.S. President,* May 1982. Supplement, July 1982.
7. Cravath, Swaine, and Moore (attorneys for Cincinnati Milicron). *Computer-Aided Manufacturing: The Japanese Challenge.* December 1982.
8. Dyck, Richard. *A Sociological Analysis of Japan's Research and Development System.* Ph.D. Thesis, Harvard University, 1975.
9. Hutchinson, G. K. "Flexible Manufacturing Systems in Japan." Unpublished manuscript, November 1977.
10. Inaba, Seiuemon. *Robotto Jidai o Hiraku.* PHP Kenkyujo, 1982.
11. Japan Machine Tool Builders' Association. *Machine Tool Industry: Japan.* Annual.
12. Japan Metal Forming Machine Builders Association. *Japanese Metal Forming Machinery.* 1982.
13. Kogyo Gijutsuin, ed. *Arata na Kenkyuu Kaihatsu ni Mukete.* Nikkan Kogyo Shinbunsha, 1982.
14. Mechanical Engineering Laboratory, AIST (Japan). *"Flexible Manufacturing System Complex Provides With Laser"* Project, July 1982.
15. Machine Tool Panel of the National Academy of Engineering. *The Competitive Status of the U.S. Machine Tool Industry.* National Academy Press, 1983.
16. National Machine Tool Builders' Association Japanese Study Mission. "Meeting the Japanese Challenge." September 14, 1981 (mimeo).
17. *Nikkei Mechanical.* "FMS Tokushu." August 2, 1982, pp. 59–86.
18. Nikui, Ken. *Kiiroi Robotto: Fanakku no Kiseki.* Yomiuri, 1982.
19. Office of Technology Assessment, *Automation and the Workplace.* U.S. Congress, March 1983.
20. U.S. International Trade Commission. *Competitive Assessment of the U.S Metalworking Machine Tool Industry.* September 1983.
21. Wender, Murase, and White (On Behalf of the Japanese Machine Tool Builders Association). *Comments in Opposition to the Houdaille Petition.* July 1982.
22. Yamazaki Tekko. *Kanreki Mukaeta Wakaki Mazakku no Kino to Asu.* Yamazaki Tekko, 1979.

Chapter 4. KYUSHU

1. Broadbent, Jeffrey. *State and Citizen in Japan.* Harvard Ph.D. Thesis, 1982.
2. Chiiki Shinko Seibi Kodan. *Kogyo Danchi no Goannai.* 1982.
3. Chiiki Shinko Seibi Kodan no Gaiyo. *Chiiki Shinko Seibi Kodan no Gaiyo.* 1982.
4. Chiiki Shinko Seibi Kodan. *Chiiki Shinko Seibi Kodan no Genkyo.* 1982.
5. Hiramatsu, Morihiko. *Tekunoporisu e no Chosen.* Nihon Keizai Shinbun, 1983.
6. *Kyukeiren 20 nen no Ayumi.* Fukuoka: Kyukeiren, 1981.
7. Kyushu Economic Research Center. *Outline of Kyushu Economy.* Fukuoka, Annual.
8. Kyushu Keizai Chosa Kyokai. *Kyushu Keizai Hakusho.* Annual since 1967.
9. Kyushu Keizai Chosa Kyokai. *Kyushu Keizai.* Gaikan, 1981.
10. *Kyushu Keizai Tokkei Gekkan* (monthly). Kyushu Keizai Chosa Kyokai.
11. National Land Agency. *Sanzenso: The Third Comprehensive National Development Plan.* Tokyo, 1977.

12. Nihon Kaihatsu Ginko, Fukuoka Shiten. *Kyushu Keizai no Hatten to Tomo ni*. Fukuoka, 1982.
13. Santan Chiiki Shinkoka, Shigen Enerugicho Sekitanbu, MITI. *Santan Chiiki Shinko Taisaku no Gaiyo*. 1982.
14. Santanbu Santan Chiiki Shinkoka, Fukuoka MITI Bureau. *Kyushu Santan Chiiki no Genkyo*. 1981.
15. Sekitan Kogyo Gorika Jigyodan. *Sekitan Kogyo 35 nen no Ayumi*. 1980.
16. Yada Toshifumi. *Sekitan Gyokai*. Tokyo: Kyoikusha, 1977.

Chapter 5. INFORMATION REVOLUTION

English language publications:

1. Abegglen, James C., and Akio Etori. "Japanese Technology Today," *Scientific American*, 1982, pp. J5–J30.
2. Boston Consulting Group, "The Development of the Japanese Computer Industry," in Eugene J. Kaplan, *Japan: The Government-Business Relationship*. U.S. Department of Commerce, February 1972.
3. *Business Week*. "Japan's Strategy for the '80s," December 14, 1981, pp. 53–92.
4. Dolen, Richard. "Japan's Fifth Generation Computer Project." *Scientific Bulletin* (Department of the Navy, Office of Naval Research Far East), October-December 1982, pp. 22–54.
5. Feigenbaum, Edward A., and Pamela McCorduck. *The Fifth Generation: Artificial Intelligence and Japan's Computer Challenge to the World*. Addison-Wesley, 1983.
6. *Financial Times* (London). "Japan: The Information Revolution," July 6, 1981.
7. Hilton, Barry. "Government Subsidized Computer, Software, and Integrated Circuit Research and Development by Japanese Private Companies," *Scientific Bulletin* (Department of the Navy, Office of Naval Research Far East), October-December 1982, pp. 1–21.
8. International Business Information. *The Information Processing Industry in Japan*. February 1983.
9. International Business Information. "Strategies of Japan's Computer Industry," *Japan Strategy Resources*, vol. VIII, no. 2, February 1982.
10. Kitazawa, T., ed. *Japan Annual Reviews in Electronics, Computers, and Telecommunications: Computer Sciences and Technologies*. Tokyo: OHM, 1982.
11. Kitahara, Yasusada. "Information Network System," *Japan Telecommunication Review* 24 (1982): 96–103.
12. Kitahara, Yasusada. *Information Network System*. London: Heinenmann Educational Books, 1983.
13. Lindamood, George E. "The Rise of the Japanese Computer Industry," *Scientific Bulletin* (Department of the Navy, Office of Naval Research Far East), October-December 1982, pp. 55–72.
14. Office of Technology Assessment, *International Competitiveness in Electronics*. U.S. Congress, November 1983.
15. Okimoto, Daniel I. *Pioneer and Pursuer: The Role of the State in the Evolution of the Japanese and American Semiconductor Industries*. Stanford: Northeast Asia-U.S. Forum on International Policy, April 1983.
16. Okimoto, Daniel I. Takuo Sugano, and Franklin B. Weinstein, eds. *Competitive*

Edge: The Semiconductor Industry in the U.S. and Japan. Stanford University Press, 1984.

17. Shinn, James. "Yokon, wasai: Lessons from Japan in the IC Business." Unpublished manuscript.
18. Silin, Robert. *The Japanese Semiconductor Industry, 1981/1982.* Bank of America Asia Ltd., 1982.
19. Welke, H. J. *Data Processing in Japan.* Amsterdam: North-Holland Publishing Co., 1982.

Japanese language publications:

1. Fujitsu Inc. *Ikeda Kinen Ronbunshu.* Fujitsu, 1978.
2. Komatsuzaki, Seisuke. *Joho Sangyo.* Tokyo: Toyo Keizai, 1980.
3. NTT INS Working Group. *Kodo Joho Tsushin Shisutemu.* NTT, 1982.
4. MITI, Kogyo Gijutsuin, ed. *Chokoseino Denshi Keisanki: Ogata Purojekuto ni yoru.* Nihon Sangyo Gijutsu Shinkokai, 1972.
5. MITI, Machinery and Information Industries Bureau. *Joho Sangyo no Genkyo.* May 1982.
6. MITI, Machinery and Information Industries Bureau. *Yutaka naru Johoka Shakai e no Dohyo.* May 1982.
7. *Sekai Konpyuta Nenkan, 1982.* Nihon Joho Shori Kaihatsu Senta, 1982.
8. Shirane, Reikichi. *Shin Comyunikeeshon Kakumei.* Toyo Keizai, 1983.

Chapter 6. NASA

1. Bainbridge, William Sims. *The Spaceflight Revolution.* John Wiley, 1976.
2. Bauer, Raymond A. *Second Order Consequences.* MIT Press, 1969.
3. Brooks, Harvey. *The Government of Science.* MIT Press, 1968.
4. Brooks, Harvey. "Motivations of the Space Program, Past and Future." 1982 (mimeo).
5. Doktors, Samuel I. *The NASA Technology Transfer Program.* Praeger, 1970.
6. Doktors, Samuel I. *The Role of Federal Agencies in Technology Transfer.* MIT Press, 1969.
7. Gansler, Jacques S. *The Defense Industry.* MIT Press, 1980.
8. Ginsberg, Eli, James W. Kuhn, Jerome Schnee, and Boris Yavitz. *Economic Impact of Large Public Programs: The NASA Experience.* Olympus Publishing Co., 1976.
9. Levine, Arnold S. *Managing NASA in the Apollo Era.* NASA, 1982.
10. Logsdon, John. *The Decision to Go to the Moon.* MIT, 1970.
11. NASA. *Productivity in Aerospace Research and Development.* NASA, 1980.
12. Nelson, Richard R., ed. *Government and Technical Progress.* Pergamon Press, 1982.
13. Newell, Homer E. *Beyond the Atmosphere.* NASA, 1980.
14. Norman, Colin. *The God that Limps: Science and Technology in the Eighties.* Norton, 1981.
15. Price, Don K. *Government and Science.* New York University Press, 1954.
16. Rosholt, Robert L. *An Administrative History of NASA, 1958–1963.* NASA, 1966.

17. Sayles, Leonard, and Margaret Chandler. *Managing Large Systems.* Harper & Row, 1971.
18. Schoettle, Enid C. B. "The Establishment of NASA," in Sanford Lakoff, ed., *Knowledge and Power.* Free Press, 1966.
19. Webb, James E. *Spage Age Management.* McGraw-Hill, 1969.

Chapter 7. AGRICULTURE

1. Austin, James. *Food For Peace.* Harvard School of Public Health, February 1977.
2. Barnet, Richard J. *The Lean Years.* Simon & Schuster, 1980.
3. Bolling, Richard, and John Bowles. *America's Competitive Edge.* McGraw-Hill, 1982.
4. Castle, Emery N., and Kenzo Hemmi, with Sally A. Skillings. *U.S.-Japanese Agricultural Trade Relations.* Resources for the Future, 1982.
5. Cochrane, Willard W. *The Development of American Agriculture,* University of Minnesota Press, 1979.
6. Johnson, David Gale, and John A. Schnittker. *U.S. Agriculture in a World Context.*
7. Mayer, Martin. "Our Butter and Egg Men Are Winning Big Abroad," *Fortune,* May 19, 1980.
8. Rasmussen, Wayne D., and Gladys L. Baker. *The Department of Agriculture.* Praeger, 1972.
9. Schertz, Lyle P., and others. *Another Revolution in U.S. Farming?* U.S. Department of Agriculture, 1979.
10. U.S. Department of Agriculture. *Fact Book of U.S. Agriculture.* November 1980.
11. U.S. Department of Agriculture. *Foreign Agricultural Trade of the U.S.* Monthly, passim.
12. U.S. Department of Agriculture. *A Time to Choose.* January 1981.
13. World Food Institute (Iowa State University). *World Food Trade and U.S. Agriculture, 1960–1980.* May 19, 1980.

Chapter 8. HOUSING

1. Aaron, Henry J. *Shelter and Subsidies.* Brookings, 1972.
2. Congressional Budget Office. *Federal Housing Assistance: Alternative Approaches.* Congressional Budget Office, May 1982.
3. Eichler, Ned. *The Merchant Builders.* MIT Press, 1982.
4. Frieden, Bernard J. *American Housing Policy since World War II.* MIT-Harvard Joint Center for Urban Studies, September 1978. Document 07A.
5. Kaiser Committee. *A Decent Home: The Report of the President's Committee on Urban Housing.* Government Printing Office, December 1968.
6. Keith, Nathaniel S. *Politics and the Housing Crisis since 1930.* Universe Books, 1973.
7. Meyerson, Martin, Barbara Terrett, and William W. C. Wheaton. *Housing, People, and Cities.* McGraw-Hill, 1962.
8. *Report of the President's Commission on Housing.* Government Printing Office, 1982.
9. Solomon, Arthur P. *Housing the Urban Poor.* MIT Press, 1974.

10. Starr, Roger. *Housing and the Money Market.* Basic Books, 1975.
11. Struyk, Raymond J., and Marc Bendick, Jr., eds. *Housing Vouchers for the Poor.* Urban Institute Press, 1981.
12. Tuccillo, John A., with John L. Goodman, Jr. "The U.S. Housing Finance System and the Reagan Program." Unpublished manuscript, May 1983.

Chapter 9. NORTH CAROLINA

1. Employment Security Commission of North Carolina. *Manufacturing Employment in North Carolina, 1969 to 1979.* Raleigh, 1980.
2. Hamilton, W. B. "The Research Triangle of North Carolina: A Study in Leadership for the Commonwealth," *S. Atlantic Review,* Spring 1966, pp. 254–278.
3. Herzik, Eric B., and Sally Branch Teater, eds. *North Carolina Focus.* North Carolina Center for Public Policy Research, Inc., 1981.
4. Hodges, Luther. *Businessman in the Statehouse.* NC Press, 1962.
5. North Carolina Citizens Association. *North Carolina,* vol. 38, no. 6, June 1981.
6. *North Carolina Insight* (quarterly journal, North Carolina Center for Public Policy Research, Inc.), passim.
7. North Carolina State Board of Education. *1976–1978 Biennial Report.* North Carolina System of Community Colleges. 1978.
8. Sanford, Terry. *But What About the People?* Harper & Row, 1966.
9. Stuart, Brad. *Making North Carolina Prosper: A Critique of Balanced Growth and Regional Planning.* North Carolina Center for Public Policy Research, Inc., 1979.
10. Wilson, Louis R. *The Research Triangle of North Carolina.* Colonial Press, 1967.

Chapter 10. COMPETITIVE STRATEGY, AMERICAN STYLE

1. Abernathy, William J., Kim B. Clark, Alan M. Kantrow. *Industrial Renaissance.* Basic Books, 1983.
2. Alic, John, et al. *U.S. Industrial Competitiveness: A Comparison of Steel, Electronics and Automobiles.* U.S. Congress, Office of Technology Assessment, July 1981.
3. Alic, John. *Industrial Policy: Where Do We Go from Here?* Office of Technology Assessment. Unpublished paper, April 1982.
4. Bluestone, Barry, and Bennett Harrison. *The Deindustrialization of America.* Basic Books, 1982.
5. Bolling, Richard, and John Bowles. *America's Competitive Edge.* McGraw-Hill, 1982.
6. Bower, Joseph L. *The Two Faces of Management: An American Approach to Leadership in Business and Politics.* Houghton Mifflin, 1983.
7. California Commission on Industrial Innovation. *Winning Technologies: A Strategy for California and the Nation.* September 1982.
8. Congressional Budget Office. *The Industrial Policy Debate.* U.S. Congress, December 1983.
9. Congressional Quarterly, Inc. *Employment in America.* 1983.
10. Data Resources, Inc. *Report on U.S. Manufacturing Industries.* January 1984.
11. Department of Commerce, International Trade Administration. *An Assessment of U.S. Competitiveness in High Technology Industries.* February 1983.

12. Freund, William C. *U.S. Economic Performance in Global Perspective.* New York Stock Exchange, February 1981.
13. Industrial Policy Study Group. *Promoting Economic Growth and Competitiveness.* 1984.
14. *International Competitiveness in Electronics.* U.S. Congress, Office of Technology Assessment, November 1983.
15. Johnson, Chalmers, ed. *Industrial Policy Debate.* San Francisco: Institute for Contemporary Studies, 1984.
16. Lodge, George C. *The American Disease.* Alfred A. Knopf, 1984.
17. Lodge, George C., and Bruce Scott, eds. *U.S. Competitiveness in the World Economy.* Harvard Business School, 1984.
18. Mason, Edward S. *"Industrial Policy in the U.S."* Development Discussion Paper No. 157. Harvard Institute for International Development, November 1983.
19. National Research Council. *International Competition in Advanced Technology.* National Academy Press, 1983.
20. Office of Technology Assessment, *Computerized Manufacturing Automation.* U.S. Congress, April 1984.
21. Phillips, Kevin P., *Staying on Top.* Random House, 1984.
22. Porter, Michael E. *Competitive Strategy.* Free Press, 1980.
23. Public Policy Analysis Service, *Policy Trends in the Mid-Eighties: A Survey of American Attitudes.* Somers, CT, Spring 1984.
24. Reich, Robert B. *The Next American Frontier.* Times Books, 1983.
25. Reich, Robert B., and Ira C. Magaziner. *Minding America's Business.* Harcourt Brace Jovanovich, 1982.
26. Rohatyn, Felix G. *The Twenty-Year Century.* Random House, 1983.
27. Servan-Schreiber, Jean-Jacques. *The World Challenge.* Simon and Schuster, 1980.
28. Sorensen, Theodore C. *A Different Kind of Presidency.* Harper & Row, 1984.
29. Thurow, Lester C. *The Zero Sum Society.* Basic Books, 1980.
30. Thurow, Lester C. *Dangerous Currents.* Random House, 1983.
31. Zysman, John. *Governments, Markets, and Growth.* Cornell, 1983.
32. Zysman, John, and Laura Tyson. *American Industry in International Competition.* Cornell, 1983.

INDEX